19 STARS OF INDIANA

19 Stars of Indiana

Exceptional Hoosier Men

Michael S. Maurer

Foreword by Michael A. McRobbie

Published in association with IBJ Media, Indianapolis

Indiana Historical Society
Indianapolis

Also by Michael S. Maurer

Water Colors (2003)

19 Stars of Indiana—Exceptional Hoosier Women (2009)

This book is a publication of
Indiana Historical Society Press
Eugene and Marilyn Glick Indiana History Center
450 West Ohio Street
Indianapolis, Indiana 46202-3269 USA

http://www.indianahistory.org

Telephone orders	1-800-447-1830
Fax orders	1-317-234-0562
Online orders	http://shop.indianahistory.org

Published in association with IBJ Media, Indianapolis
41 East Washington Street
Indianapolis, IN 46204

The paper in this publication meets the minimum requirements of American National Standard for Information Sciences—Permanence of Paper for Printed Library Materials, ANSI Z39.48–1984

Manufactured in the United States of America.

Library of Congress Cataloging-in-Publication Data

Maurer, Michael S.
19 stars of Indiana : exceptional Hoosier men / Michael S. Maurer ; foreword by Michael McRobbie.
p. cm.
"Published in association with IBJ Media, Indianapolis."
ISBN 978-0-87195-291-2 (cloth : alk. paper) 1. Indiana—Biography. I. Title. II. Title: Nineteen stars of Indiana.
F525.M38 2010
977.2'0430922—dc22
2010045122

1 2 3 4 5 14 13 12 11 10 09

For my children,
Todd, Jill and Greg

★ Contents ★

FOREWORD

A *mericans consider society as a body in a state of improvement,*
humanity as a changing scene, …; and they admit that what
appears to them today to be good, may be superseded by something
better tomorrow.

—Alexis de Toqueville, Democracy in America

With these words, French historian and keen observer of American democracy Alexis de Toqueville could have been describing the nineteen Hoosier stars about whom Mickey Maurer has so eloquently written in this volume. With this volume he has turned his Protean talent to documenting in his graceful but personal way, the accomplishments and careers of nineteen remarkable Hoosier men who reflect what is best in America as a great democracy and a great meritocracy.

Each demonstrates the ability to rise to the top from the most humble beginnings, the virtues instilled by fine education, the opportunity to prosper through ingenuity and energy, deep commitment to public service and philanthropy, and above it all, moderation and common sense. All these are, of course, classic Hoosier values. They are also the virtues of the Midwest, a fact that underscores how this region is, in so many ways, the Heartland of America.

In reading these biographical essays, one is struck by the range of areas in which these nineteen Hoosier men have excelled: in the arts, business, education, medicine and science, politics and public service, and sports. One is also struck by how nearly all of them came from modest backgrounds. By sustained effort and excellence, all reached the peaks of their areas of endeavor. Most received education through the great public universities of America, some triumphed over prejudice in the most resounding ways, and a number served their country with distinction in the gravity of war.

Through all these essays another characteristic emerges. That is the essential modesty and moderation of all these men. I know nearly all of them—some are good friends—and in spite of their remarkable achievements, pretension and ostentation are completely alien to them.

Modesty and moderation are certainly not inconsistent with vision and imagination though. To see this, one only has to reflect on the world-class accomplishments of Bill Cook in medical devices, Father Ted Hesburgh in education, Senator Richard Lugar in civic reform and statesmanship, Joe Mamlin in medicine, among the remarkable accomplishments of many of the others. And in spite of the heights of achievements they have already reached, nevertheless for some of these men, their finest accomplishments may still be in front of them.

And who better to write about this diverse group of outstanding Hoosier men than Mickey Maurer, truly a modern Renaissance man. In every field to which he has turned his restless virtuosic talents, Mickey has excelled. He has been a highly successful entrepreneur in banking, media and publishing; a skilled and award-winning television commentator; an energetic and highly effective public servant; and an enthusiastic sportsman. Add to that his maybe unexpected achievements as a woodworker, mountain climber, and designer of crossword puzzles. And his beautiful book *Watercolors*, highlights another great talent as an underwater photographer with the aesthetic judgment of an impressionist painter. He has also been a munificent Indiana philanthropist: from the ingenuity of Mickey's Camp to his magnificent gift to his alma mater Indiana University, to name the law school at IU's Bloomington campus the Michael Maurer School of Law.

Mickey Maurer's *19 Stars of Indiana: Exceptional Hoosier Women*, the companion volume to this one, contains luminous biographical essays on some remarkable Hoosier women and demonstrates his great skills as an author.

It has been said that the art of reading learned texts in the Middle Ages required the ability to understand and appreciate not only what was said but also what was left unsaid. And what is left unsaid in *19 Stars: Exceptional Hoosier Men* is how the virtues and all that is admirable about these nineteen Hoosier men, are also the virtues and all that is admirable about Mickey Maurer. In this regard, he is very much the 20th Star of this fine book.

Michael A. McRobbie
President
Indiana University

PREFACE

I love biographies. One of my favorite books as a child was *Fifty Famous Americans* by Ward Griffith, published in 1946. That volume is still in my library. I also enjoyed biographies written by local author Guernsey Van Riper. I reread them to my children.

When I researched *19 Stars of Indiana, Exceptional Hoosier Women* in 2009, I enjoyed learning about more than 100 extraordinary Hoosier women. With this in mind, I accepted the challenge to write the "soul brother" to the women's book, *19 Stars of Indiana, Exceptional Hoosier Men*. The men chronicled in this book share aspects of the lives of the nineteen women – success, courage, leadership; however, their experiences were more life-threatening. You will read about Hoosiers shot out of a fighter jet, liberating a concentration camp, subjected to court-martial, knocked cold in front of twenty thousand fans, facing bigotry, and caught in the middle of ethnic slaughter—lives full of excitement, adventure and achievement.

Essentially the same criteria were used in this book as the prior effort:
- Is he living? I prefer this current collection to a historical accounting.
- Is his story inspirational?
- Did he make it on his own?
- Did he sacrifice?
- Was he faced with tough choices?
- Does he demonstrate character and class?
- Is he a Hoosier? Many well-known men including Bob Knight, Will Shortz, David Wolf and Oscar Robertson have had a connection to Indiana. They were not profiled herein because I was looking for men who call Indiana home today.

The final selection was not easy. There is no scarcity of qualified men in Indiana and this book presents only a representative sample, not a comprehensive list. It was a shame to exclude so many highly qualified men who deserve a chapter. Like all-star team selections, there is room for debate.

I am pleased to note that Indiana cities not represented in the first book are represented herein. They include Gary, Muncie and Anderson.

Although each of the men profiled has a unique story, there are common threads:

• Each man expressed profound humility—sometimes wonderment—for the position the world placed him in and his ability to not only cope but to excel.

• Each freely offered advice.

• None ducked responsibility regardless of the difficulty.

It was my goal to write both "19 Stars" books in order that our children will have access to positive Hoosier role models and dare to believe they can achieve at a high level—in the words of Angelo Pizzo in his profile, "Never be defined by someone telling you what you can't do."

ACKNOWLEDGMENTS

Thanks to editors Andrea Davis, associate editor at *Indianapolis Business Journal*, and Ray Boomhower, senior editor and Kathy Breen, editor at the Indiana Historical Society. Andrea provided many hours of assistance converting the drafts into readable text. Ray refined and polished the manuscript, adding life to the text. I appreciate their patience and careful attention to detail.

It is an honor to be among the titles published by the Indiana Historical Society. I am in debt to John Herbst, executive director and Stephen Cox, executive vice president.

I am extremely grateful for the hard work of the bright and creative writers who contributed chapters. Nancy Baxter (Gene Glick) and Bob Hammel (Bill Cook) are professionals whose work has elevated the quality of this volume.

Completing the team are general advisor Ann Finch and experts at the Indianapolis Business Journal Book Publishing Division—Pat Keiffner, director of the Book Publishing Division, Deb Strzeszkowski, creative director and Jodi Belcher, production coordinator and at the Indiana Historical Society, Paula Corpuz, former senior director, Jeanne Scheets, vice president, marketing and public relations, Stacy Simmer, senior graphic designer and Becke Bolinger, national sales coordinator. Thank you all.

Many thanks to the people who helped arrange interviews and fact-checked manuscripts, especially Kim Campbell (Jim Davis), Deborah Daniels and Maggie Ban (Mitch Daniels), Hank Johnson and Clarence Doninger (Marvin Johnson), Fran Quigley and Sally Shapiro (Joe Mamlin), Melanie Chapleau (Theodore Hesburgh), Vic Lechtenberg and Jay Akridge (Gebisa Ejeta), Dane Starbuck (Larry Einhorn) and Tim Sanders (Quentin Smith). In the chapter on Theodore Hesburgh, I borrowed freely, with permission from his autobiography, "God, Country, Notre Dame," written with Jerry Reedy.

A note of appreciation goes to Alvin H. Rosenfield, director of the Institute of Jewish Culture and the Arts, Borns Jewish Studies Program at Indiana University, and Holocaust expert Juergen Matthaus of the Holocaust Museum in Washington, D.C., for vetting the chapter on Stephen Beering.

I gratefully acknowledge the valuable research, insightful observations and cheerful support of my executive assistant, Susan Roederer.

Thank you, Janie Maurer, my wife, who is always my collaborator.

Finally, an extraordinary debt of gratitude is owed to the nineteen remarkable Hoosier men whose lives are probed in this volume. Their collaboration was essential to the success of the project. Their stories are inspirational and their impact on all of us will be felt for years.

MEN PROFILED

Baker, David *(Bloomington)*: Jazz composer; performer; Distinguished Professor of Music, Jacobs School of Music, Indiana University

Beering, Steven, M.D. *(Indianapolis)*: Physician; President Emeritus, Purdue University

Bepko, Gerald *(Indianapolis)*: FBI Agent; Dean, Indiana University Law School; Chancellor Emeritus, IUPUI

Carter, David *(Indianapolis)*: Mountain climber; conqueror of Mt. Everest

Cook, William *(Bloomington)*: Industrialist; philanthropist; historic landmarks preservationist

Daniels, Mitch *(Indianapolis)*: Indiana governor

Davis, Jim *(Muncie)*: Syndicated cartoonist

Einhorn, Lawrence H., M.D. *(Indianapolis)*: Physician; scientist; Distinguished Professor Department of Medicine, Division of Hematology/Oncology, IU Simon Cancer Center

Ejeta, Gebisa *(Lafayette)*: Geneticist; Distinguished Professor Plant Breeding and Genetics, Purdue University

Erskine, Carl *(Anderson)*: Major League Baseball player; banker

Glick, Eugene B. *(Indianapolis)*: Real estate developer; philanthropist

Hesburgh, Rev. Theodore M., C.S.C. *(South Bend)*: Priest; President Emeritus, University of Notre Dame

Johnson, Marvin *(Indianapolis)*: Light heavyweight champion of the world; Sgt. Marion County Sheriff's Department

Kernan, Joseph *(South Bend)*: South Bend mayor; Indiana governor; President, South Bend Silverhawks

Lugar, Richard *(Indianapolis)*: Indianapolis mayor; United States senator

Mamlin, Joseph, M.D. *(Indianapolis)*: Physician; Professor Emeritus of Medicine, School of Medicine, IUPUI

McGinnis, George *(Indianapolis)*: Professional basketball player; businessman

Pizzo, Angelo *(Bloomington)*: Screenwriter; movie producer

Smith, Quentin *(Gary)*: Tuskegee airman; educator

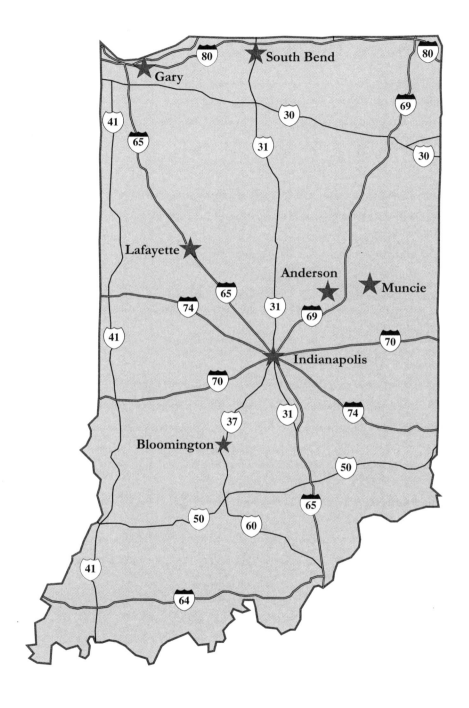

19 STARS OF INDIANA

Joseph Kernan

Honored Warrior/Civic Leader

At 4:30 on the sunny afternoon of May 7, 1972, naval flight officer Joseph Kernan and pilot Ron Polfer lifted off in an RA-5C Vigilante from the aircraft carrier USS *Kitty Hawk* stationed off the coast of Vietnam. It was Kernan's twenty-sixth reconnaissance mission. Their assignment was to take pictures of the target objective after the last bomber had dropped its load.

Kernan observed the damage below from 4,500 feet as the Vigilante flew at a speed of 563 knots (just under 650 miles per hour.) Suddenly, the plane was hit by antiaircraft fire—right up the rear end. The nose pitched down. Polfer leveled the wings and turned toward the safety of the water. Just ten miles from the beach, less than a minute away, the jet began to plunge to earth. Polfer struggled with the controls as the plane dropped below 3,200 feet. The altimeter was unwinding but it could not keep up with the dive.

Kernan had to bail out. He braced himself and pulled the ejection handle on his seat. The cockpit filled with light as the canopy jettisoned. He blacked out from the force of the ejection. At the descent speed of the disabled jet—a mile every five seconds—a delay of one more second would have meant certain death.

Joseph E. Kernan III was born April 8, 1946, the oldest of nine

children and one of only two boys. He was raised in Chicago by his father, Joseph E. Kernan Jr., who was a naval aviator during World War II and later enjoyed a career in government service. His mother, Marian Powers Kernan, worked a number of jobs but was most proud of her tenure with C&P Telephone, where she ascended to communications representative. One of her important accounts during that time was the Pentagon. She was particularly proud of her top-secret security clearance.

The family moved to South Bend when Joe was ten. Kernan played all sports in high school, but he loved baseball and dreamed of wearing the blue-and-gold varsity uniform of the University of Notre Dame. After a season as a walk-on on the freshman team, he accomplished his goal when he made the varsity squad as a sophomore utility infielder. He was used sparingly—not enough for young Kernan.

By the time Kernan was a junior, he realized he was not going to crack the infield as a starter. He beseeched Coach Joe Kline to grant him permission to switch to catcher. Kernan began winter practices that year as third-string catcher, but he had a plan that included good friend and neighbor Jim Gibbons, who had played and coached basketball and baseball at Notre Dame and was an outstanding student of the game. Gibbons had earned a World Series ring in 1960 as a member of the Pittsburgh Pirates coaching staff. Every night after practice, Gibbons and Clay High School coach Jim Reinbold worked with Kernan on footwork, getting rid of the ball, blocking pitches, and all the other skills that a varsity catcher needed to perfect. By the time the season began, Kernan was squatting behind home plate. He earned a scholarship his senior year.

Kernan majored in government, since those were the classes he enjoyed the most. He had no idea how important that decision would be to his future career. When Kernan graduated in the summer of 1968, the United States was embroiled in the Vietnam War. Kernan knew that he would be required to serve his country. He had already passed his preinduction physical and his draft orders were imminent. Kernan wanted to fly, perhaps because of the influence of his father. He applied to the navy for acceptance as an aviation officer. His admission tests were administered at Andrews Air Force Base in Washington, D.C., where his family had moved during his sophomore year at Notre Dame. He was confident that he would be accepted into the navy but in early December 1968, while waiting for those orders to come through, he received a notice to report to South Bend for induction into the U.S. Army.

About to surrender his dream of flying, Kernan had a serendipitous discussion with First Class Petty Officer Nickelson, the sailor who had administered his tests at Andrews Air Force Base. Nickelson suggested that Kernan inform his draft board in South Bend that he was living with his family in Washington, D.C., and that his records should be sent there. Nickelson calculated that the delay would give Kernan enough time to join the navy. The ploy worked. Kernan's army induction was rescheduled for January 20, 1969, but he was sworn into the navy at 4 p.m. on January 19. The navy had gotten him first.

Kernan wanted to be a pilot, but he knew that he could not because of his poor eyesight. He settled for becoming a naval flight officer, which he said was the next best thing. He went to officer candidate school and the initial phases of flight training in Pensacola, Florida. After flight school, Kernan was assigned to Brunswick, Georgia, the final stop in jet training where he was attached to the RA-5C Vigilante reconnaissance aircraft. Kernan was responsible for radio, radar, navigation, and other equipment, including a viewfinder that enabled him to see the ground and a television camera that transmitted images from the front of the airplane. Originally planned as a nuclear-weapons platform, the Vigilante was a highly advanced supersonic bomber that was modified to fill a reconnaissance role and redesignated the RA-5C. Because the aircraft's hollow fuselage was designed to hold bombs, there was plenty of room for the vast array of reconnaissance equipment. At school, naval flight officers were not taught to land the airplane in an emergency. Navy protocol stated that if the pilot was disabled, eject and hope for the best. Kernan earned his wings in February 1970 and was assigned to the Replacement Air Group, a training squadron for Vigilantes in Albany, Georgia. After training, Kernan was reassigned to Reconnaissance Heavy Attack Squadron 7, also based in Albany. That squadron was comprised of some Vietnam veterans who were preparing to return to sea duty.

Kernan sailed in January 1972 out of San Diego on the USS *Kitty Hawk*, an aircraft carrier named after the North Carolina town near where Orville and Wilbur Wright flew the first successful, controlled powered aircraft. The *Kitty Hawk* was the last of the nonnuclear fleet. En route to Vietnam, the *Kitty Hawk* made port in the Philippines to take on provisions, then sailed to the Gulf of Tonkin in the South China Sea and prepared for battle.

The orders were routine for Kernan's twenty-sixth reconnaissance mission. He was responsible for taking photographs of the target after the last of about thirty-three bombers had dropped its load, waiting at least thirty seconds to give the smoke time to clear, but no more than sixty seconds because after that the enemy would be crawling out of foxholes, literally shooting mad. The target that day was a truck park, a staging area located on the main drag of North Vietnam's Highway 1 at the beginning of the Ho Chi Minh Trail.

Each reconnaissance flight was escorted by an F-4 Phantom jet. The Phantom was not quite as quick as the Vigilante, but it could keep up. The Phantom's role was to fly above and slightly to the side and behind the Vigilante during its reconnaissance work in order to protect it from antiaircraft and surface-to-air missiles. If the Phantom crew detected a missile launch, it broke radio silence and transmitted a warning. When he got the message, the Vigilante pilot usually turned into the direction of the missile and veered left, allowing the projectile to hurtle by. Antiaircraft artillery typically consisted of four or five weapons in a radar-controlled battery. Normally the first round missed but as the Vigilante flew straight and level, the radar automatically calculated adjustments and locked in on the aircraft's tail. The Phantom's responsibility was to advise when the lock was set so that the Vigilante could break left or right. The violence of that motion fractured the radar lock, and the Vigilante could then return and finish its mission. With such advance notice, the Vigilante was a difficult target.

Something went awry on that May afternoon. The Phantom that was supposed to be on the tail of Kernan's Vigilante was actually flying ahead. Knowing that out of formation his Phantom was useless, the pilot waggled his wings to reduce the jet's speed and fell back in formation. But he was unable to regain visible contact with the reconnaissance plane. The Vigilante continued on its mission down Highway 1 but had lost its protection. As Kernan took pictures of the truck park that the strike team had just annihilated, he and Polfer were unaware of their vulnerability.

After taking pictures of the target, Kernan's orders were to proceed along the main highway to the Thanh Hoa Bridge in order to gauge the flow of traffic. It was a dangerous area. In many previous runs over a period of seven years, the United States had lost more than forty aircraft around the bridge—said to be the heaviest defended turf on the planet, second only to the Kremlin. When the United States dispatched more airplanes, the Vietnamese installed more antiaircraft batteries. One might question the wisdom of his assignment, but Kernan never did. While flying to the bridge, Polfer did not make any evasive maneuvers because the Phantom never told him he should.

When the Vigilante was hit by an antiaircraft round, its nose pitched down, flinging loose equipment into the air. Kernan noticed the fire-warning light in the cockpit. He was trained to disregard that signal without confirmation. His hopes rose briefly as the pilot leveled out and turned toward the water and possible rescue. Then the nose pitched down again.

Kernan broke radio silence, declaring, "Flare 4 has been hit." The only person who heard that fervent message was Kernan himself. The regular radio, the auxiliary radio, and the emergency radio had all been disabled. The plane was pointing to the ground and the altimeter was spinning. Kernan had no recourse. He ejected and immediately blacked out. A little more than a one-second delay and there would not have been enough altitude for his parachute to deploy. Polfer also ejected after the hydraulic system failed, rendering the control stick nonoperational. The pilot did not have the chance to properly position himself in the seat, and as a result broke his back, his shoulder, and his arm rocketing out of the airplane. Kernan's seat worked as advertised.

Kernan awoke on the ground late Sunday afternoon, just a half-dozen miles from the beach, surrounded by hundreds of women and children. His uniform consisted of a helmet with the visor down, a G-suit and vest, and a thirty-eight-caliber revolver loaded with flares but no bullets. He was stripped to his skivvies and a T-shirt. Kernan understood that for the first twenty-four to forty-eight hours after a traumatic event such as an emergency ejection, he would be in shock whether he realized it or not. He remained quiet and outwardly calm.

Three men in uniform appeared and tied him to a stick behind his back. An argument ensued with the local citizenry about who had custody of the prisoner. Kernan was pleased that the men in uniform won the altercation. As they ran him toward a river, a child threw a rock that hit him in the back of the head. Kernan remembers turning around, looking at the young man and thinking, "What a good toss. Could have used him at Notre Dame."

Kernan was taken by boat to a small village. The "imperialist" had his picture taken with the mayor and president of the town council. He was put on display for a brief time, after which he was confined in a dark and damp basement with a dirt floor. Nursing cuts and bruises including the gash on his head, Kernan wondered if he had ejected from a plane that Polfer had somehow brought back to the *Kitty Hawk*. He thought that perhaps Polfer was back in the chow line while he was a prisoner of war. His thoughts were interrupted by a voice somewhere in that basement, complaining profanely in very clear English. It was Polfer.

Both prisoners were placed in a truck bound for Hoa Lo Prison in Hanoi. Hoa Lo, commonly translated, means "Hell's Hole." The prison complex was sarcastically nicknamed the "Hanoi Hilton" by the American prisoners of war. When Polfer and Kernan arrived, they were again separated. Kernan spent four days at the Hanoi Hilton before being transferred to a nearby prison called The Zoo, where he remained for most of his captivity. At The Zoo, Kernan was held in solitary confinement for a month, then shared his cell with one other prisoner for another month. For the rest of his imprisonment, his cell was occupied by eight to twelve prisoners at a time. They had cards and Kernan played bridge every chance he got. In the last two months of his internment, he was allowed to receive a package from the Red Cross. At that time most of the prisoners were treated humanely, a change in philosophy since the death of Ho Chi Minh on September 2, 1969.

Peace agreements were signed on January 27, 1973, and within sixty days Kernan was released. The injured were released first and then other prisoners on a first-in, first-out basis. As a late arrival, Kernan was among the last group to be set free. While a POW, Kernan ate pumpkin soup twice a day—every day. It is no wonder that Kernan dislikes anything to do with pumpkins: pumpkin pie, pumpkin seeds, pumpkin anything.

Kernan received the Navy Commendation Medal, two air medals, a combat action ribbon, two Purple Hearts, and a Distinguished Flying Cross. After a few days of debriefing and physical examinations at Clark Air Force Base in the Philippines and Bethesda Naval Hospital in Maryland, Kernan was granted ninety days' leave. Before long, he flew to Atlanta to rekindle a romance with his college sweetheart, Maggie McCullough. They married in April 1974. Kernan mustered out of the navy eight months later.

The Kernans moved to Cincinnati, where he worked for Procter & Gamble, making Zest and Camay soap. He hated it. It did not take long for the young couple to return to South Bend. After more than four years in South Bend—first working for the South Bend Community Schools and later in sales—Kernan's good friend Pete Mullen suggested that he inquire about becoming the city controller. Kernan was ready to try something new, and he was curious. Although not a bean counter, Kernan talked to the recently elected mayor, Roger Parent, and landed the job. It was his first taste of public service and he enjoyed it. He held the job of city controller for a full term before returning to a business career as vice president and treasurer of Mac Williams Corp. But Kernan missed public service.

In December 1986, after learning that Parent had opted against running for a third term, Kernan decided to run for mayor. He secured the nomination in the Democratic primary with 51 percent of the vote and won the November election by a slim 53 percent to 47 percent margin. In 1991 he was reelected with 76 percent of the vote and four years later captured a third term by a record 82 percent of the popular vote. Kernan was pleased and gratified in the job, and obviously the city of South Bend returned that affection.

As the newly elected mayor of South Bend, Kernan had rejected advice to unlist his telephone number to avoid being pestered to death. A year and a half later, the phone rang at his home on a Saturday morning. Maggie answered the call from a South Bend resident who explained that her son was in the army in Germany and that he was very sick. The army advised her to come see him right away, but she had no passport, no birth certificate, and no proof of citizenship and, therefore, could not leave the country. The frantic mother did not know where to turn. Maggie, with the help of her husband's aides, put the paperwork together for a voter's registration. With that certificate in hand, the mother was able to board an airplane that same afternoon. She arrived at her son's bedside five hours before he died. "We have an extraordinary capacity to do good things. It doesn't have to take years to accomplish, to involve complicated negotiations or demand an advanced degree," Kernan said. "It's most often just a simple act of kindness." His telephone number is still in the book.

In 1990 Kernan and other Indiana mayors joined Lieutenant Governor Frank O'Bannon on a seventeen-day trade mission to Poland, Russia, the Ukraine, and Yugoslavia. Kernan had known O'Bannon through politics, but not well. On the trip, he and O'Bannon established a friendship. In 1996 O'Bannon was the odds-on favorite to win the Democratic nomination for governor. He needed a running mate, but Kernan made it known to mutual friends that he did not want the job. He loved South Bend and wanted to finish his term as mayor. Kernan said he would rather that O'Bannon not ask him to run because he did not want to be put in the position of saying no to a good friend. By the end of May, O'Bannon still had not made his choice. Kernan and a persuasive O'Bannon met. Before he left, Kernan attempted to make his position clear. "I love what I do. I'm happy," he said. "If you ask me to do it, I'll do it. I'll give it everything I've got, but you know how I feel." When he got back to the hotel, he told Maggie what had happened and she said, "Thank God it's finally over." The following Monday, Memorial Day, the phone rang and it was O'Bannon. He asked. That November the O'Bannon/Kernan ticket was elected in a close vote.

In 1998 Lieutenant Governor Kernan was chosen as Notre Dame's commencement speaker and was awarded an honorary doctorate. In his address he cited an incident on the Notre Dame campus in 1922, when the Ku Klux Klan rallied in South Bend to show contempt for the Roman Catholic nature of the community and the university. Advising the graduates to confront this form of hatred, Kernan shared his belief that bigotry is the greatest barrier to living a life recognizing that we are all God's children, equally, every day.

The O'Bannon/Kernan collaboration worked well. As lieutenant governor, Kernan's assignments included commerce and agriculture. He also administered veteran affairs and played a meaningful role in a tax-restructuring initiative. In 1999 Lieutenant Governor Kernan launched the Veterans Outreach Initiative, which encouraged veterans to take advantage of the state and federal benefits they earned by serving their country.

Kernan, a reluctant candidate, was elected lieutenant governor of Indiana with the expectation that he would run for governor after O'Bannon had served his maximum eight years. It was therefore a surprise when Kernan announced in December 2002, midway through O'Bannon's second four years in office, that he would not be a candidate for governor in 2004. Instead, he would return to South Bend when his term was completed.

On September 7, 2003, Kernan and O'Bannon were in Chicago for a convention of Japanese businesses that had invested in the Midwest. O'Bannon was to attend the opening ceremonies the following day. But that Monday morning, Kernan received a call from O'Bannon's aide asking him to stand in for the governor. She said, "He's fine. They can hear him snoring, but he's got the door bolted. We're having trouble waking him up." Kernan felt something was wrong and went directly to O'Bannon's room. He got there just after hotel security personnel had called 911 and gained access to the room. O'Bannon was on the floor, having suffered a stroke. Although he was still alive, he never regained consciousness. O'Bannon died on September 13.

The world had changed for Kernan. On September 13, 2003, after being sworn in by Indiana Supreme Court justice Theodore Boehm, the man who did not even want to be lieutenant governor became the state's forty-eighth governor. Once again Kernan enjoyed public service. He relished using the office of governor to help others. His love of community stretched from Lake Michigan to the Ohio River. Shortly thereafter he announced that he would, in fact, run for governor in 2004.

Kernan had precious little time to establish his administration before he was faced with an election campaign in 2004. One of the decisions he is most proud of was the appointment of his lieutenant governor, Kathy Davis, the first woman to hold that office in Indiana. Davis had earned a bachelor's degree in mechanical engineering from the Massachusetts Institute of Technology and a master's degree from the Harvard Business School. She had served in the administrations of both O'Bannon and his predecessor, Evan Bayh, and had worked closely with then Lieutenant Governor Kernan to set up the 21st Century Research and Technology Fund to provide an economic incentive to fledgling companies. Her appointment was unanimously confirmed by the Indiana General Assembly in October 2003.

After losing a hard-fought election to Mitch Daniels and completing O'Bannon's term, Kernan returned to his beloved South Bend in 2005 with a new cause: Save the Silver Hawks, the Single A professional baseball team in his adopted hometown. The former owner had arranged to move the team to Marion, Illinois, before Kernan convinced him to sell to local ownership. Kernan formed an investment group to purchase the team, which he serves full time as president—a return to his lifetime love, baseball. He is also an adjunct professor in the political science department at Notre Dame.

Although no longer an elected official, Kernan returned to public service in June 2007 when Governor Daniels asked him and Indiana Supreme Court chief justice Randall Shepard to cochair a commission to examine the state's current system of local government and to make recommendations on reforming and reshaping it. The governor and Kernan agreed that Indiana needed to break the shackles of redundant government entities and emerge with an efficient plan to carry out the responsibilities of government. In making the appointment, the governor cited Kernan as a "distinguished and respected Hoosier." After hearing testimony and weighing various options, the commission made recommendations to streamline government that were heartily endorsed by the governor. If they had been enacted by the Indiana legislature, the proposals would have significantly reformed state government. But political reality is such that most of these reforms have not passed.

Kernan has always been willing to serve his fellow man. Although initially reluctant to enter political life, he has enjoyed it and is proud of his accomplishments. He advises our youth to find something they love and do it. "People are good at things they like to do," he said. Always in good humor, Kernan added, "smile when you are not laughing." Kernan, the warrior turned civic leader, loves America and Indiana. The feeling is mutual.

MARVIN JOHNSON

A Fighter and a Gentleman

Market Square Arena was rocking on Sunday afternoon, February 9, 1986. Spectators had turned out for the fight of the year, a battle for the World Boxing Association light-heavyweight championship of the world. It had snowed the night before and earlier that morning, and travel to downtown Indianapolis was a treacherous journey. No matter. A near-capacity crowd of more than ten thousand braved the winter chill. Seven bouts were scheduled, but few fans really cared about the undercard. They came to cheer hometown hero Marvin Johnson in the title bout. And cheer they did. Boxing fans are like no others, howling, jostling, and draining Budweisers. It warmed up quickly in MSA.

Twice before Johnson had reigned as light-heavyweight champion, only to lose each time in his first title defense. Johnson hungered to regain this championship and at age thirty-one—old for a boxer—he knew this could be his last opportunity. "That was the most important fight of my career," he recalled decades later. Johnson was ranked number one by the WBA and his opponent, Leslie Stewart, known as the Tiger from Trinidad, was ranked second. The title had been vacated by Michael Spinks in September when he had upset previously undefeated Larry Holmes to become the first light-heavyweight champion to win a heavyweight title.

15

In his dressing room Johnson went through his prefight routine, including getting rubbed down and dressed by his corner man and cousin, Willie Ray Johnson, known as Fab after a short-lived career as an entertainer. Fab began to put on Johnson's right shoe, but the southpaw stopped him. "Fab, you know how I like to do this. Put my left shoe on first: left shoe, right shoe, left glove, right glove." Fab did as he was instructed and laced it all up.

At 3:30 p.m. the fighters were summoned to the center of the ring as ABC commentator Al Michaels readied himself for the nationally televised fight. Johnson's hooded satin robe—sewn by his wife, Delores—was adorned with royal blue and white sequins, and as he moved around the ring they cast reflections of the arena lights over the partisan assemblage. The crowd rose in anticipation. The introduction of the fighters was followed by a frenzied chant, "MAR-VIN, MAR-VIN, MAR-VIN." Johnson's brother, Hank, commented that the emotion was so thick it felt like you could walk on it. The fight was scheduled for fifteen, three-minute rounds but not many expected the fight to go the distance. Of the combatants' combined sixty-four bouts, forty had ended by knockout.

Johnson, a gentleman on other occasions, was an animal in the ring. He charged out of his corner at the opening bell in search of a quick kill and pounded Stewart's face and body with numerous jarring blows that drew blood over his right eye. In the second round, Johnson used his right hand to force Stewart to the ropes, where he deployed a barrage of combination punches. Rhythmic drums from Trinidad were barely discernable over the electrified fans shouting "MAR-VIN, MAR-VIN, MAR-VIN."

Stewart, a confident fighter with fast hands and quick feet, came into the fight with a record of 18-0, including thirteen knockouts. The ordeal of the first two rounds left him undaunted. In the third round, Stewart rocked Johnson with a series of headshots that appeared to buckle the hometown hero's knees as he staggered back to his corner at the bell. Johnson said later, "He hurt me. I thought I had better start defending myself." In the fourth and fifth rounds, the boxers fought feverishly. Michaels wondered to the national audience whether Johnson, who had acquired the nickname "Pops" in deference to the seven-year age difference of the fighters, had the stamina to keep up the pace. Johnson answered that question by resuming the more aggressive role in the sixth round. He opened up a cut over Stewart's left eye. Both cuts bled profusely. Referee Frank O. Priami of Italy, who spoke no English, signaled a halt to the round while the ring physician wiped the bloody face of Stewart and examined the cuts. He allowed the fight to continue. Both fighters were relentless—Johnson sensing victory and Stewart, with limited vision, desperately searching for a knockout. Then, fifty-six seconds into the blood-splattered seventh round, Priami stopped the fight. It was Johnson by a technical knockout. With a record of 42-5, he became the first man to ascend to the light-heavyweight throne on three separate occasions.

Marvin L. Johnson was born on April 12, 1954, in Indianapolis to R. L. and Ruthie Mae Massey Johnson. R. L. never learned to read or write and worked construction most of his life as a hod carrier. Even his family did not know his given name. In spite of the fact that he did not finish elementary school, he was bright and respected by his peers. According to his oldest son, Hank, he loved the law and could have been an attorney. On days with bad weather, he enjoyed sitting in the courtroom and listening to lawyers arguing a case. Neighbors often asked him for legal advice. Ruthie was a housewife who was fully occupied with her nine children.

Johnson, who was fifth in line, was not as much introduced to boxing as he was initiated. The teenaged Hank would get on his knees and force seven-year-old Marvin to spar with him. Three of the five boys were boxers, and all three—Hank, Marvin, and Fenton—won local Golden Gloves championships as teenagers. Only Marvin became a professional.

Johnson attended Crispus Attucks High School, an all-black school in central Indianapolis. Named for the African American who died in the infamous Boston Massacre and became a martyr in the American Revolution, the school is most famous for its Oscar Robertson-led state championship basketball team of 1955. More importantly, Crispus Attucks earned national recognition for educational excellence and produced a number of business leaders and professionals in many fields. Johnson enjoyed Crispus Attucks and earned good grades. He wanted to play football for the high school team, but his social studies teacher, Graham Martin, discouraged him from participating for fear that he would incur an injury that would end his quest to make the Olympic boxing team.

On most afternoons after school, Johnson hung around the gym at Saint Rita's Police Athletic League Club, which adjoined the Saint Rita Catholic Church in the heart of the inner city. Johnson entered his first amateur tournament, the Indianapolis Golden Gloves, at age fifteen. Although sixteen was the minimum age for participants, they were not required to produce birth certificates. He entered in the light-heavyweight (178-pound limit) subnovice division and won. The following year he won the light-heavyweight open division, where the reward was a jacket with "Indianapolis Golden Gloves" written on the back. He proudly wore it to Attucks. That win also earned Johnson a trip to the nationals in Fort Worth, Texas, where he prevailed. Although Golden Gloves bouts consist of only three rounds of three minutes each, he won three of the five bouts by knockout. That same year he won the national Amateur Athletic Union light-heavyweight championship. He won several other amateur championships before turning professional.

After graduating from Attucks in 1971, Johnson devoted himself to the Saint Rita program under the tutelage of Colion "Champ" Chaney. Chaney was a professional heavyweight boxer during the Joe Louis era. He knew boxing and loved it. Johnson was confident that Chaney was the best fighter and the best teacher in the city. "I believed he was a man I could trust, and he had the experience to teach me all I needed to know," Johnson said. "He also had the ability to demonstrate his points, rather than just talk about them. He could teach you to slip or roll with a punch, show you why and how you got hit as you moved in or out on your opponent, and the thing I liked best—he did not try to change any boxer's natural style. I'm an aggressive fighter, and he did not change that or attempt to. He took what I had, and added to it."

Under Chaney, Johnson began to refine his distinctive style, a relentless attack meant to wear down, dominate, and beat up the opponent. Johnson always came to fight. He was an explosive puncher who could light it up for the entire round, as Hank said, "from ding to dong." A Chaney sign in the PAL Club dressing room said, "Be nice before and after the fight—not during."

In order to prevail the Johnson way, he had to be in better shape than his opponent. He was in the gym every day punching the bag for six to ten rounds, jumping rope, boxing, and running. In the mornings he ran up to twelve miles. In preparation for a bout, his routine would be to run in the morning, eat breakfast, and rest until it was time to go to the gym at midday. In the gym he followed Chaney's regimen, which included the speed bag, the heavy bag, jumping rope, sparring, and general exercise.

Johnson fought nineteen times before he lost as an amateur. In 1971, at the age of seventeen, he was defeated by Johnny Conteh in a three-round decision. Johnson was devastated. He ached for a rematch but it was never granted. Conteh, from Liverpool, England, was one of Britain's most successful boxers. He won the World Boxing Council light-heavyweight crown in 1974 and held it until 1978. According to Conteh's own account, his high living, excessive lifestyle brought about a premature decline in his talents.

A year after his first defeat, Johnson qualified for the U.S. Olympic team in the 165-pound class. The team was coached by Bobby Lewis, who had coached heavyweight George Foreman to a gold medal in the previous Olympiad. The 1972 Games were held in Munich, West Germany. Johnson was housed in the Olympic Village and remembered that access was unsecured. The West German Olympic Organizing Committee had encouraged an open and friendly atmosphere in the village to help erase memories of the militaristic image of wartime Germany, and, specifically, of the 1936 Berlin Olympics, which had been exploited by Nazi dictator Adolf Hitler for propaganda purposes. But the open access had a price. Members of the Israeli Olympic team were taken hostage and eventually murdered by Black September, a militant group of Palestinians. By the end of the ordeal, the terrorists had killed eleven Israeli athletes and coaches and one West German police officer. Five of the eight members of Black September were killed by police officers during a failed rescue attempt. At the time of the hostage-taking, the Munich Olympic Games were well into their second week. In the wake of the disaster, competition was suspended for the first time in modern Olympic history.

When the games resumed, Johnson earned a bronze medal, defeating Cuba's best fighter. He lost by a decision to the eventual gold medal winner, Vyacheslav Lemeshev of the Soviet Union. Johnson had bested the Russian six months earlier in a United States/Russian meet and was named the event's outstanding fighter. He was disappointed when he lost the rematch and had to settle for bronze, but he made no excuses. On his return home he received the key to the city from Indianapolis mayor Richard Lugar. Johnson turned pro the following May.

Family friend and fellow Attucks alumnus Hallie Bryant had been a professional athlete himself with the Harlem Globetrotters. He felt that Johnson needed mentors and referred him to Clarence Doninger, an attorney who assembled a cadre of Indianapolis businessmen to manage Johnson and support him through the early stages of his professional career. The group included Jack Appel, an amateur boxer who owned a successful insurance agency. Johnson readily accepted the arrangement.

As a professional, the first objective is to be noticed—ranked in the top fifty by a sanctioning body. In 1973, there were two, the WBA and the WBC, that performed the same function in direct competition with each other. Johnson's management group was ineffectual. They knew little of the "fight game" and failed to arrange bouts that would move their boxer up in the rankings. Doninger said, "I learned very quickly that this is the most unusual business, indeed. Some people are competent and trustworthy—many are not. It became apparent to us right away that the field was controlled by a few promoters who had access to the top contenders and you had to have a connection with somebody who could put on fights on a regular basis. We did not have it and failed." The group disbanded after a few local fights.

Johnson spent a frustrating year fighting a few small-time "club" bouts and just punching the bag. In desperation, he drove to the training camp of his favorite fighter, Muhammad Ali, in Miami to discuss his career with him and his trainer, Angelo Dundee. Ali, a fellow Olympian, was familiar with Johnson's success in Munich. He advised Johnson to work on his opposite side—to change his stance and fight like a right hander, mastering a left-hand lead. "When you get as good at fighting with the right hand as you are left-handed, then you and me will be the baddest men in the world," Ali told him. Johnson did not take that advice. He preferred the advantage accorded to southpaws, whose opposite attack side generally befuddles opponents.

Dundee was considered one of the greatest trainers of all time. He had trained World Welterweight Champion Carmen Basilio and was in the midst of a relationship with Ali that lasted until Ali's retirement in 1981. Dundee helped Johnson forge a relationship with J. Russell Peltz, a successful promoter and boxing director at the Philadelphia Spectrum, who in 2000 was inducted in the World Boxing Hall of Fame. From the time the Indianapolis group disbanded until the end of Johnson's career, Peltz promoted or was otherwise involved in almost every one of Johnson's fights. Under his tutelage Johnson began to move up in the rankings. But he was paid just $1,000 per fight, even after he broke into the top fifty. One reason for the meager pay was that light heavyweights did not attract the interest of the heavyweight bouts, and thus few were televised. Johnson fought every two to three months and was bothered by the fact that he did not fight more often. He needed to stay sharp. He trained hard during the interim and relied on the financial support of friends and family. According to Doninger, "Johnson did not get fights because guys did not want to fight him. He was one tough guy. I did not see anyone who was tougher than Marvin." At age twenty-one, Johnson broke into the top ten of light heavyweights, but still only made between $1,000 to $2,500 per fight.

In 1977 Johnson sustained his first professional loss when he was knocked out in the twelfth round by Matthew Franklin, later known as Matthew Saad Muhammad. The following year, after winning six of his next seven bouts, Johnson earned a date with Mate Parlov of Yugoslavia, the newly crowned WBC light- heavyweight champion. The bout was staged in Marsala, Italy. Parlov, also a southpaw, had won a gold medal in the light-heavyweight division in the 1972 Olympics. He was no match for Johnson. Johnson won by a knockout in the tenth round, earning his first championship and a purse of $50,000. That same year, he married his high school classmate, Delores. They have five children—none of whom became professional boxers.

Johnson was anxious to defend his title in front of his hometown fans. He granted the opportunity to Matthew Franklin before a home crowd in 1979, making $75,000. He lost his crown by knockout in the eighth round, and "just like that I was back to fighting for chump change," Johnson recalled. Still, he maintained his position as a top-ranked fighter and later that year was offered an opportunity to fight Victor Galindez from Argentina for the WBA light-heavyweight championship. It was a close fight until the tenth round, when Johnson caught Galindez with his favorite knockout combination: a right hook followed by an overhand left. Johnson knocked Galindez to the canvas and his corner surrendered. In March 1980, again on his first title defense, he lost to Eddie Gregory, later Eddie Mustafa Muhammad, in the eleventh round by a TKO.

After a fourth-round knockout loss to Michael Spinks in 1981, Johnson was depressed and needed to regroup. He did not fight for more than a year. Many observers thought he had quit the arena, but Johnson was not finished. He reeled off ten wins, most by knockout, through 1984 and was named comeback fighter of the year by *Ring* magazine, the so-called Bible of boxing. He won all four of his bouts in 1985 by knockout, setting up the fight with Leslie Stewart for the WBA light-heavyweight championship. Johnson tried to find videotapes to study Stewart but as he said then, "There's not much tape available on Stewart because he's not a real popular guy. I don't plan for him to be any more popular when he leaves town." At five feet, ten inches tall, Johnson gave away two and one-half inches of height and almost as much reach to the undefeated Stewart. After his seventh-round victory, Johnson embraced the losing fighter in the middle of the ring and wished him well. Stewart was not quite so gracious, claiming his cuts were the result of head butts. Johnson replied, "The cuts were caused by a left hook and a short right. When I land those left-right combinations sometimes fighters feel like they were hit with baseball bats, hammers, trucks or pick axes and who knows what." He was paid $100,000 for his efforts.

Johnson successfully defended his title in Indianapolis later that year, a thirteen-round TKO of Jean Marie Emebe of Cameroon. On May 23, 1987, Johnson granted Stewart a rematch in Port-of-Spain, Trinidad. It was to be Johnson's largest payday—$265,000. The match was staged outdoors on a hot, muggy Caribbean night. Announcing for the television audience again, Michaels confided to the eight or ten Johnson fans in attendance that he was worried that if Johnson won they would have difficulty exiting the stadium through a belligerent crowd. Johnson did not win. The fight was stopped on a TKO in the ninth round. Some commentators contend that Johnson overtrained for the bout. As Bruce "Mouse" Strauss, an All-American wrestler and nutrition expert quipped, "Strain on a young body builds; strain on an old body destroys." Indianapolis boxing promoter Fred Berns, who was in attendance at the bout agreed. "If Johnson did no training for three to six months and came off the street to fight Stewart in a six-rounder, it would be Marvin in three or less," said Berns. After the fight ended, a mob charged into the ring, threw beer cans, and taunted the ex-champion. He required a police escort to his locker room. On the Monday following the bout, Johnson met with the prime minister of Trinidad, who praised him for being a fine athlete. Johnson, the gentleman, replied that he appreciated the prime minister's hospitality and the hospitality of his people.

After that defeat, Johnson retired from boxing with a professional record of 43-6, including thirty-five knockouts. Boxing fans lamented his decision. Johnson's bouts exhilarated fans who knew that win or lose, someone was going to get hurt. Of his six losses he was knocked out five times. Chaney, who had never boxed for a championship, lived his dreams through Johnson and was especially sad. Johnson talked to Chaney many times before his coach died of Alzheimer's disease in May 2005. Chaney called Johnson just before he went into a nursing home and tried to convince him to come out of retirement and do it one more time.

Johnson does not dwell on his past as many retired athletes do. He does regret that he did not praise God for his success, saying "I think God should have been recognized more in my life during that time and I did not do it." When he was not in the ring, Johnson was employed at the Marion County Sheriff's Department as a corrections officer and later promoted to the rank of sergeant. When he retired from boxing, he said he wanted to get out of the fight business and turn his attention toward "making Indianapolis a better place to live," as a full-time member of the sheriff's department. He did exactly that. He also has been a television spokesman for various commercial enterprises including Eastgate Chrysler Plymouth, for whom he has appeared for almost thirty years.

After more than twenty years in retirement, Johnson remains a hometown hero. The Attucks High School museum honored him with a display that includes two of his championship belts and the blue-and-white sequined robe Johnson wore when he won the light-heavyweight championship for the third time—testimonies to a champion and a role model for Attucks students. According to Berns, the Indianapolis promoter, "No fighter was ever more loyal to his people and no fighter lived a cleaner life than Marvin."

Johnson advises those who aspire to become a professional boxer to work as hard as they can to get their bodies in tip-top condition because, "once your career is over, if you have taken care of your body like you should, then your body will take care of you in your older years. But if you go out there and fight those hard fights and you are not in the best of condition, then when you get to be an older man you are going to be a lot like those punch-drunk people who cannot half talk, cannot half walk. So be in your best condition or do not do it at all."

In 2008 Johnson received one of boxing's greatest recognitions—inclusion in the World Boxing Hall of Fame. At a ceremony in Los Angeles, he was inducted along with other boxing greats Lennox Lewis, Greg Haugen, and Parnell Whitaker. Always soft spoken, Johnson humbly accepted the honor, thanking those who helped him in his career, especially Delores. He said his wife was always there for him with encouragement and undying love and support—a love that has endured for almost forty years. It is Indiana who should thank this fighter and gentleman for representing the state with ferocity and grace.

EUGENE B. GLICK

Born to Build

Dumped in the Epinal commune on the northeastern coast of France with no prior combat experience, twenty-three-year-old army infantryman Eugene B. Glick found himself in one of the most intense campaigns in history. The assignment was to recapture several small villages, which had to be taken yard by yard in some of the fiercest fighting in World War II. The mission was clear to Glick: "Do my duty and avoid death."

Glick remembers November 11, 1944—Armistice Day—as particularly awful. "The shells were coming in thick and fast, and I saw a slit trench nearby, two feet deep. I figured it had ice on it, about two or three inches thick. A shell came in and I dove in," he said. "But the ice was only a half-inch thick, and I plunged through it into three or four inches of water. I lay there flat belly, face down, in the freezing water. Shells rained down and I was terrified that the shrapnel hitting in the trees would fall and kill or maim me. It seemed to last for hours, but I suppose it was only ten or fifteen minutes. When the shelling died down, I looked at my watch. Ten minutes to eleven. . . . I remember thinking, 'Wouldn't it be wonderful if World War II could end as World War I did, November 11, 1944?' Of course, it did not happen."

Still, he never forgot that day. And anytime he thinks he has it tough or things are not going well, he says to himself, "Glick, how does this

26

compare with November 11, 1944?" That day became the guiding star to him, the point of comparison for his life.

Eugene Biccard Glick was born on August 29, 1921, to Ruben "Ruby" Frank and Faye Biccard Glick. He came from an Indianapolis Jewish family that encouraged him in both entrepreneurialism and helping others, living the life of a normal midwestern teenager until he was drafted into the second great conflict of the twentieth century.

His desire to build—if only his own business future—got its start during his school years. In elementary school, Glick built one of the largest *Indianapolis Times* newspaper routes in the city, and at Shortridge High School in Indianapolis he was an ace advertising salesman for the *Daily Echo*, one of the nation's preeminent high school papers. "I canvassed the school to find out where the students' relatives worked. These were prime prospects, along with the recent grads of the school, or parents whose kids had just graduated or were soon to come into the school," Glick recalled. "We put a little tag onto the ad which let students purchasing things at advertisers' stores get a gift for coming in. You have to develop a unique selling proposition in any sales enterprise. Find out why you are different, better than the others and emphasize that." He further developed his business skills at Indiana University by setting up a bus shuttle service.

Glick began college as the Nazis invaded Poland on September 1, 1939. News of the growing turmoil bombarded even the fairly isolated college campus: the fall of France, the German invasion of Russia, and the attack on Pearl Harbor. Glick accelerated his class work, graduating in December 1942 and reporting for duty at Fort Hayes in Columbus, Ohio. After basic training and stints as a combat instructor, Second Lieutenant Glick was assigned to F Company in the Seventh Army and sent overseas in June 1944. For the rest of that year, he was in constant contact with the enemy.

At the end of April 1945 Glick and his fellow soldiers liberated Dachau, the Nazi concentration camp outside Munich, Germany. By the time he arrived, the German guards had fled and Russian soldiers were en route. "I had known in general how cruel the Nazis were to certain segments of the human race, to Jews in particular, and I certainly did not want to be captured by them," Glick remembered. "But almost no one in that advancing force knew what we, the first group to liberate Dachau, would find there. Russian prisoners were in the camp, and they tried to tell us about the mass murders there." He saw the ovens and the crematoria. He saw the gas chambers, where Nazi guards herded masses of people into make-believe showers. Russian prisoners took him to a huge pit, and in sign language and charades showed him how their captors shot prisoners at the pit's edge and pushed them in. Worst of all were the railroad coal cars, still on the tracks. They were filled not with coal, but with human bodies overlapping, limbs sticking out, and heads hanging over the edge.

The next day, when the Jeeps arrived with the soldiers' backpacks, Glick grabbed his, removed his camera, and returned to photograph what he had seen the day before. He resolved to have the unspeakable scene recorded, for himself and the outside world. When he took the film—lots of it—to a Munich shop to be developed, a pretty German girl was behind the counter. She was very upset with the pictures. "Why did you take such terrible pictures?" she asked. "They would show the German people in a bad light." She wanted to destroy the photographs rather than returning them to him. He was just short of threatening her when she finally handed them over.

Glick sent the photos home to his parents. In 1977 the U.S. Memorial Holocaust Commission, the U.S. Information Agency, and Emory University all wrote to Glick, stating they had found his name in the army archives as a liberator of the concentration camp and asked if he had any pictures of Dachau. He sent photos to Emory and to the Holocaust Commission, but received no response from either. Years later, Glick was alone, watching a World War II documentary on late-night television, when a story came on about the liberation of the concentration camps. There were pictures of Dachau. Glick exclaimed to himself, "My God, those are my pictures!" His name was listed in the credits, confirming the origin.

After victory in Europe, Glick returned to Indianapolis as a proud veteran. Deciding he had done enough to contribute to tearing down, even in a good cause, he resolved to commit himself to the process of building not only his own future but America's for the better. He was introduced to Marilyn Koffman, who lived down the street. After an eighteen-month courtship, they married in January 1947. She became his business partner as well, helping him start his building business. They had four daughters.

While working at a bank, where he helped returning veterans finance new homes through the GI Bill, Glick visited a building site with one of his loan customers. "It was a day in spring, and I had been walking around the site, watching the progress of the home," he recalled. "The earth was freshly turned, beautiful, with a wholesome scent to it. Lumber was there, freshly sawn in big piles. It looked so neat and so new and so promising." He looked at the blueprints for the home, thought about the young, newly married couple who would be occupying it with so many dreams forming themselves there on that building site, and decided he wanted to build homes.

In 1947 the young Glicks formed Indianapolis Homes, a small company that began by building one-story, affordable dwellings. Soon it was developing streets of houses, and even total neighborhoods, all over the city. Later Glick built and managed apartments. What followed had its roots in the unique Glick personality and business mission. His success boils down to his adherence to five guiding principles, which he set forth in his autobiography, *Born to Build*:

• True entrepreneurship requires a total commitment of time, resources and energy. "Entrepreneurship is second nature to me," he said. "I'd loved it as a paper boy, as a high school ad salesman, and as a bus travel agent. I knew that whatever I did, I was going to give it all I had, and I was destined to love it or whatever I went into, and never to consider it as work."

• Success in business can best be judged by the contribution one makes to society. "There is no doubt that I was an idealist; many in my generation were and are," Glick said. "The contribution I wanted to make to society was part of the everlasting thrill. And my own ability to help some of my fellow travelers on planet Earth to achieve better lives has rewarded me greatly."

• Quality matters. Glick believes a business person should always deliver a bit more than is required. If the young people whose homes he was building wanted special touches—a brick façade, stone walk, or extra space in the bedroom, for example, he found a way to design them inexpensively. In fact, he began outthinking his customers and providing amenities and luxuries before they asked. Shoddy workmanship and employees who shirked their duty were never allowed.

• Expect excellence. As he built and managed properties, Glick always had his eyes open for improvements in the operation. He attended tenants' meetings and acted on their concerns. He inspected and graded his properties regularly and later he instituted hotlines and e-mail comment systems to help deliver the best results in the business. Glick's intense focus on excellence in all things was clearly demonstrated during the marathon Monday-night management meetings he instituted in the 1960s. After eating steaks, department heads participated in a carefully orchestrated free-for-all exchange of ideas on business problems and issues. The group included Bernard Landman, a brilliant lawyer and tactician aptly named "The Wizard;" Max Thurston, the company's chief financial officer; and Jim Bisesi, who was well seasoned despite his youth. The maestro himself, Glick, led the discussions, which sometimes lasted until 1 a.m.

• The true meaning of a business experience is reflected in the faces of individual men and women whose lives are improved or uplifted or changed by what you do. One of Glick's greatest joys has been to go to birthday parties at the subsidized apartment units his company has built, helping elderly residents blow out their candles and seeing the pleasure of these folks who now have comfortable homes with bright, modern kitchens—and helpers at hand if they need them.

Glick recalled the initiative of Lyndon Johnson's Great Society to finance affordable and decent housing for the poor and elderly. He wanted to erect apartment units supported by the subsidy, but Indianapolis did not accept the federal government's largesse. Glick met with Indianapolis mayor John Barton, who explained that he was so short staffed there was nobody to write the enabling legislation. So the businessman hired an attorney to write the necessary provisions, which the city council passed into law. "You should never be afraid to take a lead, blaze a trail, think of unusual solutions to perplexing problems and follow through like a bulldog until you get results," Glick said. He is proud that he was willing to think beyond the norm to settle a problem, even pursuing heel-dragging government officials into their hotel rooms and confronting them in restaurants to sign papers as they had promised.

Still, Glick's sense of humor has not allowed him to get carried away with all this idealism. He is the first to acknowledge that his service to mankind through affordable housing has truly enriched him in multiple ways. He achieved great wealth, for one thing, which has allowed him to do all he ever wanted to do. And for that he is immeasurably grateful. "I don't want to discount the wisdom of comedian Joe E. Lewis, who would look out at the audience and say, 'Folks, I've been poor and I've been rich, and I want to tell you that rich is better.' And I can say the same," said Glick. His financial success came through a combination of the on-site construction supervision that resulted in a high-quality product and Glick's own shrewd business acumen. The formula served him well as the company produced an increasingly sophisticated housing mix, progressing from those small box houses just after the war to national homes in the 1950s and 1960s and to large-scale cooperatives and apartment complexes in the 1970s and 1980s.

Another quality that has helped assure Glick's success has been his ability to remain calm in the face of the many adversities and even calamities of the typical business life. Perhaps reflecting upon his experience on November 11, 1944, he is absolutely placid when confronting setbacks or insults that would adversely affect the demeanor of most businessmen. One day, seven women demanded to see Glick and complained that their move-in dates were six weeks behind schedule. They were livid and let Glick know it. He was unflappable, replying calmly, "You know, you ladies are absolutely correct. If I were in your place I'd be even more vociferous than you have been. I want to tell you that we are going to do everything in our power to get you in just as soon as possible. I am sincerely sorry for what has happened." The ladies looked at each other before one finally spoke up, "We wanted to be mad at you when we came over here. You've taken the wind out of our sails."

Looking back at the building phase of his life, Glick considers the most stimulating and rewarding projects to be the government-subsidized apartments that he built—scores of them around the country, many financed through the government's Housing and Urban Development program. He changed the model for low-income housing nationally by innovatively placing his units in suburban areas close to amenities and cultural opportunities, instead of in the inner city. He wanted these modest living units to "take care of people well." Focusing on the disadvantaged was a choice; many in the construction business at the time were building elegant luxury apartments. As Glick recalled, "We did not yearn to put up fancy apartments—there were plenty of people to build deluxe units. I was not interested in the marble bathroom trade. And my interest was not piqued just because the government was giving money for subsidies. I wanted to see those who never had advantages finally have a few."

The results were impressive. By the time the last building project was completed in 1991, Glick had constructed thirty thousand housing units. Although the company stopped major new construction then, it continued to manage apartments. At the end of 2010, the Gene B. Glick Company managed approximately eighteen thousand units in ten states.

Today, the Glick Company stands as a model for the successful creation of both market-rate and subsidized housing. Although the bricks-

and-mortar building effort was remarkable, the community building that has come from their philanthropic efforts is the ultimate payoff for Glick and his wife and partner of more than sixty years. Eugene and Marilyn are unparalleled donors to the growth of agencies that work for the public good. Buildings and institutions all around Indiana bearing the Glick name are testaments to the charitable instincts of a couple that has given more than $150 million to charity.

The Eugene and Marilyn Glick Family Foundation, formally established in 1982, was a direct outgrowth of years of an ever-developing philosophy of giving. When Glick was a boy he used to watch his mother and father "take care" of people. Even during the Great Depression, when Ruby Glick did not have money to pay some of his own bills, he covered the rent for others. "My mother was a champion of the disadvantaged," Glick recalled. "She believed pure and simple that all people are created equal, and that they should have equal chances to succeed in life." When the foundation was established, helping the disadvantaged was one of its primary goals. In its early years the foundation contributed to Big Brothers and Big Sisters of Central Indiana, Boys and Girls Clubs of Indianapolis, United Way of Central Indiana, and the Children's Bureau.

Many other charitable projects were directly connected with Glick's boyhood joys. One of his happiest memories of childhood was the management of a pickup baseball team composed of neighborhood boys, including his own relatives. It seemed a natural evolution that when he had the means to help boys and girls develop character, he funded a much-needed Little League field on the far east side of Indianapolis. He also leased a helicopter to take the team members for rides. Later, Glick chaired the successful campaign to raise funds for a central regional Little League headquarters. Glick also had enjoyed art and music projects in his school, and he was pleased to support the arts in Indianapolis through contributions to groups, including the Indianapolis Symphony Orchestra, Indianapolis Museum of Art (on whose board Glick also served), Indianapolis Art Center, Indianapolis Opera, Indiana Repertory Theatre, and Young Audiences of Indiana.

Glick's pet project in the 1980s and 1990s was one that combined his interest in sports and entrepreneurship with his desire to help the disadvantaged. In the 1980s city leaders noticed a problem with unemployed teenagers getting into trouble and drafted Glick to help. He and the foundation set up Pro-100, an on-the-job training program for high schoolers. Youths were hired to do landscaping at public golf courses and schools, and they also were taught how to apply for jobs and handle business procedures. "I took a lot of pride in those early days," Glick said, "meeting with the young workers and maybe coaching them on how to apply for a job. And later, I've loved hearing how some of them went to West Point, joined the police force of big cities, or got other good jobs and found meaningful places in society." The Pro-100 program has served more than two thousand teens.

Although it is difficult to fully recount the broad array of the Glicks' giving to causes of all kinds in Indianapolis and elsewhere, several remarkable examples demonstrate their commitment to health care, education, and the arts.

The Glicks have given to hospitals, medical research centers, and community health services alike. A $30 million donation to IU to establish the Eugene and Marilyn Glick Eye Institute will fulfill their dream of helping understand the causes of blindness. Marilyn was a founder of People of Vision in Indianapolis, and both Glicks have been particularly active in blindness-prevention research.

In the past ten years the Glick Foundation has donated to the Children's Museum of Indianapolis, public broadcasting station WFYI, Brebeuf Jesuit School, Ball State University, Butler University, Purdue University, Ivy Tech State College, and Marian University. Support for the Arthur Glick Jewish Community Center in Indianapolis perpetuates Glick's love of and respect for his older brother, who died of meningitis as a child. Another favorite among the scores of educational institutions benefiting from his generosity is the Gene B. Glick Junior Achievement Education Center. Glick, an inductee in JA's Central Indiana Business Hall of Fame, takes pride in visiting the Indianapolis center and chuckling at children who arrive on buses, role playing quite seriously in jobs as artisans, bankers, and newspaper reporters. He is particularly gratified that others also have supported the JA project. "We want to aid causes that reflect our own interests and to do unique projects that won't get done in any other way," he said, "but we also want to be sowing seeds that others can cultivate. Let those that come after us take these efforts up. That is the only way these good causes will continue."

Glick also appreciates his personal history as a member of one of the city's respected Jewish families. A recent $8 million gift to the Indiana Historical Society established the Eugene and Marilyn Glick Indiana History Center. Part of the center's active program is the Indiana Experience, which allows visitors to travel back in time to relive Indiana history, complete with three-dimensional sets and interactive activities.

The Glicks also played a major role in the development of the downtown Indianapolis Cultural Trail. Glick explained his single-minded goal, one he had thought about for years: "I am proud of my service in World War II. We did our job and did it well. To honor that and the service of other veterans, we have impressive world war memorials in Indianapolis's downtown. But, I asked myself, where are the tributes to the progress of mankind?" So, working with the Central Indiana Community Foundation and city leaders, the Glicks helped scope out the trail, contributed $15 million to its development, and funded architectural and construction expenses for twelve special sculptures honoring "luminaries" who have worked for the world's betterment. Glick and his family enjoyed choosing those contributors to peace and the good of the world. The statues will be placed at key points along the trail, running for eight miles through downtown Indianapolis and passing various cultural and historical places of interest. "My favorite for the list of contributors to mankind is Jonas Salk," Glick said. "Just think of what he did with the polio vaccine. But we also listed Martin Luther King Jr., Andrew Carnegie, Thomas Edison, and Susan B. Anthony among our choices." In honor of the Glicks' contribution, the trail officially is named Indianapolis Cultural Trail, A Legacy of Gene and Marilyn Glick.

This man who, with Marilyn, is probably the most generous philanthropist in recent Indianapolis history, remains understated about the foundation's contributions but realistic about the responsibility it bears. "Of course it is satisfying, but it is also a lot of work," Glick said. "I've always liked the wise man's saying: 'To amass a sum of money is in any man's power; to give it away intelligently is very difficult.'"

The foundation's assets exceed $150 million, but Glick feels Indianapolis has given to him far more than he can ever give back. "I am so full of gratitude. I can start by expressing my thanks to all the people in our business," he said. "There is no real way to thank adequately all of the officers and workers in the Glick Company, who have dedicated their hearts to our projects. Beyond that, there are the folks in Indianapolis who are honest, decent, full of appreciation for services and blessings, and heartwarming in their personalities. Indianapolis is a fine place to build a life."

When NBC News anchor Tom Brokaw was interviewing prospects for what would become his best-selling book on everyday heroes of World War II, his representative picked up *Born to Build* and said, "I think Mr. Brokaw ought to take a look at this man's story." The tale she was reading, a part of the description of the post-Normandy campaign across Germany, sold Brokaw on using Glick as an example in *The Greatest Generation*. Brokaw's 1998 narrative became one of the most popular nonfiction books of the decade.

From the years when he helped dismantle Nazi Germany to today, when he is completing a career of business achievement and giving, Glick's life has always been active and full. He is grateful to his town. But the town he so commends also should give him a tip of a construction worker's hard hat for being one of its master builders.

Richard Lugar

Statesman

History wrote a shameful chapter on April 4, 1968, the thirty-sixth birthday of Indianapolis mayor Richard Lugar. The young mayor had intended to celebrate with his family, but Democratic presidential candidate Robert F. Kennedy made a campaign stop in Indianapolis that evening. Just after 6 p.m., civil rights leader Martin Luther King Jr. was felled by an assassin's bullet. King, at thirty-nine, was not much older than Lugar. In 1964 he had won the Nobel Peace Prize for his leadership of the non-violent protests in the civil rights movement. The prize citation praised King as the first person in the Western world to have shown that a struggle can be waged without violence, yet he died a violent death and that death sparked waves of violence throughout the country.

After learning of King's death, and in spite of the fact that Lugar expressed concern for his safety, Kennedy insisted that he keep his appointment with the citizens of Indianapolis at Seventeenth and Broadway Streets in the heart of the community, an area with a high crime rate and a potential sparking point for racial tension. Kennedy exhorted the predominately black audience to "replace that violence, that stain of bloodshed that has spread across our land, with an effort to understand, compassion and love." In his brief speech, he lauded King and compared the pain that his audience was suffering to that which filled

his heart on the assassination of his brother, President John F. Kennedy.

In the aftermath of the assassination, civil unrest affected more than 110 cities throughout the United States. Kennedy's speech, no doubt, had a calming effect on the black community in Indianapolis that night, but it was also through Lugar's efforts that the hostility that plagued the rest of the nation did not erupt in the Indiana capital in the days to come.

Shortly after his election, Lugar had befriended and established a close working relationship with a number of local black activists. Those activists witnessed Kennedy's speech and, in deference to the mayor, ensured that Indianapolis acted in a sophisticated, peaceful manner. They corralled other young activists and persuaded them that the black community would be better served by working with this charismatic mayor. The day after King's death, Lugar implemented a strategy that he characterized as a street corner/church basement campaign. He met with the pastors of the black churches. He walked the streets with the people, visiting, greeting, and reassuring them that peaceful dialogue would prevail. For the next ten days he appeared on television every evening. As the United States was set on fire, Indianapolis was calm. The statesmanship evidenced by Lugar in response to this catastrophic event has characterized him throughout his career as one of the most lauded and trusted members of the U.S. Senate.

Richard Green Lugar, a fifth-generation Hoosier, was born on April 4, 1932, the oldest of Marvin and Bertha Lugar's three children. Marvin, a graduate of Purdue University's School of Agriculture and a farmer, also earned a living as a livestock broker at the Indianapolis Stockyards, facilitating the sale of cattle and hogs in exchange for a fee. Bertha was a housewife whose father, Thomas L. Green, was an entrepreneur and inventor who founded a business on the west side of Indianapolis that manufactured bakery machinery. Marvin and Bertha were interested in politics, although neither of them ever ran for office. Lugar remembered listening to the radio with his father early one morning in 1940 as Wendell Willkie won the Republican nomination for president of the United States.

The year before Lugar was born, his father purchased the family farm, 604 acres in Decatur Township that represented Lugar's first introduction to capitalism. Years later, Marvin offered young Dick and his brother, Thomas, an investment opportunity. For thirteen dollars, they could plant an acre of winter wheat and reap the profits when the wheat was harvested. Six weeks after the wheat was in the ground, untimely rains caused the White River, which formed the eastern boundary of the farm, to rise over the levy and engulf the wheat field. Marvin informed the boys one Sunday afternoon that they had been wiped out. The crop and the thirteen dollars were lost.

The following year, Marvin suggested that the boys could raise money toward their college education by investing in a sow that would have pigs that could be sold at a profit. The brothers were skeptical. They had been down that trail before. Nevertheless, they went through with the investment of less than ten dollars and watched the sow very carefully. When the sow had piglets, the boys counted them all and made sure they stayed alive. Lugar does not recall the return on that successful endeavor, but he does remember that it was a valuable lesson—and an experience from which Lugar could draw while serving as chairman of the U.S. Senate Committee on Agriculture, Nutrition, and Forestry.

At Shortridge High School in Indianapolis, Lugar participated in many sports, including freshman football, quarterbacking the team that won the city title. As a sophomore reserve, he weighed a scant 135 pounds and was called by the coach "Little Elusive" because he dodged, weaved, and otherwise escaped the grasp of larger opponents. Lugar confided that fear was a motivating factor. He also ran track and played on the golf team. Lugar began piano lessons at age five and while in high school became proficient enough to improvise and compose. He loved music and regularly attended performances of the Indianapolis Symphony Orchestra with his family. He also was an Eagle Scout and the valedictorian of his 1950 graduating class.

Lugar always sought to imagine improvement in any situation and was eager to lead—to bring about change. He ran for junior class president and lost. Undaunted, he ran again his senior year and lost once more. In his later quest for public service, Lugar lost more elections but always demonstrated the resilience and perseverance that ultimately took him to victory.

When the time came, Lugar looked for a liberal arts college of medium size where he would be able to participate in athletics, journalism, debate, and musical performance. He needed to find a college that was within driving distance to Indianapolis because of his father's poor health. When he received an offer of a full tuition, four-year scholarship from Denison University in Granville, Ohio, the choice was made. With potential business and political careers in mind, he chose a major in economics and a minor in political science. Lugar graduated first in his class from Denison in 1954, earning Phi Beta Kappa recognition. At Denison he rekindled his taste for elected office. During his junior year, Lugar was voted co-president of the student body—a co-presidency of one man and one woman. His counterpart was Char Smeltzer, who was quoted as saying to friends that she fully expected to exercise her co-partnership in this endeavor. It was the beginning of a long romance. They were married in 1956 and had four sons: Mark, Bob, John, and David.

The year he graduated from Denison, Lugar was named a Rhodes Scholar at Oxford University. He spent two years at Pembroke College in Oxford, England. Toward the end of his Oxford experience, Lugar had an abundance of personal time. He wrote a novel but failed to find a publisher. (He later said that was a good thing and that he made sure he had all of the copies.) Lugar also thought about the world and its many talented citizens—and contradictions. He felt a growing desire to enter politics and perhaps one day run for Congress. He also thought about his 2-S student deferment—which spared him from military service as long as he remained in school—the uneasy Korean War armistice, and his country. And he made a thoughtful decision, to go to the American Embassy in London to enlist in the armed forces. With eagerness to see much more of the world and anticipation of substantial sea duty, he volunteered to serve in the U.S. Navy. After earning an honors degree in politics, philosophy, and economics in 1956, he was accepted for officer's candidate school. A few weeks later, his father died. While awaiting his induction, Dick and Char Lugar occupied one of the old houses on the Lugar farm, chased mice, made sure that the livestock did not run over the road and generally tried to hold the farm together.

After completing officer candidate school with a rank of ensign, Lugar entered the Navy Intelligence School. In 1957 Admiral Arleigh Burke, chief of naval operations, established a briefing theater on the "E" Ring of the Pentagon, to which he invited fifty admirals, members of Congress, the cabinet, and others to attend an intelligence briefing at 8 o'clock every morning. A number of aides were plucked from the navy, including Bobby Ray Inman and Don Harvey, both of whom became admirals, and Lugar. Their job was to come in after midnight, read what Lugar referred to as "the secrets of secrets" of the country, and prepare for the intelligence briefing. Occasionally, after a briefing, he was ordered by Admiral Burke to brief President Dwight Eisenhower by remote control from the White House room where Franklin Roosevelt had held fireside chats. It had space for graphics and maps and other materials that were made available to the President. This was a heady assignment for a lad in his twenties, and he preformed it well. Burke was impressed.

Burke believed that Lugar had a promising career in the navy and implored him to extend his enlistment, but Lugar was compelled for family reasons to accept an honorable discharge at the end of his hitch. His grandfather's factory was losing money and was threatened with potential bankruptcy, and the family farm was burdened with debt left over from Marvin's last days. So in 1960, after more than three years of active duty, Lugar mustered out. His relationship with Burke endured, however. When Lugar was elected to public office, Burke was counted on as a mentor in world affairs.

Lugar, pressed into running the family business with his brother, Tom Lugar, and saving the farm, had no professional education for either endeavor. He had not contemplated this career turn. Liberal arts and military service did not prepare him for manufacturing baking machinery and the science of agriculture—growing corn and beans. Nevertheless, he persevered.

In 1963 a group of citizens from the west side of Indianapolis implored Lugar to run for the Indianapolis Public Schools board. The group was concerned that west-side schools were not receiving their fair share of revenue and attention. The citizens group did not inspire confidence in making their pitch. They closed their appeal with some brutal honesty for their would-be candidate: "You are probably far too young but you are about all we've got." Lugar was thirty-one. He was not even sure where the school board met, not to mention what they did. He had no idea how to go about getting elected, if one had such an ambition. He knew that although business at the factory and farm were improving, it was not exactly the right time. Nonetheless, after talking to Char and realizing that one of his sons was about to enter Indianapolis Public Schools, he accepted the challenge. In the midst of this consideration, President John F. Kennedy was assassinated. This was a traumatic period for most Americans, and certainly for Lugar. With the same sense of patriotism that drove him to enlist in the navy, he felt that he was meant to do his share in Indiana. In the school board election of May 1964 the winners were the top seven vote gainers. Lugar came in second behind Gertrude Page, an African American widow. He became passionately involved and spent an abnormal amount of time in school board work.

Lugar's first controversy on the school board was the federally supported school breakfast program. Many latchkey children attended school with nothing to eat. Lugar felt that a school breakfast program was necessary to nourish the children, but Indianapolis had an absolute doctrine of refusing federal aid for any program. By a bare majority, the school board adopted the breakfast program and bore harsh criticism, particularly from the Chamber of Commerce, which acted as though this was unconscionable—but the students got breakfast.

In 1966 popular *Indianapolis Times* columnist Irving Lebowitz wrote that it would be wonderful if someone like Lugar were mayor of Indianapolis. Lugar began to think "Why not?" and declared himself a candidate. He articulated his image of a great Indianapolis in the future, a city attractive to students, businesses, and tourists with a unified outlook in the central city and the suburbs. Republican Party committee chairman Keith Bulen chastised Lugar, "Dick, you should never, never admit that you have ambition to run for office. You wait to be asked." Lugar nevertheless survived the GOP primary against former mayor Alex Clark and struggled to victory against incumbent John Barton, 53 percent to 47 percent. He resigned his school board position and took office in 1968 at the age of thirty-five.

The most significant achievement of the Lugar administration was Unigov, a concept that extended the borders of the old city of Indianapolis to the Marion County line and unified the city and county into one government. Needing legislative approval and the signature of the governor, Lugar undertook a vigorous campaign throughout the state, meeting with most members of both houses of the legislature. Unigov was passed and signed by Governor Edgar Whitcomb in 1970. It proved to be a boon for the growth of the city. Indianapolis vaulted from twenty-sixth to the twelfth-largest city in the country. Once outlying buildings became part of Indianapolis and were placed on the tax rolls. In five of the eight years that Lugar was mayor, he reduced property taxes. According to Lugar, the only way a city can remain whole is with a vital center, as well as vital suburbs.

In 1970, at the invitation of President Richard Nixon, Lugar attended an international conference at NATO headquarters in Brussels, Belgium. Energized and enriched by the conference, Lugar invited the mayors of the world to come to Indianapolis the following year for the first international conference on cities. Planeloads came from Europe, Japan, and Mexico. The ethnic groups in Indianapolis entertained the dignitaries from around the world. Reflecting his growing national reputation, Lugar was elected president of the National League of Cities in 1971 and was chosen to be the keynote speaker at the 1972 Republican National Convention.

Lugar was reelected mayor in 1971, but because Indiana law limited the mayor's office to two consecutive terms, he could not run again. He began to think about his lifelong ambition to serve in Congress, but he had learned his lesson and kept a low profile. It worked. Party regulars "persuaded" Lugar to run for the nomination that was decided via convention in 1974. The fortunes of Republican candidates for Congressional races were largely tied to Nixon's travails about Watergate. A poll had shown that if Lugar would run in the 1974 election, he would lose by eight percentage points to incumbent Senator Birch Bayh. When

Nixon resigned the polls showed Lugar and Bayh even, but when President Gerald Ford pardoned Nixon, Lugar's number nosedived. The election was a setback. Lugar failed to carry Marion County and lost by four points to Bayh.

Still, the 1976 senatorial election was on the horizon. The incumbent, Vance Hartke, also a naval veteran, stood for reelection. Gene Sease, president of Indiana Central University (now known as the University of Indianapolis) invited Lugar to teach courses in political science and ethics in the morning, enabling him to campaign the rest of the day and the evening. Lugar defeated former Governor Whitcomb in the primary and won the general election with 59 percent of the vote. Lugar packed up his family, which by then included Char and the four boys, and moved to Washington, D.C. He took with him a trusted member of his mayoral administration, twenty-seven-year-old Mitch Daniels, who signed on as chief of staff. Lugar's popularity with Hoosiers grew. In 2006 he was elected to an Indiana-record sixth term with 87 percent of the popular vote.

Throughout his career, Lugar's daring and innovative leadership has rallied his colleagues on the important issues of the day. In 1985, as chairman of the Senate's Foreign Relations Committee, Lugar offered legislation that imposed sanctions on South Africa during its time of apartheid. He met with President Ronald Reagan, who reluctantly indicated that he would not sign the bill. He offered no explanation. It was the only Reagan veto on a foreign policy question that was overruled by Congress. Nelson Mandela, an antiapartheid activist who became president of South Africa after twenty-seven years in prison, delivered a dramatic and touching speech to a joint session of Congress in 1990. At a lunch afterwards, he reminisced, "I was sitting in my cell. I realized I was losing my wife and my marriage. I was losing the affection of my children. I was losing everything. I thought [English Prime Minister Margaret] Thatcher was going to help, but she turned her back. . . . Only the United States' Congress came to the rescue and saw South Africa and the future." According to Lugar, one of his crowning achievements as a senator was to help bring down apartheid, free Mandela, and preserve the relationship between the United States and South Africa. "It put the United States on the right side of history," he said. The rift with Reagan did not endure. In 1988, his last year as president, Reagan referred to Lugar in a recorded endorsement as the Senate's leading intellect, a great Hoosier, and a great American.

Lugar also played a pivotal role in the 1986 Philippine election that brought Corazon Aquino to power. As the head of the American election-observation team, he recognized Aquino as the legitimate winner and spotlighted corrupt activities of supporters of former president Ferdinand Marcos, ultimately convincing Reagan to back Aquino.

But perhaps the most important legacy of Lugar's senatorial career is the partnership with then-Senate Armed Services Committee chairman Sam Nunn (D-Georgia) that resulted in the 1991 Nunn-Lugar Cooperative Threat Reduction Program. It would seem unusual only to those who are not familiar with the statesmanship of Lugar that an Indiana Hoosier with agricultural roots should be on the forefront of nuclear weapons containment. Lugar was alerted to this issue while serving on an arms-control observer group in Geneva, Switzerland, in 1986. With the fall of the Soviet Union in 1991, Lugar saw the grave proliferation risk presented by its vast arsenal of nuclear, chemical, and biological weapons. In the old Soviet Union no one attempted to invade the nuclear spaces, but with the threat of anarchy in the early 1990s there were potentially renegade military personnel who might know how to deliver nuclear weapons to places that would pay them a fortune.

Nunn and Lugar went to see Russian president Boris Yeltsin. According to Lugar, Yeltsin ordered them to tell Ukrainian president Leonid Kravchuk that "he was going to bomb the hell out of them if they didn't give up their nuclear weapons." At the time, Ukraine was estimated to be the third-largest nuclear power in terms of weaponry. Lugar estimated that under Nunn-Lugar, the United States spent about $750 million for technicians, armed forces for security, and foreign aid in the Ukraine to remove nuclear material. Today the Ukraine is nuclear free. Lugar witnessed the Ukraine administration blowing up a thirteen-story silo that housed missiles and vividly remembers that on the fifth floor there were pictures of cities in the United States, perhaps targets. Nunn-Lugar initiatives have deactivated about six thousand nuclear warheads. The Nunn-Lugar program was nominated for the Nobel Peace Prize.

Stimulated by his experiences as chairman of the Senate Foreign Relations Committee in 1985 and 1986, Lugar wrote, *Letters to the Next President*, in which he offered guidance on numerous issues, particularly foreign policy. In 1995 Lugar placed himself as a candidate for the Republican nomination for president. The announcement of his candidacy on April 19, 1995, coincided exactly with the bombing of the federal building in Oklahoma City, one of the most significant acts of terrorism on American soil. It erased Lugar from the front page of the newspapers. He looks back at his failed bid as a beneficial experience that gave him the chance to meet people throughout the country for the better part of a year. His high-water mark was the 14 percent of the vote he received in the state of Vermont. Although Lugar has been mentioned as a potential candidate in subsequent presidential campaigns, he has politely declined to run again.

Lugar believes that the reliance upon foreign oil is one of the greatest challenges the United States faces, calling Americans' excessive reliance on oil "the albatross of national security." In fact, he sees energy dependency as one of the biggest threats—if not the biggest threat—to our environment, our economy, our way of life, and our position in the world. Lugar advocates a difficult but necessary transition to alternate energy sources, including solar, wind, nuclear, and water power, and he has supported a number of policies to stimulate this transition. He feels that he needs to be a continuing outspoken critic of our energy policy for the rest of his career.

In 1991 Lugar received the Outstanding Legislator Award from the American Political Science Association. In April 2006 *Time* magazine designated him as a wise man and named him one of the country's ten best senators. In 2008 he was named by the Council for Excellence in Government as one of the twenty-five greatest public servants of the last twenty-five years. He has received forty-one honorary degrees.

During his career, Lugar has participated in more than 12,000 votes in the Senate. Only ten people in the history of the U.S. Senate have voted more often. When asked about retirement, Lugar stated, "It depends largely upon how you are feeling about your health and whatever else surrounds you at this point but I thoroughly enjoy what I am doing and am excited every day about the activities we have." Exercise is an important component in Lugar's daily regimen. Every year Lugar, an avid jogger, is involved in the Dick Lugar Health Fair and Fitness Festival at Butler University.

Lugar often speaks to students, advising them to "to do everything possible as a young person to learn to speak well and to write well. These are the elements of power and persuasion. If you are of high school age, join the debate team. Learn how to make points. Express yourself concisely in the three-minute, five-minute, or ten-minute discipline that might be required. Take every opportunity that you have to publish your work in your school paper or your church paper to actually see your words in print." Lugar speaks from experience. At Shortridge, he was on the state championship debate team and he wrote a weekly column for the school newspaper called, "Shooting the Works." He also wrote a weekly column in the Denison paper.

Lugar is an elder statesman, a powerful member of the Senate, and adviser to presidents—a very prestigious position in life, and one that was well earned. He is an independent thinker, someone who is not bound by party lines but tries to think through what needs to be done. He is a proud American. "No nation is more closely associated with a set of historical moral precepts and for better or worse no nation is judged more meticulously according to its own articulated values," he said. "Our democratic institutions and political and social freedoms have been models for the world, and we have actively helped to nurture democracy in numerous nations. Even Americans themselves do not fully appreciate the international impact of the example set by our transparent political debate and the extraordinary degree of self-examination that accompanies American policy decisions."

Lugar spends about half of his weekends and about half of the congressional recess and vacation time in Indiana. He has often proudly proclaimed, "Indiana is my home." How fortunate we are to have Richard Lugar representing us in the U.S. Senate and throughout the world.

DAVID BAKER

Reinvention/Resilience

I n the Indiana winter of 1952, Fred Dale Band drummer Ray Churchman fell asleep at the wheel while driving his fellow performers back to Bloomington after a gig at Lake Hamilton just outside of Fort Wayne. The ensuing crash propelled the front-seat passenger through the windshield. His body was ripped and broken as he bounced along the pavement. An ambulance rushed him to the hospital in Huntington. In spite of a poor prognosis, the band's trombonist survived.

Amidst the trauma and masked by the pain of other injuries, an important diagnosis was overlooked: a dislocated jaw. Left ticking, this time bomb finally exploded less than a decade later. Suffering from jaw pain and weakness, the musician could hardly sustain a note. He tried acrylic braces and other remedies, but in 1962—the year he won the New Star Award for trombone in a *Down Beat* magazine jazz critic's poll—David Baker was forced to lay down his horn.

Despite this setback Baker summoned the inner strength to persevere and reinvent himself. It was determination born of desperation. Sustained by a wondrous musical talent and a prodigious work ethic, he earned acclaim with a new instrument, the cello, and achieved world

51

renown as a musician and jazz composer.

David Baker Jr. was born December 21, 1931. His father, who hailed from Kansas City, had moved to Indianapolis in 1927 and practiced carpentry. He later worked for the U.S. Postal Service. David Jr.'s mother, Patress, died when the boy was four years old. He and his sister, Shirley, acquired a stepbrother and half-sister through their father's remarriage.

As an elementary school student, the junior Baker wanted to play a musical instrument. He chose trombone—or rather, it chose him—because it was the only instrument left when the music teacher reached his classroom. After a few lessons, his teacher failed to recognize Baker's extraordinary potential and asked him to surrender his trombone, unceremoniously ending his earliest musical career.

Baker attended Crispus Attucks High School, an all-black school in central Indianapolis. Named for the African American who died in the infamous Boston Massacre and became a martyr in the American Revolution, the school is most famous for its Oscar Robertson-led state champion basketball team of 1955. More importantly, Crispus Attucks earned national recognition for educational excellence and produced a number of business leaders and professionals in many fields, including the performing arts. Baker took a streetcar across town every day to attend school. "It was a curse and it was a blessing," he recalled. "All the student talent at any level was funneled to the same high school if you were black and the same thing with teachers. We probably had more doctorates and master's-degreed teachers than almost any school because in racially segregated Indianapolis it was the only place they could teach." In 1968 Baker was inducted into the Crispus Attucks Hall of Fame.

In high school Baker again picked up an instrument—this time the tuba. He joined the marching band because, as he admitted, "I liked marching behind drum majorettes more than any other reason," and he took to the tuba quickly. His music teachers at Attucks included Laverne Newsome, who later received an honorary doctorate from Wabash College, and Russell Brown, who became a major influence in his life. "Brown charged a quarter for a lesson, but taught students even when they could not pay," said Baker who sought to emulate Brown. Baker's senior yearbook listed his future occupation as music teacher.

By the time Baker joined his first band, an after-school jazz group called the Rhythm Rockets, he had switched back to his favorite instrument, the trombone. Enthusiasm did not necessarily equal excellence. "We were sad," Baker recalled. "We could empty a gym pretty quick at a dance by the way we played." The band varied in size from six to thirteen. Baker's mentor played whatever instrument anybody else did not play. Brown could play them all.

Baker graduated from Attucks in 1949 and attended Arthur Jordan Music School, now known as the Butler University School of Music, part of the Jordan College of Fine Arts. His tuition was paid in part through a hundred dollar scholarship from a local jazz club. Baker made up the difference by working as a busboy at LaRue's Supper Club, a local eatery.

In the early 1950s Indiana Avenue on the near-northwest side of downtown Indianapolis boasted more than a dozen jazz venues. Many of the talented musicians allowed recent Attucks graduates to sit in on jam sessions, particularly on Tuesday and Thursday nights. The teenagers would play one tune and then move on to the next club. When he was not sitting in, Baker listened outside the clubs on the Avenue and throughout downtown. He often stood outside the Sunset Terrace or Cotton Club near racially segregated Lockfield Gardens and enjoyed the music of great musicians, including Slide Hampton, a left-handed trombonist not much older than Baker. At twenty, Hampton already had performed at Carnegie Hall. Baker was entranced by self-taught bassist Leroy Vinnegar and the Indianapolis Montgomery family: Monk (string bass and electric bass), Buddy (vibraphone and piano), and Wes, who many musicians consider the greatest influence among modern jazz guitarists.

All the clubs required patrons to be twenty-one years old. That was the law. Baker used an eyebrow pencil and wore a disguise that included a tam and glasses—without lenses—in order to look older. "We would have to hope that it did not rain and wash the mustache down your throat," Baker remembered. It was a vibrant scene. Music was everywhere. Baker loved it and his trombone that he played incessantly, "enough to drive my folks crazy."

Radio station WIBC-AM dominated the airwaves. Baker listened to disc jockey Easy Gwynn, who aired the popular music of the day: Bing Crosby, Nat King Cole, and the still-popular Louis Jordan, the number one rhythm and blues artist of the 1940s. Reflecting the laid-back attitude of the music world, Gwynn often signed off with, "If you're going to take it son, take it easy."

Baker attended music school in Indianapolis for a year and a half until he was in a sense discovered by Roscoe Poland, president of the National Negro Association of Musicians and the first African American to earn a doctorate in music from Indiana University. Poland, also a denizen of the club scene, felt Baker belonged on center stage. He brought the young musician to his alma mater and insisted that Baker apply for admission. Poland was instrumental in his acceptance at IU. Baker majored in music education and specialized in the trombone under the tutelage of Aaron Copland protégé Thomas Beversdorf, who had joined the faculty as a professor of trombone and composition. Beversdorf was a prolific composer who taught at IU until his death in 1981. He encouraged his pupils to "keep it simple" and not sacrifice the musical goal by focusing on the physical means of producing it.

It was a time of stinging segregation. At IU Baker lived in Mays House, a dormitory that was also the college residence for African American athletes, including George Teliaferro, an All-American quarterback who in 1949 was the first African American drafted into the National Football League, and IU track star Milt Campbell, who became the 1956 Olympic decathlon champion. Baker was denied access to restaurants and barbershops and was accorded standing room in the balcony at only a few movie theaters. But much like the environment at Attucks, the music school was a safe haven. There, Baker felt at home and comfortable. It started with the teachers. "People would put their arms around you and it was a great place to grow up," said Baker. He earned his tuition and living expenses by playing with the

Fred Dale Band and other gigs, including a stint with a band led by saxophonist Al Cobine, a Richmond, Indiana, native.

Baker also played the baritone horn in IU's concert band and the bass trombone in the university orchestra. The baritone horn resembles a baby tuba and sounds much like a trombone, with which it shares range and sound. The bass trombone is not a musician's favorite instrument since it keeps the rhythm at the bottom of the brass section, instead of carrying the melody.

In spite of the prolonged recuperation from the automobile accident during his junior year, Baker graduated on time with two degrees: a bachelor's in music education in 1953 and a master's in music education the following year. In 1954 he also was presented with the IU Scholarship Achievement Award. It was the cusp of the age of rock and roll, a phenomenon so markedly unique that it literally threw the music world off its beat. Unsure whether his education and talent were sufficient to render him employable in this new era, Baker remained at IU and began working on a doctorate, which he did not complete. According to Baker, "It would have finished me quicker than I could have finished it."

In 1955 Don Kelly, a bass trombonist Baker had met in Indianapolis, recommended that he take his place in the Stan Kenton Orchestra while Kelly took a short vacation. His stint with the national touring group gave Baker wanderlust. On an impulse, he boarded a train bound for Los Angeles with his trombone and meager wardrobe. He had been living in Los Angeles for just a few months—and not enjoying the new venue much—when he received a call from a trombonist who was teaching at Lincoln University in Jefferson City, Missouri, a school that was in the process of integrating. He implored Baker to take his place for one year while he worked on a doctorate. Although Baker had never taught before, he leapt at the opportunity.

At Lincoln Baker was introduced both to teaching and his future wife: a white coed who was a talented singer. Because he had crossed the "color line" and laws preventing such a union were rigidly enforced in Missouri, the couple drove to Chicago at the end of the school year to wed. In 1957 the newlyweds moved to Indianapolis, where Baker played six nights a week at The Topper, a club at Thirty-Fourth and Illinois streets. It was a good living, but the marriage was not as successful. Before they divorced, the couple had one child, April Elaine, who is a professional violinist and violin teacher who lives in Bloomington, Indiana with her husband. Baker married his current wife, Lida, in 1979.

In the late 1950s a mentor of Baker's, George Russell, assembled a sextet to play in New York at the Five Spot, a highly desirable venue. The group included Baker, Joe Hunt from Richmond and David Young from Indianapolis. Opening night at the Five Spot was overwhelming for the group, many of whom were in their twenties. Jazz greats J.J. Johnson (fellow Attucks graduate), John Coltrane, and Miles Davis all were in attendance. Surprisingly, the George Russell Sextet, although relatively unknown, lasted two years touring the country and recorded a number of albums for Riverside Records, a prestigious house that counted Cannonball Adderley, Thelonious Monk, and Wes Montgomery in its stable. A big band that Baker formed and led, consisting of a mixture of college students and young professionals, was named Best Band at the first Notre Dame Jazz Festival in 1959. Baker was often asked to write music for the group. He also wrote a few pieces for others, including one for Quincy Jones, but he was not serious about composing. Baker's first serious composition was not written until 1964, after the death of his father.

In 1959 Baker and a number of others in the band were invited to attend the Lenox School of Jazz in Lenox, Massachusetts, near Tanglewood, the summer home of the Boston Symphony Orchestra. Baker's tuition was partly underwritten by a Dizzy Gillespie Scholarship. Russell taught at Lenox, which ran from 1957 to 1960 and was one of the first programs where the world's greatest jazz artists were enlisted as faculty to teach promising young musicians. Baker learned and played at Lenox with Johnson, the Modern Jazz Quartet, and Dizzy Gillespie. Other lecturers included ragtime pianist Eubie Blake and composer/conductor Leonard Bernstein. Concerts, a major part of the Lenox education, were presented every Thursday and Saturday evening. Students usually stayed for three weeks and were encouraged to develop as composers and present their work at term-end concerts.

Throughout the 1950s and early 1960s, Baker was constantly fighting pain. Because his dislocated jaw had never healed properly, one side grew stronger as the other side became very weak. The result was extraordinary discomfort that was impossible to abate. In 1961 Baker accompanied Quincy Jones and his orchestra on a European tour. Upon returning to America, Jones worked as an arranger for some of the most important artists of the day, including Frank Sinatra, Ella Fitzgerald, and Dinah Washington. Baker's career went in a different direction. When the tour ended, Baker's jaw hurt so badly that he realized he had to give up the trombone. "If I put metal like a mouthpiece anywhere near my face, I could feel the spasms," Baker said. In order to ease the pain caused by his trombone addiction, Baker's jaw was wired shut for ninety days. He had to eat through a straw.

When Baker resigned himself that his career with the trombone was over at the age of thirty, he was devastated. "All of a sudden, you wake up one morning when . . . you're winning polls and placing high according to all measuring mechanisms and then you find out you can no longer play. I died," Baker said. "I tell you, I used to sit there and think why me? Why me?" His high school teacher, Brown, played a big role in Baker's transformation. He jolted Baker back to reality, asking him, "How often did you say 'Why me?' when you were winning awards?" Together, they decided that Baker should play the piano.

"I was so inept that I should have known after the first week that I was not going to be a piano player, but I persevered for several months," Baker recalled. He practiced all day and banged the keys most evenings in a band at The Topper. One day an exasperated Brown asked why he did not just choose another instrument. Baker replied, "Well, what?" They purchased and assembled a fifteen dollar cello from a pawn shop. Brown showed Baker some basics of the instrument and Baker taught himself more. He was not much better at the cello than he was at the piano, but he enjoyed the instrument and made the switch.

Baker credits Norma Woodbury, a cello teacher whose husband, Max Woodbury, was the principal trumpet player in the Indianapolis Symphony Orchestra, for improving his cello skills. Baker realized his self-taught method was not going to achieve greatness and asked her for help. It was not enough, though, so in the summer of 1964 he requested lessons with Leopold "Terry" Teraspulsky, a world-famous cello recitalist and concert soloist on the IU faculty. According to Baker, "I had no illusions about my playing. I played coffee houses." Baker added, "I remember playing for Teraspulsky during my first lesson. He was sitting on a hassock. I was playing a piece with my eyes shut but I remember looking up and seeing him sitting there with his hands over his ears rocking on the hassock as he was saying to himself, 'Oh, my God, how can you play like that?' I was so discouraged I couldn't play for a week." Teraspulsky accepted him as a student but told Baker, "I'm not going to even let you put your left hand back on your instrument until Christmas." By Christmas Baker was playing with both hands and delighting his instructor.

In 1966 Baker was invited to join the faculty at IU's School of Music and was charged with building a degree-granting jazz program. Two years later, Indiana became the first Big Ten School to offer a jazz degree. Baker has been on the faculty ever since, currently serving as the distinguished professor of music and chairman of the jazz department. His courses include the History of Jazz, the History of Soul and Jazz, the History of Bebop, and the History of Duke Ellington. He also teaches improvisation. He received the President's Award for distinguished teaching at IU in 1986. He has performed and taught throughout the world. Baker also is the artistic director of the Smithsonian Institution Jazz Masterworks Orchestra, which he conducts once or twice a month.

Baker is credited with pioneering the use of cellos in jazz. In the late 1960s, IU professor Josef Gingold, the eminent violinist, asked him to write a piece for violin and jazz band. Shortly thereafter the renowned musician, teacher, and recording artist Janos Starker asked for a piece. Baker remembered his collaboration with Starker as exacting. Once when Starker objected to the length of the orchestral introduction to a cello concerto he had written, Baker cited the Dvorak Cello Concerto in B Minor, the most often performed and recorded cello concerto, as an example of long introductions, to which Starker replied, "You ain't Dvorak." Starker encouraged him to draw from the music of his own cultural background. Baker listened, and Starker was pleased with the final result. The work with Starker enhanced Baker's reputation as a composer and created a large demand for commission work. After much travail and many instruments, after learning and teaching and performing—and after many years—Baker finally had found his niche: composing. It was his gift.

In 1971, after nine years without jaw pain, Baker could no longer resist the trombone and within months regained his mastery. He recorded albums including 1972's *Living Time* with George Russell and the great jazz pianist Bill Evans, but the intense pain returned and before the end of the year Baker had to put down his trombone once more—this time forever.

Baker does not write lyrics, preferring to collaborate with others to put words to his music. He is particularly fond of his collaboration with Indianapolis native Mari Evans, the author of many poems, including "I Am a Black Woman." Baker wrote *Alabama Landscape*, a classical work for orchestra and voice, from an Evans poem of the same name about a slave escaping from the South. In 1986 Baker wrote "Through This Vale of Tears" about the assassination of Martin Luther King Jr. In 2008 he finished a work for the Abraham Lincoln bicentennial that premiered at the Indiana Historical Society—where Baker himself had been honored as a Living Legend in 2001. A piece called "The Underground Railroad" also premiered in 2008. Baker sometimes uses the Bible for lyrics, saying, "it is a source for which I pay no royalties nor do I have to secure permission." A spiritual man, Baker has put expression to his religion in many compositions.

Baker has been honored to serve many times on the Pulitzer Prize Music Jury. He stated, "It was a wonderful experience to be able to sit in judgment of great pieces." Baker was inducted into the National Association of Jazz Educators' Hall of Fame in 1981 and received *Down Beat* magazine's lifetime achievement award in 1987. He was presented the Arts Midwest Jazz Masters Award in 1990 and the National Endowment for the Arts Jazz Master Award in 2000.

In 2003 Baker won an Emmy for his musical score for the PBS documentary *For Gold and Glory* about another Hoosier, Charles Wiggins, the first African American to be a professional racecar driver. Wiggins, although ostracized from the esteemed Indianapolis 500 in the 1920s and 1930s because of his ethnicity, still managed to become one of the best drivers in America. In 2007 Baker was recognized as a Living Jazz Legend by the John F. Kennedy Center for the Performing Arts for lifetime achievement. Among the other honorees that night were Dave Brubeck, Ahmad Jamal, Al Jarreau, and Wynton Marsalis. "It was a staggering sight to see all those people on stage together, representing what must be a hundred years of the world of jazz. I feel blessed to have been with them all," Baker said. His achievements also have been acclaimed at ceremonies conferring an honorary doctor of humane letters from Wabash College in 1993, an honorary doctor of music from Oberlin College in 2004 and an honorary doctorate from the New England Conservatory of Music in 2006.

Baker advises others to have a passion for what they do—all the time. According to Baker, "Someone might out-talent me, but nobody is going to out-work me." Indeed, he has been prolific. Baker has written more than four hundred articles and more than seventy books, including *How to Learn Tunes, Jazz Improvisation* and tomes on playing the bass and cello. As a composer he contributed a broad range of works from small ensemble to orchestral. Baker has been commissioned to write for more than five hundred individuals and ensembles. His compositions total more than two thousand in number, including jazz and symphonic works, chamber music, and ballet and film scores.

Baker often thinks about the accident that cost him his trombone. He feels that God intervened because until his debilitating injury, he played the trombone to the exclusion of all other activities. He feels that if it had not been for accident, he never would have achieved success as a composer, conductor, and teacher.

Today Distinguished Professor Baker can be found in his studio practicing, writing, composing, or teaching—all a testimony to resilience and courage, to reinvention and faith. His legacy not only can be played note by note, but also can be enjoyed day by day and year by year in the music he has composed and in the hundreds of students that he has mentored.

QUENTIN SMITH

A Well-Grounded Airman

In March 1945 U.S. Army pilot Quentin Smith was reassigned to Freeman Field near Seymour, Indiana. The twenty-six-year-old was a first lieutenant and a certified bomber pilot, but despite his rank and the fact that money was deducted from his pay to support the officers' club, he was not allowed to use the facility. Neither could any of the other proud Tuskegee Airmen—the celebrated group of black aviators that served during World War II.

Base Commander Robert Selway, a strict segregationist, had designated members of the unit—all either qualified pilots or seasoned support personnel—as "trainees," then issued an order prohibiting trainees from using the officers' club. It was a flimsy ruse for de facto segregation, sparking racial tension on the base. That order was struck down by U.S. Army Air Corps legal officers hastily dispatched to the scene, so Selway recast his policy in the form of a directive outlining when "trainees" could use certain facilities, effectively prohibiting the black officers from using the officers' club during leisure times. Selway ordered Smith to sign a directive indicating he had read and fully understood its contents. Smith refused.

The commander told him failure to obey the order would be a violation of Article 64 of the Articles of War, which stated: "Any person subject to military law who . . . willfully disobeys any lawful com-

63

mand of a superior officer, shall suffer death or other such punishment as a court martial may direct." Selway repeated the order. Smith was reluctant to answer. He was angry, but he also possessed good sense. Finally, he shook his head and in a very high voice said, "No sir." He was immediately placed under arrest and, along with one hundred others who refused to sign the directive, was confined to quarters for four days until he was moved to Goodman Field at Fort Knox, Kentucky. There, the black officers were locked in a stockade with barbed wire, dogs, and guards.

Their heroic stand was brought to the attention of President Harry S. Truman, who responded, "Turn them loose." A defense team captained by Thurgood Marshall, a brilliant lawyer and future Supreme Court justice, was retained by the National Association for the Advancement of Colored People (NAACP). In addition to securing releases for all of the officers, Marshall obtained honorable discharges for those who wanted to leave the military, including Smith. Although Smith never had an opportunity to prove himself in combat, his brave action and that of his comrades garnered national attention and forced the armed forces to rethink its policy of segregation. Two years later, Truman signed an order desegregating the military.

Quentin Paige Smith was born July 30, 1918, near Huntsville, Texas, in the community of Weldon, population less than 200. According to Smith, "Down in Texas folks say that Huntsville is famous for three things: the Texas State Penitentiary, Bonnie and Clyde, and Quentin Smith. That's Huntsville." Quentin's father, Paige Smith, headed north to Chicago in 1923 after breaking a deputy sheriff's arm during an altercation. Given the racial environment in Texas at the time, he had no choice but to get out of town. He grabbed the first train that was moving. He ended up in Chicago, finding work in a cement plant before landing a job in the steel mills of East Chicago, Indiana. After about eighteen months, he sent for his wife, Ione, and his five children, including six-year-old middle child Quentin.

Smith attended high school at East Chicago Washington, a partially integrated institution. Smith was bright and enjoyed his studies. He loved to read. He earned top grades at Washington but felt he was unfairly denied the honor of valedictorian when he graduated. At school, he was not allowed to swim in the pool or join the wrestling, tennis, and golf teams. He could participate in football, basketball, and track but opted out, choosing instead to play in the band. Smith became so proficient on the clarinet that he was selected to play in a 150-piece Chicago orchestra for the 1933 World's Fair. Dubbed A Century of Progress International Exposition, the fair was conceived to celebrate the city's centennial and as a testament to "modern" industrial and scientific achievements. Smith made friends with the piano player, Nat King Cole, and persuaded Cole to play at his high school prom—the black students' prom, that is. Cole was a year younger than Smith, but he already led a twelve-piece band that charged seventy-five dollars per performance. More than six decades later, Cole was inducted into the Rock and Roll Hall of Fame as one of the major influences on early rock and roll.

Spurred by his mother's insistence that he continue his schooling, Smith was determined but unable to afford college after graduation in 1935. He secured employment as a crusher operator at a brickyard in East Chicago, working twelve hours a day, seven days a week. In a series of operations, crushers reduced massive 500-pound blocks of stone to the dust from which bricks were made. Eight months after he began working, a large black man named Shelby approached Smith and asked what he was doing there. Smith replied, "I'm saving money to go to school." The man scoffed. "You're not going to make it. Do you know what you are sucking in every day?" Shelby asked, referring to the silica in the dust that was damaging workers' lungs. Smith answered by asking Shelby why he was there. His response: "I've got five kids. I'm stuck." Smith ran into Shelby just a few weeks later, finding the man emaciated and suffering from silicosis, an often-fatal lung disease caused by prolonged inhalation of silica dust. Shelby warned the young man, "This is what you're going to look like if you stay here." Smith quit the next week and found a job at his father's employer, Inland Steel Company, hauling brick to the furnaces. He chose Inland Steel because it gave each new employee a physical examination and Smith wanted someone to check his lungs. Shelby had scared him to death. Smith also worked part time at a funeral home. One evening while on duty, he picked up a corpse whose lungs were as hard as concrete. It was Shelby. Smith decided it was time to go to college.

Smith was accepted at Indiana State Teachers College (now Indiana State University) in Terre Haute, where he enrolled for the 1936 fall semester. He had saved money but was unsure how long it would last. His tuition was paid in part by a federal grant and in part by Inland Steel, a forward-thinking organization with a policy that assisted all employees who wanted to attend college, regardless of color. ISU did not allow African Americans to live in the dormitories. Smith found room and board in the home of a wealthy white family in exchange for manual labor. He lived in the basement and tended to the furnace all winter long.

At ISU, Smith signed up for the marching band. The bandmaster eyed Smith, who had reached his adult height of six feet, two inches and had filled out to a muscular one hundred ninety pounds, and inquired, "Do you play the tuba? The big bass drum?" When he learned that Smith played the clarinet, he was surprised to find out that Smith did not own an instrument. He loaned Smith a clarinet for the audition and was so impressed that he gave it to him afterward. Smith played in the ISU band for three years.

By his senior year, Smith's physical stature did not go unnoticed by the athletic coaches. He was enticed to give up his horn and play varsity football. Varsity athletics, one of the first places on the college campus to recognize and accept individuals no matter their race, was undergoing a transition. When ISU played the University of Kentucky, Smith was not allowed to dress for the game, even though the contest was played in Terre Haute. At Illinois his team stayed in the college dormitory; Smith was forced to bunk for the night with a black family. He nevertheless became a football hero and was elected vice president of the senior class.

During the summer of 1937, while working at Inland Steel, Smith joined a strike initiated at U.S. Steel South Works, the largest steelmaking operation in Chicago. Smith was upset that white employees at Inland Steel were promoted over his father, and he wanted a fair seniority system established. (Everybody struck—both blacks and whites—as part of a union-organized action in steel mills throughout the country.) Violence ensued. The strike lasted one week and won the union many concessions. More than a decade later, Smith drew on this experience to organize a teachers' union.

Smith graduated from ISU in the spring of 1940 with a bachelor's degree in education, certified to teach English, Latin, and political science. The Indiana Department of Public Instruction issued his first teacher's license in September and that same year he began his career at Gary Roosevelt School, teaching fifth- and sixth-grade English. In this era of segregation, Gary Roosevelt was exclusively black. During the summer months Smith continued working at Inland Steel.

At a party for friends of Gary Roosevelt, Smith met Willa Brown, a transcontinental pilot who often was hailed as the foremost female pilot in the country after the 1937 death of aviatrix Amelia Earhart. Brown, who was black, also had graduated from ISU and taught business education at Gary Roosevelt before quitting to establish a flying school on the southwest side of Chicago in 1938. Brown predicted that there was "going to be a war and pilots are going to be in it." Smith replied, "Willa, I believe in terra firma. The firmer the ground, the less terror." But when his younger brother, Grady, an infantryman in the U.S. Army, returned on leave from basic training and complained about lying on his belly in the mud, Smith changed his mind.

Knowing he would be drafted, Smith enlisted in the army in 1942 and passed the test for assignment to flight school. The United States had no separate air force. Until 1944 one of the prerequisites for black soldiers to become army pilots was a college degree, even though whites only needed to graduate from high school. The army awarded Smith a bonus for enlisting: two cartons of cigarettes. Smith was not a smoker. He was sent for nine months of training at Brown's flight school, the only such program in America for aspiring black army pilots. Smith was exhilarated in the air and relished in the knowledge that he was among a select few who could command a flying machine.

According to Smith, opportunity in the armed services for pilots and other skilled positions opened up for blacks because President Franklin Delano Roosevelt, who was eager for a third term, met with black leaders and promised that chance in exchange for black political support. Roosevelt delivered, creating separate combat forces to avoid integration.

The black air force was informally referred to as the Tuskegee Airmen because they trained at Tuskegee Army Air Field in Tuskegee, Alabama. Brown's school sent about two hundred certified pilots to Tuskegee. They were the first black aviators in the segregated army of World War II and served their country in the face of discrimination with pride. Tuskegee Airmen of the 332nd Fighter Group were cited for valor. They flew escort for heavy bombers and were reportedly referred to by Germany's Luftwaffe as "Schwarze Vogelmenschen" (Black Birdmen). The Allies called the airmen "Redtails" because of the distinctive crimson paint on the vertical stabilizers of the unit's aircraft.

In addition to basic pilot training, Smith was trained by Brown as an instructor. There were no white instructors for blacks. As a private in the army air corps, Smith earned fifty dollars per month plus an additional twenty-five dollars hazardous-duty pay because he was a pilot. It was a fair wage in the 1940s. The students learned in small sixty-five-horsepower Piper Cubs—almost too small for Smith, who acquired the nickname "Big Q." After receiving certification at Brown's school, for no apparent reason, he was stationed and grounded in Biloxi, Mississippi, with no real duties for six months. He was transferred in 1944 to Tuskegee, where in order to qualify as an instructor he was required to complete a beginning course as though he had never flown an airplane.

It was accepted as truth that the Tuskegee Airmen had gone largely unutilized in the war effort until First Lady Eleanor Roosevelt visited the base in 1943 and flew with a black pilot. Less than one month later the Tuskegee Airmen were in combat. Smith proudly stated that many of his students distinguished themselves in combat missions over Europe. When it was time for Smith's class to be shipped overseas in 1945, his superiors realized that Smith's formidable size and the required combat paraphernalia would make it impossible for him to "ditch" from the smaller planes. So Smith was reassigned to a B-25 Mitchell medium bomber, an airplane that was used in both the European and Pacific theaters. He earned his bomber certification at Tuskegee three weeks later.

There were few pilots of that era that did not experience at least one death-defying incident. As part of the certification process at Tuskegee, pilots were required to perform aerobatic maneuvers. Protocol dictated an altitude of three thousand feet for those exercises, but Smith decided one day to perform at two thousand feet. During a loop, he blacked out due to the gravitational force. When he awoke, he was upside down fifteen feet above the treetops. It was his scariest moment in the air.

According to Smith, most of the higher-ranking officers in the army were southerners who brought their prejudice with them. That prejudice permeated the force, creating a belief that blacks could not lead, could not fight, and could not fly complicated aircraft. Nearly all of the black soldiers worked in the kitchen, dug ditches, and hauled supplies. In the marines and paratroopers, the officers were white. At Tuskegee, blacks eventually took their places as officers. As a fully trained bomber pilot of the 477th Composite Group, Smith had to wait until black personnel were trained because army brass would not allow white navigators and gunners to take orders from a black commander.

After black personnel were trained and formed up, the bomber units were sent to Fort Knox, Kentucky but the runways there were too short for the heavy airplanes. Needless fatalities ensued. In March 1945 the 477th was shipped to Freeman Field in Indiana, named in honor of Captain Richard S. Freeman of Winamac, Indiana, a 1930 graduate of West Point and one of the pioneers of the army's air mail service. Activated in 1942, the installation already had awarded wings to more than four thousand airmen. Freeman Field was ideal for training with its long runways, which allowed four-engine bombers to take off and land safely.

At Freeman Field on April 5, 1945, Smith sauntered over to the officers' club. He was refused admittance. Smith cited army regulations, which stated that any officer could go in any club in the United States or its possessions, to no avail. Additional black officers attempted to enter the officers' club but were turned away. Selway's order had barred the door. All told, 101 of the 545 black officers refused to sign Selway's segregation order. Through the efforts of the NAACP, Marshall settled the matter known as the Freeman Field Mutiny just before D-Day in May 1945, but a letter of reprimand was placed in each officer's file anyway. Knowing that the letter of reprimand in his army file clouded his future in military service, Smith requested and received an honorable discharge in November 1945.

Still interested in furthering his education, Smith took advantage of the opportunities available under the GI Bill. He enrolled in the master's program in English at the University of Chicago the following year, attending classes primarily during the summer. During the winter months, he attended IU Northwest in Gary in a quest for a master's degree in education.

In 1951 Smith was armed with an English degree from the University of Chicago plus certifications as an army air force pilot and commander. He wanted to fly but was barred because commercial airlines were not hiring black pilots. He returned to teaching school at Gary Roosevelt, where he was assigned to teach English and Latin. His Latin classes were standing-room only. While teaching he completed a master's degree in education at IU in Bloomington during the summers of 1955 and 1956.

In 1956 Smith was given the opportunity to help develop a new school. He was named the first principal of Benjamin Banneker Elementary School. It was only minimally integrated due to its location in a predominately black neighborhood. It became the number one elementary school in Gary based upon test scores and related criteria, and it is among the few public elementary schools in Indiana to have received a distinguished Great Schools rating of ten out of ten. In 1968 the Gary Community School Corporation established West Side High School, a four-year public school accommodating more than three thousand pupils. It was the largest high school in the state and was founded to integrate students within the Gary school system. Smith was named its first principal. Later, he was appointed the director of secondary education for the Gary schools, in which capacity he served for ten years. In all, he spent fifty years in education.

Smith continued to fly as a hobby. In 2009, at age ninety-one, he was still flying. He has flown all types of aircraft, anything he could get his hands on. Throughout his career he has also made time for his community. He was elected to the Gary City Council, and served as president of the Gary/Chicago Airport Authority, the Lake County Development Commission, and the Urban League of Northwest Indiana. He served on the selection committee for the Fund for Hoosier Excellence, a privately funded, not-for-profit organization created by U.S. Senator Richard Lugar in 1983 to provide scholarships and encourage outstanding minority students to excel in school and remain in Indiana as leaders.

In 1972, while a number of the Tuskegee Airmen were enjoying informal social camaraderie, an idea emerged. Tuskegee Airmen Inc. was born with a mission to honor the accomplishments and perpetuate the history of African Americans who participated in the U.S. Army Air Corps during World War II and to mentor black children and encourage them to seek careers in aviation. By 2009 there were fifty-one chapters nationwide populated by heritage members and others who believed in the mission. Smith served as an officer and director of the Chicago chapter. The organization, with the assistance of black airline pilots, flies children seven to seventeen years of age for free. In addition, it provides flying-lesson scholarships to children. "Flying is a mystery. Kids are interested in how it works," Smith said. "Once you get them started, you just have to get out of their way." Smith enjoyed the program, but at age sixty-two stopped flying the children.

In 1995 Rodney A. Coleman, assistant secretary of the U.S. Air Force, announced at a Tuskegee Airmen banquet that the letters of reprimand would be removed from the files of the one hundred one courageous officers upon request. He declared that the Freeman Field incident was a "bellwether for change with respect to integrating the U.S. military" and that the men who refused to sign the directive had taken a giant step for equality ten years before Rosa Parks refused to sit in the back of the bus in Montgomery, Alabama. "The Tuskegee Airmen paved the way for changes in the soon to be brand new service, the

U.S. Air Force," Coleman said. Smith holds no anger toward the army, the government, or the United States, saying "that's non-productive." Nor does he regret leaving the army before serving in combat. "We engaged in combat on our home soil. We stood up for the constitutional provision that 'all men are created equal.' We changed the military," said Smith.

In 2007 President George W. Bush honored Smith with the Congressional Gold Medal, the highest civilian award that can be bestowed by a legislature in the United States. Later that same year, Smith was inducted into the Northwest Indiana Hall of Fame. In 2008 President-elect Barack Obama personally extended an invitation for the nearly three hundred surviving Tuskegee Airmen to attend his inauguration. Smith joined his fellow squadron members in Washington, D.C. for the ceremony early the next year. Also in 2009 Smith was named the Lifetime Achievement Winner by the Quality of Life Council of Northwest Indiana for devoting a significant part of his life to improving the quality of life in northwest Indiana.

Smith advises children to be prepared for whatever they set out to do. "If you are not prepared, it's not going to happen," he said. He also advises them to be diligent: "Know what you can do and do what you can. Use your head." Smith lives in Gary with his dog Rusty. He is an honored elder and is active in the community. He has two sons, Quentin Jr. and Charles, both of whom reside in Scottsdale, Arizona.

Gracing the Hall of Honor at the U.S. Air Force Academy in Colorado Springs, Colorado, is a sculpture honoring the Tuskegee Airmen. The statue stands as a tribute to the bravery of the men who fought fascism overseas and racism at home. The artist incorporated Smith's features in shaping the face of the sculpture. No one could better epitomize the stature of a Tuskegee Airman than Gary, Indiana's own Quentin Paige Smith.

GEORGE MCGINNIS

A Performance of a Lifetime/ A Lifetime of Performance

Nothing much was expected on the eve of the second of two Indiana/Kentucky high school all-star games in late June 1969. Nothing much was expected, especially by Joe Voskuhl, the six-foot, eight-inch forward on the Kentucky roster who had guarded a listless George McGinnis in the first game of the series. McGinnis scored twenty-three points in the Indiana win, but that was well below his 32.5-points-per-game average that year. McGinnis had missed numerous scoring opportunities, netting only eight field goals out of twenty-six attempts, and he had committed a plethora of turnovers. "They compare him to Oscar Robertson. I played against Oscar in street ball in Cincinnati. McGinnis is not even close to Oscar Robertson," Voskuhl told the *Louisville Courier-Journal* and whomever else would listen, capping his interview with a single word, "Overrated."

Indiana All-Stars Coach Angus Nicoson made sure that McGinnis read Voshkul's postgame analysis. "I've never had anybody throw it at me like that," McGinnis recalled. The Indiana forward responded with fifty-three points and thirty rebounds in a 114-83 rout of Kentucky—two records that still stand. Rebounds came amidst competition from seven-footer Tom Payne, the first African American recruited

74

at Kentucky, and longtime teammate Steve Downing, a six-foot, nine-inch leaper. According to Hall of Fame sportswriter Bob Hammel, "Everybody just got out of the way that night." Kentucky coach Joe Harper said that as the game went on, Voskuhl was calling McGinnis, "Sir." Today, Hammel, with the perspective of more than fifty years as a sports columnist for Indiana newspapers, states flatly, "It was simply the best game I ever saw a basketball player—at any level—play."

George McGinnis was born on August 12, 1950, to Burnie and Willie McGinnis in Hoopersville, Alabama, a small farming community just east of Birmingham. The family, including older sister Bonnie, came north to Indianapolis in 1952 as part of the Great Migration. Burnie found employment in a factory and also worked construction. He was a big man, six-feet, six-inches tall and 230 pounds. McGinnis' mother, a homemaker, stands two inches shy of six feet.

As a teenager, McGinnis was an extraordinary physical specimen, a fully mature six-feet, eight-inches, 220 pounds and an intimidating athlete for the Washington High School Continentals. He played football and basketball, enjoying success in both sports. He was the first high school athlete in Indiana history to be named to *Parade* magazine's first team All American in football for three straight years. With a decided height advantage and sure hands, McGinnis was a formidable tight end. It was no wonder that he received more college recruiting offers for football than basketball. McGinnis also was a first team All American in basketball for two years and was named *Basketball News'* national high school Player of the Year in 1969. Although he considered pursuing football in college and perhaps the pros, McGinnis—like most Indiana athletes—preferred Indiana's favorite pastime, basketball.

In the high school gym, McGinnis had no peer. He fed his desire for competition during the summer with older boys, including Washington graduates Ralph Taylor and Billy Keller. McGinnis also benefited from illustrious high school coaches. Indiana Football Hall of Famer Bob Springer said McGinnis was the most dominant player he had ever seen. Hall of Fame basketball coaches Jerry Oliver, who later coached

McGinnis at Indiana University, and Bill Green, who won a record six state championships at Marion High School, were excellent role models. McGinnis credits his coaches for not only teaching him the games but also imparting many lessons in life.

McGinnis also learned important lessons from Ellie Dragoo, his high school speech teacher. She knew that he was going to be an athlete and told him he needed to learn how to respond in an interview, how to converse. She took a genuine liking to McGinnis, providing special assignments and inviting him to her house on the weekends, where they conducted mock interviews. Dragoo insisted that he be thorough and sound like he knew what he was talking about. McGinnis credits Dragoo for his confidence and comfort in the public eye. "She was a special person in my life," he said.

Hoosier hysteria was rampant in the spring of 1969. Four Indiana high school teams met at Butler Fieldhouse for the state basketball finals, and for the first time in history three of the four teams were undefeated. The unique single-class basketball of Indiana, aptly chronicled in the movie *Hoosiers*, gave small-town teams the chance to dream big. That year, the giant killer was the Alices from Vincennes Lincoln, which was 27-0 under aptly named coach Gunner Wyman. The other teams were Gary Tolleston (27-1), Marion (27-0), and Washington (29-0).

The afternoon game between Marion and Washington was the most exciting of the weekend. Marion, led by Indiana all-star Jovon Price, dominated most of the game, and led Washington 52-42 at the end of the third quarter. Then Washington took over. Led by McGinnis, Steve Downing, and guard Wayne Pack, the Continentals outscored Marion 19-8, finally prevailing thanks to a Downing basket with twenty-three seconds left on the clock. The final score was 61-60. McGinnis led the team in scoring with twenty-seven points. The other semifinal contest ended the Alices' dream with a 77-66 loss to Gary Tolleston. In the state championship game that night, a McGinnis-dominated team sent the Tolleston team back to Gary with a 79-76 defeat. Washington ended its season 31-0, only the second undefeated state champion in Indiana history. McGinnis was named Mr. Basketball, the highest honor a high school cager can attain in a state that is rabid about basketball. Years later, the undefeated 1969 Continentals were inducted into the Indiana Basketball Hall of Fame as a unit.

The Indiana/Kentucky all-star series was always electric, pitting two great programs on the hardwood. In the era before the Nike All Stars and other breeding grounds for basketball talent, this border battle was one of the few showcases for players entering college. Only the best high school seniors were selected to participate. No wonder the games drew sellout crowds in Indianapolis and Louisville.

At one time, Indiana led the series 14–1 but by McGinnis's senior year the gap had closed to 24-17. Louisville newspaperman Bob Gorham had expected the trend to continue in 1969—until he saw McGinnis in action. "We'd have whipped you again this year if you hadn't brought along one of the Boston Celtics," he told Hammel. Coach Nicoson engineered a sweep for Indiana, including the second game in Louisville's Freedom Hall witnessed by a record crowd of 17,875. The sweep was Indiana's first since 1958 and came after seven defeats in the previous eight games. Kentucky's Harper commented on McGinnis's dominance after the final game: "I've never seen someone so physically mature and so tough at his age. That was just a man against boys out there tonight."

Burnie McGinnis had driven to Louisville to attend his son's last— and best—high school game, but sadly it was his final game, too. Burnie was killed two weeks later when he fell from a scaffold on a construction site at Eli Lilly and Company. The younger McGinnis had tentatively committed to play basketball for his home fans at Indiana University following graduation, and his father's death confirmed that decision. Bloomington was close to his mother, to whom he remains devoted. He accepted a scholarship and matriculated at IU the following fall. McGinnis, who has never lifted weights, worked construction jobs the summer after he graduated and after his freshman year in college, building his muscular body along with Lafayette Square Mall. His paycheck went directly to his mother.

McGinnis was recruited to IU by Lou Watson, who had played for legendary IU coach Branch McCracken and later had been his assistant. Watson ascended to the position of head coach upon McCracken's retirement. McGinnis looked forward to playing for Watson and Jerry Oliver, his assistant coach. At IU, McGinnis, his high school team-mate Downing, and fellow Indiana all-star Cornelius "Bootsy" White, along with Jerry Memering and John Ritter, formed the nucleus of a freshman team that could have competed with any varsity program in the country. According to National Collegiate Athletic Association rules at the time, freshmen were not allowed to play at the varsity level. College players also had to cope with the "Lew Alcindor Rule," which forbid dunking the basketball. Alcindor, who later changed his name to Kareem Abdul-Jabbar, was so dominant that he could dunk the ball at will, so NCAA officials forbid dunking in college games. Although Alcindor was drafted in 1969, the rule was not rescinded for another seven years. Even so, expectations at IU ran high when hoops fans learned that during a scrimmage the McGinnis crew crushed the varsity team that later finished third in the Big Ten.

When McGinnis returned for his sophomore season in 1970—the first year of his varsity eligibility—it was obvious that some previous starters would have to watch the game from the bench, but it was a spectacle to behold. McGinnis was the first sophomore to lead the Big Ten in scoring and rebounding, averaging thirty points and fifteen rebounds per game. He garnered first team All Big Ten and All American honors. The team finished third in the Big Ten, a good season with a strong winning record but not exactly what supporters had expected given the quality of the recruiting class.

In the early 1970s the IU campus was boiling with new ideas and challenges. Black pride manifested itself in afros and bell bottoms—and racial strife. African Americans on the football team rebelled against their coach, John Pont, over a perceived decision to limit playing time based upon color and resigned en masse. When the African Americans on the basketball team were asked to support the football boycott with one of their own, McGinnis believed his coaches did not deserve that treatment. Neither he nor his teammates participated in the boycott.

McGinnis was truly a student athlete. He enjoyed his classes, especially history, studied hard and achieved good grades in college, but other forces were at work. Whether it was the IU win/loss record, racial strife, or general malaise, Watson was finished at IU—so was McGinnis.

A so-called hardship rule instituted in 1971 allowed underclassmen to be drafted by a pro team if they could demonstrate that they suffered from a financial hardship. Since McGinnis was the sole supporter of his widowed mother, hardship was not difficult to prove. That year he was drafted in the first round by the National Basketball Association's Philadelphia 76ers and the American Basketball Association's Indiana Pacers, and again chose to stay close to home. He joined the Pacers, a championship-caliber team. The entire signing bonus of $35,000 was used to purchase a home in Indianapolis for his mother—one that she lives in today. It was the proudest moment of McGinnis's life.

Watson's successor at IU, highly respected college coach Bob Knight, once commented to McGinnis that had he stayed just one more year, Knight could have added another NCAA championship to his resume. A respectful McGinnis replied, "Coach, my mother needed the money." McGinnis understood the value of a college education. As time allowed he enrolled in classes at Indiana University Purdue University-Indianapolis and at Temple University in Philadelphia. He made progress but fell one year short of a degree. McGinnis is disappointed that he missed the opportunity to continue his education at IU and to play for Knight.

According to McGinnis, Pacers coach Bob "Slick" Leonard, himself an Indiana high school all-star, was a good "X" and "O" man and a great motivator. Leonard was a two-time All American who played on IU's 1953 national championship team under McCracken and he was the first person inducted into the IU Sports Hall of Fame. McGinnis and fellow rookie Darnell Hillman, who brought his oversize afro from San Jose State University, added to a veteran team that included Roger Brown, Mel Daniels, Bill Keller, and Rick Mount. That team won ABA championships each of McGinnis's first two years, and he was named the 1972 Rookie of the Year.

The Pacers had a great connection with their fans and achieved the best attendance in the league. Much of that had to do with players contributing to their community during the summer. McGinnis has a cheerful demeanor coupled with an endearing love for his fellow man. His fans returned that affection. Fans also enjoyed the intense league competition with the Denver Nuggets, the Utah Jazz, and the Pacers' arch rivals, the Kentucky Colonels.

McGinnis enjoyed practice when he first came into the ABA, but as the years went by and the drudgery of playing an eighty-game professional schedule began to take its toll, practice became McGinnis's least favorite activity. His lack of intensity at practice did not have an adverse effect on his performance at game time.

After four years in the ABA and a string of outstanding performances, McGinnis found himself at the center of litigation between two NBA teams that vied for his services. After his Pacers contract expired in 1975, he signed with the New York Knicks, but the Philadelphia 76ers won a court challenge, claiming that they owned first rights to McGinnis because they drafted him. So McGinnis went to play in Philadelphia. The Pacers desperately wanted to resign their star, but could not afford the half-million-dollar bonus other teams offered. McGinnis's financial situation had improved, and deservedly so. He had garnered a number of honors in the ABA, including co-MVP with Julius Erving, adored as "Dr. J."

McGinnis arrived in the City of Brotherly Love in 1975, but there was no love there for professional basketball. Philadelphia was still remembering the 1972-73 season, during which the team had suffered the worst record in NBA history. That squad won a total of nine games and are still pegged as the worst team ever. The 76ers won a few more games in the season before McGinnis arrived, but they repeated as the worst team in the NBA with the worst attendance.

The first year of the McGinnis era, the team made the playoffs— a reawakening for the franchise. Billboards throughout Philadelphia proclaimed, "Let George Do It." George indeed did it. The energy was back in Philadelphia, and attendance began to rise.

Despite his success, McGinnis missed his family and friends—particularly his boyhood sweetheart, Linda Taylor, whom he had been dating for some time. After his first year in Philadelphia, they married. McGinnis did make a number of friends in Philadelphia. Among them was team owner Irv Kosloff, who became a constant companion and mentor to McGinnis. They spent evenings at dinner, shows, and plays. McGinnis refers to him as a father figure.

The summer before McGinnis's second season in Philadelphia, the ABA and the NBA merged. That offseason, the team purchased the contract of Irving. Before closing the deal, Kosloff asked McGinnis if the acquisition was acceptable. He answered an enthusiastic yes. The NBA had eliminated the hardship rule, making players eligible once their high school class had graduated. The 76ers supplemented their team with a cadre of young basketball players with great personalities: Doug Collins, Lloyd Free (who changed his name to World B. Free), and Darryl Dawkins, the first high school player ever chosen in the first round of the NBA draft. Dawkins called himself Chocolate Thunder; sportswriters tagged McGinnis "Big Mac" and "Baby Bull."

An account in *Sports Illustrated* suggested that there may not be enough room on the team for two superstars the caliber of Irving and McGinnis. Although there was always talk about their inability to mesh properly, the men were and are great friends. Their 1977 team was defeated by a Bill Walton-led Portland Trail Blazers team in the finals of the NBA championship, but it sold out every road and home game that year. The Dr. J/Big Mac collaboration lasted three years.

In 1978 McGinnis was traded to the Denver Nuggets, a team starring David Thompson and coached by Larry Brown. It was not a good fit for McGinnis. Brown was complex. "He did strange things like tell players how much he liked them and then the next day he was in his office trying to trade them," McGinnis recalled.

McGinnis suffered a major injury in Denver. While attempting to steal the ball during a game with the Buffalo Braves, he tore the ligaments in his left ankle. It never fully recovered. He was on the injury list for almost eight weeks and never returned to full playing shape. He also picked up a habit that may have shortened his career—cigarettes. Many players smoked at the time, not having full knowledge of the adverse consequence of a nicotine addiction. It was difficult for McGinnis to come back from his ankle injury and he eventually was traded back to the Pacers, where he remained until retiring from professional basketball in 1982.

During his pro career McGinnis was named an All Star numerous times in both the ABA and the NBA. He holds the record for most points scored in a Pacers game (fifty-eight versus the Dallas Chaparrals) and for most rebounds (thirty-nine versus the Carolina Cougars). He hit more game-winning shots than anyone can remember. In 2000 McGinnis was named to Indiana University All Century Team. He is also a member of the Indiana Basketball Hall of Fame.

On November 21, 1985, during halftime of a Pacers game, the jersey numbers of McGinnis (30), along with teammates Mel Daniels (34), Roger Brown (35), and Coach Slick Leonard (529, for the number of his wins) were retired before a packed house. They were the first Pacers to be so honored. The video highlights of their careers were met with monstrous applause. As their numbers were hoisted to the rafters, the players were presented with Rolex watches and other gifts. Fans were provided special programs for the event.

After retirement from basketball at thirty-two, McGinnis relocated to Denver and relaxed for six years while engaging in his hobbies, fishing and skiing. Linda grew tired of "the good life" and urged him to get back to work. "You can't do this," she told him. "First of all, the money won't last, and second you need to find something to do." With Linda's encouragement, they returned to Indiana and McGinnis was named spokesman for the Indiana Lottery and for Farm Bureau Insurance. He also did play-by-play commentary for Butler University basketball and the high school championships.

In 1992 George and Linda established GM Supply in Indianapolis. The company, capitalizing on McGinnis's knowledge of construction, originally sold supplies for commercial construction. Now named Integrated Supply, it has evolved into three lines of business: subassembly, in which the company purchases components and assembles them under contract for customers that include Fortune 500 firm Cummins Engine; materials handling for International Truck and Engine Corporation plants in Chicago and Huntsville, Alabama; and the original distribution facility serving customers including Eli Lilly, General Mills, Toyota, and Procter & Gamble.

After a few years working alongside her husband, Linda retired. The company is profitable, operating out of multiple locations throughout the country. Although the sports chapter of his life was rewarding, McGinnis said his current position as CEO is more fulfilling. He cited the fast pace of business that satisfies his competitive instincts and affords him an opportunity to approach life with a purpose. That was missing during his retirement in Denver.

Although consumed for years with his basketball career, he now realizes that athletic honors are not the essence of life. He prefers to concentrate on his future. McGinnis advises young people to stay centered and "never forget where you came from. No matter what kind of money you make, always be humble. Look at it as a blessing. Try to be helpful to others." McGinnis often is invited to talk to young athletes, including some of Knight's teams. McGinnis is thankful that he has had strong relationships with people. He relishes the times he spends working in the community, particularly with children. He continues to be involved in basketball events, including cochairing the host committee for the NCAA Final Four held in Indianapolis in 2010. "I've been pretty lucky," McGinnis said. "From where I've come from, the environment I grew up in, I could have easily gone the other way, but I had good parenting. I was lucky to have my mother and father who were hard on me and it paid off. We grow up to be our parents, so I've been blessed. I feel fortunate." Reflecting the values of his mother and father, McGinnis is a true "gentleman." He has one son, Tony, and two grandsons.

McGinnis believes playing sports gives participants the opportunity to be exposed to different kinds of people and their sensitivities. "Sometimes we get so self-centered about what we do and who we are that we forget there are other people. Sports also exposes you to the world of diversity and teaches you how to work well with others," he said. "It teaches self-confidence." McGinnis laments the fact that children try to emulate the highlights they see on television and do not concentrate on fundamentals. "Too many players never learn the whole game of basketball," he stated. McGinnis worries about the future of the NBA and the negative vibes projecting from the tattooed masses of thugs running the court, in particular his beloved Pacers who have had so much off-court trouble.

McGinnis is adamantly opposed to the idea of body art: "Tattoos? Never, never. If you want to be in a nonsports environment, tattoos are not good for business. Attitudes are changing all the time and the world is getting a bit more liberal, but I don't think tattoos will work well in an office and business environment. I would never wear a tattoo."

McGinnis is a supporter of Metro Indianapolis Coalition for Construction Safety, an organization whose most prestigious honor is the Burnie McGinnis Award (named for his father) that recognizes those who demonstrate an outstanding commitment to worker safety. McGinnis is proud to be a Hoosier, saying "Indiana is like a big family." Indiana is proud too, of George McGinnis—a success on and off the court.

STEVEN BEERING, M.D.

Doctor of Medicine/Career of Service

The World War II Battle of Hamburg, code named Operation Gomorrah, was hardly a conflict. Although the German city was fortified by antiaircraft weapons and defended by the Luftwaffe, the British-American forces wrought devastation in a series of air raids thought to be the heaviest assault in the history of aerial warfare. Incendiary bombs turned the city to hell in less than a week. Operation Gomorrah killed an estimated 34,000 people, injured more than 125,000 others, and destroyed 250,000 houses, leaving almost a million civilians homeless. Much of Hamburg, like the biblical city of Gomorrah, essentially disappeared.

On the morning of July 30, 1943, just after terror stopped raining from the German sky, a mother and her two young sons crawled through the rubble from the basement of a Lake Alster apartment building near downtown Hamburg. The building had collapsed, crushing almost everyone in the makeshift refuge. The family, devoid of all possessions, was bundled up and transported for three days in the back of a truck to a rural camp for displaced civilians near Weidensees. One of the boys, eleven-year-old Stephan Bieringer, was grateful for this miraculous gift of life and grew up determined to share it with his fellow man. He ultimately became a physician, scientist, professor, dean, university president, and above all, humanitarian whose contributions

87

have been felt throughout Indiana and the rest of the world.

Stephan Claus Bieringer was born on August 20, 1932, in Berlin, Germany. His father, also named Stephan, was an executive with Thonet Furniture Corporation, an international concern. The Bieringers lived in Berlin for a short time before moving to Hamburg, the hometown of Bieringer's mother, Alice, who affectionately called her son by his middle name, Claus. Because her husband was from Bavaria, the union was derided. In early 1930s Germany, feelings of ethnic and regional identity ran strong. Bavarians were often the butt of jokes from the northern Germans who thought themselves more elegant and better educated. The good-natured derision was similar to the ongoing Indiana/Kentucky rivalry. So the question was, "Why does your mother marry this Bavarian?"

Bieringer's parents met at a swim club, a favorite venue of his father, who later swam the breaststroke in Berlin at the 1936 Olympics. Bieringer and his younger brother, John, enjoyed a privileged life with a father who was an Olympic hero, a mountain climber of renown, and a successful businessman. Although his father was not a supporter, life was pleasant under the Nazi regime—that is, for all but Alice who was born to Jewish parents and who was compelled to wear a yellow Star of David sewn to her clothing on the left side of her chest. For her, life was tolerable.

Alice's parents, Theodore and Emma Friedrichs, owned a clothing store chain with locations throughout Europe, including France, Italy, and England. They were Jewish and prescient. In the early 1930s, smarting from persecution and suspecting the inevitability of steepening antagonism from the Nazi machine, they left everything behind, escaped to the United States, and settled in Pittsburgh. They walked away and started over. Although they beseeched other family members to do the same, their advice was not heeded, and most of the Friedrichs side of the family went up in the smoke of the Holocaust gas chambers. The Bieringers, including Alice, who had converted, were practicing Catholics.

As the Allies began to prevail and wage the war on German soil, normal civilian life grew uncertain. Just before the Battle of Hamburg, the elder Bieringer traveled to Berlin on business. Then on July 27, 1943, nearly 750 aircraft attacked Hamburg, raining bombs throughout the city and causing enormous destruction. Two nights later the city was attacked again by 700 aircraft. Eight square miles of the city was incinerated. The heat was so intense that many perished while in bomb shelters. Reports of Hamburg's utter devastation reached Bieringer's father, and he was convinced that his family had perished in the flames. It was impossible to confirm the fate of them or other Hamburg families. Likewise, Alice sensed that her husband had been lost in Berlin. She and her two young children were assigned to live with a family in a farm labor camp near Weidensees in southern Germany.

In one of many ironies of those turbulent times, the bombing of Hamburg, which brought death to so many, was probably the salvation of Alice and her boys. Perhaps her marriage to an Olympic hero had allowed her to remain free for a time. Inevitably she and her children would have been loaded in a cattle car and sent to their deaths, the fact that she practiced Catholicism notwithstanding. But for the cascade of world events, her fate—like that of much of her extended family—had been sealed.

As most of Germany was wending a miserable path to capitulation, Bieringer was learning to milk cows and to cut and bale hay. He and his brother enjoyed two years on the farm while the war ran its course. The host family was convinced the Bieringer boys would become farmers. That was not the case, but years later when Bieringer (his surname anglicized to Beering in 1948 when the family moved to America) was president of Purdue University, he participated in a milking contest on Monument Circle in downtown Indianapolis. The other contestants were the governor, lieutenant governor, and the president of Indiana University. When Beering was asked if he wanted tutoring to prepare him for the event, he replied, "I know how to milk a cow." Beering won the milking contest.

From Pittsburgh the Friedrichs provided funds to the International Red Cross to finance the search for their daughter and her family. It was not until late 1945 that Bieringer's father was located in Hamburg and informed that his family was intact. A reunion in the farming village followed shortly thereafter. The war had taken its toll. Bieringer's father had lost all of his hair and more than forty pounds. The Bieringers resettled in Hamburg, which was being rebuilt.

At an early age Bieringer was encouraged by Alice to go into the field of medicine. He yearned to become a physician. As a teenager he was concerned that the lack of schooling during his years on the farm would prevent him from reaching that goal. His father took him to the gymnasium—the German word for a fancy high school—in Blankenese, a fashionable suburb of Hamburg. Professor Herr Plewka, an Oxford graduate who taught Latin, was sure that young Bieringer would flunk out, but he had not counted on the child's determination. During the first week the students were tasked with a dictation exercise. The instructor read an excerpt from "A Christmas Dinner" by Charles Dickens about Uncle George and the plum pudding, while the students transcribed the story in English. At the end of the dictation, papers were collected. Bieringer resisted. He requested an extra day so that he could study it with his mother at home. His father and mother were both fluent in English and French. With his mother's assistance, Bieringer achieved straight As during the year he attended the gymnasium.

Alice's parents helped the Bieringer family survive in postwar Germany with care packages and money while entreating them to find a better life in the United States. In 1946 that persistence paid off. With the help of the Red Cross, the family temporarily emigrated to London, where they were supported by the love and care of relatives. While awaiting passage to America, immigrants were not allowed to attend school. For two more years Bieringer's education was interrupted. The dream of becoming a physician was slipping away. Alice took advantage of the time with her sons by educating them at museums and other cultural institutions—home schooling as best she could.

For a short time in England the family stayed with Alice's cousin, Frederick Valk, a famous Shakespearian actor and movie star. Born in Hamburg, he fled the Nazis in the 1930s and became a British subject.

According to Bieringer, one day Valk said to him, "I'm having some of my understudies in for dinner and I would like for you to meet them. They are good actors." He sat next to a man named Ollie who confided that if he ever achieved success in the Shakespearian theater, it would be due to the efforts of cousin Frederick. Ollie, later known as Sir Lawrence Olivier, was knighted for his work in the theater. But Bieringer was not bitten by the acting bug. His dedication to science was unwavering. "When we finally came to America," he recalled, "my life truly began."

On July 24, 1948, after a week's ocean passage, the ship *Britannic* arrived on the New York coast and docked at Ellis Island only a few hundred yards from the Statue of Liberty. The Bieringers disembarked and began a critical, nerve-racking test. Papers were presented to immigration authorities, who assigned doctors to perform cursory physical examinations. They were looking for anyone who wheezed, coughed, shuffled, or limped. Children were asked their names to make sure they were not deaf or dumb. In 1907 legislation barred immigrants who were physically disabled or suffering from tuberculosis or epilepsy. Of primary concern was tuberculosis. Those passengers that did not pass inspection were escorted to their ships and sent back to Europe. Because of the Friedrichses' intervention, the Bieringers were considered sponsored immigrants, and that made a difference. A new life in America beckoned. The Bieringer family passed into the arms of grandparents who were waiting at the dock.

When the family arrived in Pittsburgh, Bieringer was not quite sixteen. The transition involved adjustments that would have caused most teenagers pause, but Bieringer was driven. His dream of becoming a physician had not faded. He had fallen behind during the two years he had not been formally educated, and although he felt ready for college he was informed that he would have to attend high school. He interviewed and gained acceptance in the junior class of the largest high school in Pittsburgh, Taylor Allderdice. Due to his vast and varied world experience, Bieringer was more urbane and in a sense better educated than his classmates, but he lacked a classical education and had a large knowledge gap—particularly in subjects to which he had had no exposure, such as geometry.

Bieringer worked diligently and graduated in 1950 with a perfect record. He was offered a number of college scholarships, but because his grandfather had suffered a stroke that sapped the family finances, Bieringer was forced to attend a school close to home. He chose the University of Pittsburgh, where he majored in biology and chemistry and graduated summa cum laude in 1954.

In 1951—on the first day of class of his sophomore year—he met freshman coed Jane Pickering. Although for a time Jane lived in Washington, D.C., they dated steadily and were married in 1956, three years after he became a citizen. Jane had studied international political science in college and was fluent in Chinese. She had promise at the U.S. State Department but gave up her job in Washington, D.C. to rejoin Bieringer, now Beering in Pittsburgh.

After college, Beering attended the University of Pittsburgh School of Medicine, graduating in 1958—at last a lifelong quest fulfilled. Beering enjoyed the medical school and remains a proud supporter of the university. He has served on its board of trustees for many years, chairing the medical school visiting committee. In 2009 he was elected a lifetime trustee.

As Beering experienced medical school, every rotation excited him. Each time he was exposed to a new specialty he thought, "This is what I want to do the rest of my life." He finally decided on internal medicine because it was the broadest specialty. Within internal medicine, he opted for further training in endocrinology, explaining, "Hormones are what really regulate the body and I thought disease to be an aberration or form of hormonal imbalance. Today, cancer of the breast, an epidemic right now, may be related in part to the fact that women have been taking birth control pills and we have been prescribing estrogen to menopausal women and therefore unbalancing their hormones."

In the midst of the Korean War, young men over eighteen were called to the draft board and given a physical every six months. A sergeant whom Beering had gotten to know suggested that he could avoid this routine by volunteering. He could choose the service he wished, but he would have to serve four years instead of two. Beering was enamored with the prospect of flying and joined the U.S. Air Force in 1957, at the beginning of his senior year in medical school. He was commissioned a second lieutenant, making him eligible for a military-sponsored internship and residency, which he undertook at Walter Reed Army Hospital in Washington, D.C., and the U.S. Air Force Wilford Hall Medical Center at Lackland Air Force Base in San Antonio, Texas. After completion of residency, he was asked to join the staff of the Department of Medicine there.

Beering enjoyed the quality and diversity of his practice. He stayed at Lackland for ten years, rising in the ranks. During his tenure at Lackland, he was named chief of internal medicine and was honored to be promoted to lieutenant colonel.

In 1960 Beering was named one of the physicians for Project Mercury, the United States' first human space flight program. Its goal—achieved in 1962—was to put a human in orbit around the earth. In his capacity as a physician to the astronauts, he administered to the medical needs of the Mercury Seven: Scott Carpenter, Gordon Cooper, John Glenn, Gus Grissom, Wally Schirra, Alan Shepard, and Deke Slayton. While still at Lackland, he served on the medical support team for the subsequent Gemini and Apollo programs as well. He gave *Apollo 11* astronaut Neil Armstrong his initial flight physical. They are still friends. Many of the astronauts were graduates of Purdue, a fact that was not relevant to Beering until a later phase of his career. Beering joined the astronauts for training and was placed on flying status achieving the designation of flight surgeon. It was a thrilling time. Beering enjoyed his medical practice, teaching, and research work. He also became a family man. All three of his sons, Peter, David, and John, were born at Lackland.

Beering was slated to move to the surgeon general's office in Washington, D.C., but was resistant to the idea of a life behind a desk. Besides, after Armstrong took his first steps on the moon, the excitement was over for Beering. He resigned in 1969 and called his friend John Hickam, chairman of the department of internal medicine at Indiana University. Hickam was an air force brat whose father was the Hickam for whom Hickam Field in Hawaii was named. On Hickam's recommendation,

Beering accepted a full professorship of medicine and assistant deanship at IU's School of Medicine, with teaching assignments in endocrinology and rheumatology. He had never even been to Indianapolis.

Medical school dean Glenn Irwin and Beering became friends and colleagues. In the early 1970s, Irwin assigned Beering a project to reinvent the medical school in order to solve the doctor shortage in Indiana. Beering developed the Indiana Statewide Medical Education System, which has become a worldwide model for medical education. Through that, he established centers of education at the other major universities around the state: Purdue, Indiana State, Ball State, Evansville, and Notre Dame. The first two years of medical school take place at these centers. After two years in the system, students who do not wash out are advanced to Indianapolis in order to complete the last two years of medical school training.

When Irwin was named chancellor of IUPUI in 1973, Beering succeeded him as dean of the IU School of Medicine, for most a fitting cap to an extraordinary career. Beering was happy and content in this position and enjoyed the tangential opportunities to serve in various additional capacities, including as chairman of the Council of Deans for the Association of Medical Colleges and as an active leader in the College of Physicians. But there was more to come—much more.

In 1982 Beering fielded a call from a committee searching for a new president for Purdue. Thinking that a medical doctor was not compatible with the highly technical engineering science curricula, he rejected the overture. He also was concerned that as a physician and an administrator at rival IU, he would not be accepted by students and faculty. His middle son, David, who was a sophomore at Purdue, implored his father to reconsider. In the fall of 1982 he was visited by the chairman of the Purdue trustees, who also asked him to reconsider his decision. The dialog was restarted. Irwin, a visionary, was excited for Beering's opportunity, knowing that it would bring about a closer relationship between IU and Purdue. Beering ultimately was hired and served as the president of Purdue for eighteen years, retiring in 2000.

Beering is especially proud of the growth in research grants under his leadership. When he arrived, Purdue was the recipient of $35 million in grants a year. When he retired, that number had grown to almost $300 million. One of the highlights of Beering's tenure was the establishment of the School of Liberal Arts, which today is as large as the College of Engineering. He also established a School of Education, which is housed in Beering Hall.

While at Purdue, Beering was elected president of the Association of American Universities, an association of the leading research universities in the country. Beering also became active in the National Collegiate Athletic Association and served on its board. He was instrumental in relocating the NCAA headquarters from Kansas to Indianapolis in 1999.

In 1983 Beering was only the second physician to be appointed to the board of Eli Lilly and Company. He served Lilly until his mandatory retirement in 2007 at seventy-five. He also served on other corporate boards, including Arvin Industries, NiSource Inc., Guidant Corporation, and American United Life Insurance Company.

In 2002 Beering was appointed to the National Science Board, and later became its chair. Founded by the Harry S. Truman administration to manage science research throughout the nation, it is composed of twenty-four individuals from science, technical, and engineering disciplines who are nominated by the president of the United States and confirmed by the Senate to six-year terms. Each member is allowed two terms. The responsibilities are threefold. First, advise the president on matters of science, such as stem cell research. Second, advise the U.S. Congress. Congress has requested that the board study renewable energy, for example, and much of the committee's congressional work has resulted in legislation. Third, serve as the board of trustees for the National Science Foundation, overseeing the execution of numerous large grants. Current projects include global installation of telescopes at high altitudes and management of the U.S. Polar Research Station at the South Pole. Beering said, "The third responsibility is probably the most key. It is very difficult to invest large amounts of money and the decision of whom to grant to should not be taken lightly."

Beering is grateful for the opportunities to help others make a difference. That service has been recognized. He was awarded the University of Pittsburgh Distinguished Medical Alumnus Award and the university's Bicentennial Medallion of Distinction (1986), among the many awards and citations from his alma mater. He also is the recipient of numerous honorary degrees and has been cited by four Indiana governors with the prestigious Sagamore of the Wabash designation. In 2009 Beering was bestowed an honorary doctorate degree by the University of Notre Dame. Beering shared the platform with President Barack Obama, who delivered the commencement address.

Beering is pleased that chance brought him to Indiana because, as he said, "The last forty years in Indiana have been phenomenal." His advice to young people is to work hard and do well. Beering declares, "It doesn't make any difference what field you are in. It does not have to be science, but you have to be sincere about it and work hard and not be selfish. Be outer directed and help others without looking for any self aggrandizement, titles, or honors."

While president of Purdue, Beering attended an alumni meeting in Hamburg, much of which was rebuilt pursuant to original plans. It was an occasion to reflect. According to Beering, "I did not plan any of the things that happened to me. I just tried to do my best wherever I was." The little boy whose life was spared amidst the rubble of war torn Germany did his best as a child and as an adult. Humanity is better for those efforts.

JOSEPH MAMLIN, M.D.

Adventurer/Humanitarian

Salina Rotich stumbled into the clinic in the spring of 2002, a full grown woman in her mid-thirties weighing barely seventy pounds. Her body, under the command of the AIDS virus, was raging with infection. Doctor Joe Mamlin began a therapeutic regimen of the latest drug combination, but Rotich was not responding. Why?

Like many in rural Kenya, Rotich was mired in abject poverty, unable to afford the basic food for proper nutrition—without which the AIDS virus would almost certainly win the battle for her life. So the doctor began giving her money for food at each visit and watched her thrive. Her weight doubled. "That's when I realized nutrition was an important aspect of AIDS treatment," Mamlin said. "No one must go hungry, particularly when fighting this devastating virus."

The care program that evolved from what Mamlin learned in the city of Eldoret now feeds more than thirty thousand Kenyans—making it the largest nutritional program in the world for those infected with HIV. Every patient is interviewed by a nutritionist, and those who are not eating sufficient amounts are given enough food for their entire household. This innovative and sensible approach to the treatment of AIDS began with Rotich and perhaps will lead to the taming of HIV in the rest of Kenya and throughout Africa. It is no wonder that Mamlin

and the Indiana University-Kenya AMPATH program—for Academic Model for the Prevention and Treatment of HIV/AIDS—were twice nominated for a Nobel Prize.

The prestigious Nobel Prize nomination is not the only honor accorded to this hero. In Kenya, it is tradition to name your child after the one who does you a great honor. At last report, there are nearly two dozen Joe Mamlins in Eldoret.

Born on November 17, 1935, Indiana's Joe Mamlin started life in the mountains of North Carolina. His father, Maurice Mamlin—the son of Ukrainian immigrants—had settled in Philadelphia but was misdiagnosed with tuberculosis and strongly advised to breathe fresher air. He chose North Carolina, where he met and married Roberta Leesta, a woman Mamlin describes as a "hillbilly." Named in honor of Robert E. Lee, her history reached back to the roots of the Confederacy. Maurice Mamlin was an inventor who designed the face protector shield for firefighters and the plastic window ice scraper. Unfortunately, the elder Mamlin lacked business acumen and failed to realize the wealth that could have resulted from his innovations.

The Mamlin family was poor. Young Joe, his two brothers, and a sister worked every day after school and every weekend. He and his siblings were raised to be completely independent. There was, however, no familial expectation for higher education. His mother managed to complete sixth grade and his father stopped his schooling after high school. Mamlin's own educational future was put in jeopardy when he was thrown out of English class his junior year, preventing him from earning enough credits to graduate with his class. The details of the ejection are lost to history, but legend has it his sense of humor was not appreciated by the teacher.

While working at JC Penney, Mamlin sold clothes to the wife of the Mars Hill Junior College president and mentioned to her that he was thinking about trying to enter college despite his lack of a diploma. Recognizing his intrinsic intelligence, she invited him to visit her husband at the junior college in the western part of the state. Also impressed, the president granted Mamlin a one-semester trial admission. After the first term, all concerned made an important discovery: Mamlin was a student. He excelled at his courses and after two years enrolled at Wake Forest University in Winston-Salem, North Carolina, where he graduated in 1958 with a double major in science and philosophy. In addition to the academic load, Mamlin held three jobs at Wake Forest—assistant in the physics department, assistant in the philosophy department, and orderly in the infirmary.

Possessed—and perhaps obsessed—with a spirit of adventure, Mamlin hitchhiked to Oregon during two summers of his college years, working as a lumberjack. While traveling across the country with very little money, he discovered that he could sign in for a free night's sleep at the local jail if he promised to clean his cell before he left the following morning. Mamlin took pleasure in lumberjacking. The work was satisfying, particularly alongside men who had a profane vocabulary the likes of which he had never been exposed to in the mountains of North Carolina. "They took it to an art form," Mamlin recalled. Lumberjacks in Oregon cut Douglas fir and Hemlock trees, bucking them into logs and loading the logs onto trucks headed for sawmills.

Mamlin was a "powder monkey"—a dynamiter who removed the hundreds of stumps that were left after the trees were felled so that the trucks could transport the logs. The procedure is as follows: A metal bar is hammered into the stump to make a hole, into which one or two dynamite sticks are placed. The lumberjack then stands on the stump and triggers the dynamite below, which creates a large pocket. (The top of the stump is the safest place to be when the dynamite goes off because two sticks of dynamite are not enough to blow up the stump, but will shoot out from the sides like a bullet.) After the initial dynamite has created sufficient space, the powder monkey puts another seventy-five to one hundred sticks of the explosive inside each stump, wires all of the stumps together, yells, "Fire in the hole" three times, and hits the plunger. The stumps completely disappear.

It occurred to Mamlin that the occupation had to be dangerous, given the absence of old lumberjacks. A personal experience confirmed that perception. One day the powder monkeys noticed they had missed a stump. Mamlin inserted the two dynamite sticks and stood on top of the stump, but just before he was ready to trigger the blast, one of the powder monkeys screamed, "Hold it, perhaps we've already put one hundred sticks of dynamite in this stump and forgot to wire it in." Mamlin dismounted and noticed that was in fact the case. He retreated to a safe place and triggered the blast. Sure enough, the stump disappeared. That would have been the end of Mamlin and countless Kenyans whose lives have been saved by this adventurous humanitarian.

While Mamlin was hitchhiking back to North Carolina one evening in 1955, the vehicle he was riding in collided with a tractor-trailer near Albuquerque, New Mexico. There were no seat belts in those days, and he suffered a broken right hip and severe cuts to his arm. He was taken to Saint Joseph Hospital in Albuquerque, where a skilled surgeon operated on him. Mamlin spent more than six weeks in the hospital and had two more surgeries. He returned to school with a vision. Until the accident, he was a philosophy major who had never thought of medicine as a career but the experience enthralled him. He yearned to join the legion of men and women who could mend people's bodies and restore them to health.

After graduating from college in 1958, Mamlin was accepted to medical school at Wake Forest. That same year, R. J. Reynolds of the RJ Reynolds Tobacco Company created a scholarship program covering all expenses at the Wake Forest School of Medicine. Mamlin was named the first Reynolds scholar. The program allowed Mamlin to finish medical school in 1962, debt free.

That year Mamlin accepted an internship and residency in internal medicine at the Indiana University School of Medicine, choosing the school because a well-known physician from Duke University in North Carolina, John Hickam, led the medical department. Mamlin had married in between college and medical school, so he moved his growing family to Indiana. In 1965 he accepted a cardiology fellowship at Duke to begin the following year. IU would pay him a salary while he attended Duke on the condition that Mamlin would return and serve on its faculty. But his plans changed. After completing the residency at IU, Mamlin and his wife, Sarah Ellen, who had earned a nursing degree, decided to join the Peace Corps. "I just heard that the Peace Corps was going to try to start a medical school in Afghanistan," Mamlin recalled. "I had to choose between a bicycle and seventy-five dollars a month in the Peace Corps . . . or go to Duke in cardiology. It was a no brainer. My wife, three children, and I took off for Afghanistan."

Residents of Afghanistan speak two languages: Pashto, the language of the Pashtun people now associated with the Taliban community, and Dari, a Persian dialect that uses different accents and word usage than Iran. Typical of government ineptitude, the Peace Corps taught Dari to Mamlin and his wife and then placed them in a community that spoke Pashto. He adjusted and during his two-year stint in Afghanistan he and his colleagues wrote the first Pashto medical textbook. Although Mamlin was the only fully trained internist for fifteen million Afghans, he enjoyed his experience there and he loved the Afghan people. Mamlin referred to the Afghanistan of those two years as Shangri La instead of today's hell.

In 1968 Mamlin returned to Indiana and accepted a position on the IU Medical School faculty. He was assigned to Marion County General Hospital, now Wishard Memorial Hospital, a major trauma center and one of the oldest hospitals in Indianapolis. While at Wishard he continued to travel to Afghanistan in a collaborative effort with other Big Ten schools to support the medical education system there—all that ended when the Russians invaded in 1979. Mamlin contented himself with the challenges presented by his promotion to chief of medicine at Wishard.

In 1988, with the assistance of Indianapolis philanthropist Marty Moore, Mamlin joined three other IU faculty colleagues to investigate strengthening a young medical school in a developing country. Or as he puts it, they sought to find out "what mischief we could create on the world scene." He knew it would not be in Afghanistan, but where? After researching worldwide, they decided upon three possibilities: Katmandu, Nepal; Kamasi, Ghana; and Eldoret, Kenya. Rugged Nepal had appeal since it reminded him of Afghanistan, but the group was concerned that its xenophobic culture would make it difficult to welcome visiting students and doctors from IU on a regular basis. There also was a problem with Ghana. Although the people are remarkable, many of their graduates leave the country. Mamlin did not want to contribute to the brain drain. That left Kenya. The Kenyan doctors by and large were staying in the country, the climate was hospitable, and English was spoken among the educated classes. Eldoret, the fifth-largest city in Kenya with a population of about four hundred thousand, was chosen.

In 1990 the IU team helped Kenya establish the Moi University School of Medicine—the second medical school in the nation. It was a collaboration of multiple universities from around the world including Sweden, the Netherlands, Canada, and the United States. IU agreed to assign one member of its medical school faculty to Eldoret on one-year rotations. Student exchange was an integral part of this program: Hoosier medical students would come to Eldoret for short visits, and upperclassmen from Eldoret would in turn visit IU. As part of the faculty commitment, in late 1992 Mamlin and his wife began a year in Kenya.

At Wishard Mamlin was engrossed with providing relief for the poor who were left out of the healthcare system. He spent years as its chief of medicine and played a significant role in creating a network of community health centers before retiring in 1999, at sixty-four. What would have been the end of an extraordinary career for most only signaled a new direction for Mamlin.

Upon his retirement from IU, Mamlin and his wife returned to Kenya for an anticipated two-year sojourn. It quickly became a lifetime commitment. Soon after their arrival, he realized the relatively quiet city of Eldoret had become a center of the world's greatest challenge—plague. Perhaps because of a lack of education, the AIDS epidemic sweeping through Africa was especially prevalent in Kenya. During his first stint in 1992, Mamlin had experienced the death of eighty-five patients on the adult medicine wards. They lived until their fifties, on average. In 2000 Mamlin was overwhelmed with the loss of more than a thousand patients on those same wards. They only made it into their thirties. "I thought the world was coming to an end in Kenya," Mamlin said. He decided he could not practice medicine in a country where all the young people were dying unless he could effect a significant positive change. At the time, no one was providing lifesaving drugs to the poor dying of HIV. He told the leadership at IU that in his opinion the program should either play a significant role in fighting the epidemic or close down and come home.

Among the young patients dying on Mamlin's ward was Daniel Ochieng, a twenty-four-year-old, fifth-year medical student suffering from a myriad of afflictions related to AIDS and literally wasting away. Once again, Mamlin wrote to IU. This time he told Ochieng's story. The response was immediate. Funding was made available from a member of the IU faculty to offer Ochieng modern antiretroviral therapy. He was the first patient ever treated for AIDS on the public wards of Moi Teaching and Referral Hospital. For a month Ochieng was too weak to leave his bed but then his recovery was dramatic. Nine years later, healthy and vigorous, he became AMPATH's director of outreach, ensuring that HIV patients comply with their treatment protocol.

Later in 2000, AMPATH secured enough medicine to treat forty additional patients. The $40,000-per-month cost was underwritten by Indianapolis donors. With this modest support, Mamlin began a clinic that has since spawned forty-five additional treatment centers. AMPATH has received $65 million in grants and has treated approximately a hundred thousand patients, making it the largest program in East Africa. Financial support has come from the United States through a program directed by another Hoosier, former Eli Lilly and Company CEO Randall Tobias, who served in President George W. Bush's administration as the director of the President's Emergency Plan for AIDS Relief. "When history writes this story, it is going to rival the Marshall Plan and be considered one of the great positive legacies of the Bush administration," said Mamlin. AMPATH has responsibility for an area populated by two million people. "We are going after that two million like it was family," Mamlin said. "We started in hospitals, then clinics, and now we're going door to door, hut to hut, doing our testing inside the home. It is probably the only program in Africa that's doing that." Mamlin and his wife work sixteen hours a day, seven days a week, with little respite.

According to Mamlin, one of the biggest threats in the pandemic is posed by HIV-infected Kenyan women who are pregnant. Left untreated, half of those babies will be born infected and 95 percent of those infants will die. Mamlin laments the time and resources expended on treating infected babies and asks the question, "Why not just not have any infected babies?" AMPATH is now screening more than forty thousand pregnant women a year. Every HIV-infected woman who is pregnant is brought to a clinic and placed on a triple therapy regardless of whether she is sick. This therapy drops the virus to an undetectable level that is not likely to be passed to the infant at the time of delivery. The mother is maintained on the antiretroviral drug regimen until her baby is weaned so the virus will not invade her breast milk. There are 1,200 caregivers engaged in this initiative, and Mamlin is the only white face practicing clinically on a full-time basis. He is proud to stay behind the scenes and let Kenyans administer what has become their program.

In addition to the medicine, nourishment, care, and attention, AMPATH clinics educate patients to use good sense in sexual relationships. "Infections generally come from someone not on therapy, unaware of his or her disease, who is sexually active with multiple partners. The infectivity of someone on antiretrovirals with fully suppressed virus and with the wisdom of having faced death is very low," said Mamlin.

In 2002 Mamlin realized that so-called food insecurity was widespread and felt that in order to ensure the proper nourishment of its patients, AMPATH needed to raise its own food. He enticed a Welsh farmer to join the program and develop a farm on ten acres donated by a local high school. Together they grew green vegetables and made their own yogurt. They also acquired chickens, adding protein-rich eggs to patients' diets. Some patients helped with the farming. Today, AMPATH farms year-round and produces more than thirty tons of fresh produce every month—all for consumption by patients. It also receives 120 tons of food every month from the United Nations' World Food Program.

In 2004, concerned that AMPATH was unintentionally creating a disease perhaps just as bad as HIV—dependency—program leaders initiated an income-generation program that aims to help provide income security for patients who strive for the independence to purchase their own food and drugs. It includes work in farming, factories, and craft shops. Purdue University joined the endeavor, and the Japanese government assists by providing fertilizer.

AIDS is just one problem that must be dealt with in Kenya. In December 2007, just after Christmas, a national election was held. When candidate Mwai Kibaki from the Kikuyu tribe was declared the winner, the populace—expecting the winner to be his opponent, Raila Odinga—accused Kibaki of fixing the election. Rioting ensued, centered in Eldoret. Suddenly all roads were closed, stores and banks were shut down, gas was impossible to purchase, and roving gangs controlled the populace. Automobiles were stopped and passengers with a Kikuyu accent were pulled from the cars and killed. The Kikuyu retaliated. Tribal warfare flared.

Almost immediately, the hospital's quiet little mortuary took delivery of 120 mutilated bodies that nobody could identify. It continued to receive twenty-five to thirty additional bodies per day. The need to treat the sick and wounded escalated. Mamlin did not stand idly by. He asked a local Eldoret pharmacist to open his store for Mamlin to collect his inventory of intravenous fluids and suture material and took them to the hospital. He then joined a police escort to safely transport a truck to the airport, where the Red Cross was able to fly in additional supplies. When he was on the tarmac at the airport, he looked around. It seemed as though houses were burning in every direction. He arranged to evacuate all the Americans—that is, everyone but him and his wife.

Mamlin hid 150 Kenyans, mostly Kikuyu, in the IU compound. A representative of the U.S. Embassy flew to Eldoret and advised him that he was risking his life concealing these people and that they should be turned away. "I thought, 'Go to hell. We are not turning anyone away,'" Mamlin said. "I looked at the children playing in the family room and said, 'What is going to happen to these children?' You do what you have to do." During that time there were no workers available to farm, so AMPATH recruited convicts from the local prison to harvest the crop in exchange for food.

After two months of war, former UN Secretary-General Kofi Annan negotiated a cessation of hostilities, putting an end to the anarchy. Kibaki was allowed to remain president and Raila was made prime minister with substantial executive power. The balance of power and the mutual naming of administrative cabinet posts created an uneasy peace. AMPATH operations returned to relatively normal. Mamlin realized that AMPATH should have stockpiled drugs at every clinic in anticipation of delivery interruptions. He lamented the fact that many of his patients fell out of remission because they had no access to drugs.

Mamlin now lives eleven months of the year in Kenya, returning to Indianapolis for the remaining month. He envisions the Kenya project lasting for the rest of his life. "I'll leave Kenya when they carry me out," he said. "That is my life and that is what I will do until I am unable to do it."

In 2004 Mamlin received IU's John W. Ryan Award for exceptional contributions to the university's international programs and engagement. Commenting on the award, medical professor and AMPATH cofounder Robert Einterz praised Mamlin: "He is a man of the highest integrity, with uncommon charisma, unquenchable energy, insatiable optimism, and exceptional vision."

Mamlin believes it is critically important for people—in whatever profession—to be superbly trained and to pursue the best education possible. But, he added, "That's only half the ticket. Learning your specialty is only a box of tools and if all you have is a box of tools you're going to get hurt later in life. Tools are not worth much if they never are used to make something." Mamlin believes too many doctors have become cynical and frustrated, dropping out of the profession early. "The problem with medicine is you go from college to medical school, medical school to residency, residency to subspecialty and then you crank, crank, crank and before you know it, life is over," he said. "Hello, what was that all about? If you can take all the wonderful skills and embed them in something perhaps a little more meaningful, life is more fun. If what you do during the day is in absolute harmony with who you really are, that's about as good as it gets."

According to Mamlin, "Life has dealt me some interesting twists and turns: A lumberjack and adventurer turns to medicine literally by accident, accepts a cardiology fellowship but diverts to Afghanistan to help build a medical school, is upended by a Russian invasion and ends up in Kenya, the epicenter of the greatest pandemic of recorded history. None of this is cited as part of a brilliant strategic plan, just following life along." When students come to Mamlin for advice, he recommends they do the same: "Why don't you spend 10 percent of your time being the best doctor you can be and 90 percent of your time figuring out who you are, and what your values are?" Mamlin knows who he is and undoubtedly, this humble world servant is the best doctor he can be.

Rev. Theodore M. Hesburgh, C.S.C.

Priest

On December 9, 1999, upon the unanimous vote of both houses of Congress, the Congressional Gold Medal was bestowed upon Father Theodore Hesburgh. Since the American Revolution, Congress has commissioned gold medals—the United States' highest civilian award—to express national appreciation for distinguished achievements and contributions. Hesburgh joined the ranks of a select few that began with George Washington in 1776 and also includes Thomas Edison, Irving Berlin, and Jonas Salk.

The award was presented by President Bill Clinton in a ceremony at the U.S. Capitol. Before he approached the podium, the president was provided a folder containing a speech written by the White House staff. He flipped through the pages before dropping the folder under his chair. When he rose, he spoke from the heart. He cited Hesburgh for his contributions to civil rights and higher education and his service to the global humanitarian community. He then declared that Father Ted may think the award is something special, and while there is something special about the medal that now hung around his neck, the best thing he has around his neck is that small white collar that enables him

to spend his life in the service of his fellow man.

Theodore Martin Hesburgh was born in Syracuse, New York, on May 25, 1917, in a world on fire—a fire that threatened to consume the energy, resources, and lives of its most peaceful nations, a fire that was aptly named World War I. He was named for his grandfather, Theodore Bernard Hesburgh, except that his middle name was given in honor of his Irish maternal grandfather. His mother, Ann Marie Murphy Hesburgh, had leveraged her lovely soprano singing voice to win a four-year scholarship to study at La Scala in Milan, Italy, but gave up her career aspirations in order to marry his father, a salesman also named Theodore Bernard Hesburgh. Both parents were religious and, in contrast to the world outside, filled their home with a sense of love and faith. Hesburgh, the second oldest, had three sisters and a brother. The children attended Catholic schools and rarely missed Mass. At Most Holy Rosary High School, Hesburgh enjoyed sports and interaction with his fellow classmates, including the girls he dated. But as early as elementary school, he knew his calling in life was to become a priest. "I can simply say that from the time I began to think about life and its meaning, it was obvious to me that I wanted to be a priest and nothing else," Hesburgh said. With the support of his family, he never wavered. After graduation from high school, he entered the Order of the Congregation of the Holy Cross and began his undergraduate studies at the University of Notre Dame.

Most of his curriculum was prescribed for him. It included basic college disciplines—English and chemistry, for example, but whenever possible Hesburgh chose courses in philosophy, Latin, and Greek. Between his first year as a postulant and his second year as a "professed religious"—one who has taken his vows—he spent a year at Rolling Prairie with twenty-eight other novice seminarians. Rolling Prairie was a small village located about thirty miles west of Notre Dame. It is also the name of the nearby farm owned by the Holy Cross Order. In many ways, Rolling Prairie was a boot camp, not unlike the marines'

Parris Island, with rigorous physical training and a hard-nosed routine intended to prepare the incoming class for the rigors of the priesthood by exposing them to physical labor and mental discipline. It was a test designed to weed out those young men who thought they wanted to be priests, but did not have the stamina and will to stay the course. At the end of the year at Rolling Prairie, only nine of the original twenty-nine remained.

The seminarians rose at 5 a.m. and spent the morning in meditation and religious observances. After household chores including cleaning rooms and washing dishes, they spent the rest of the day farming. Hesburgh learned an important truth: "The best way to handle a disagreeable job was to do it as fast as you could." As part of the mental discipline, Hesburgh was allowed to break silence only two hours a day—the hour after lunch and the hour after dinner. Despite all the farm work and house duties, Hesburgh read, in his estimation, more than a hundred books. The work at Rolling Prairie taught him how much can be accomplished if one focuses on the task at hand without interruptions and without distractions. He also learned that whatever life held for him he would never be a farmer.

After his sophomore year, Hesburgh was assigned by the Order to study for eight years in Rome for a doctorate in theology in order to prepare for the priesthood. Living and studying in Rome presented many challenges for a student from Syracuse, New York, who literally had just come off the farm. One of the challenges was language. His host home was managed by Father Savage, a Frenchman who expected that while in his home the students would converse in French, read lessons in French, and even pray in French. At the university, classes were taught in Latin: chemistry, calculus, anthropology, philosophy—all in Latin. On the streets of Italy, Hesburgh was expected to speak Italian. While mastering these languages, he also learned Spanish from a fellow student. The following summer, he mastered German. Hesburgh believes that the fluencies he acquired in Rome helped him in the work he was to do the rest of his life.

In May 1940, toward the end of Hesburgh's third year in Rome, the American counsel announced in class that the Nazis had invaded the Low Countries and that all Americans would have to evacuate in exactly one week. Hesburgh's peaceful academic sojourn in Rome was cut short by a world once again in turmoil.

Hesburgh returned to Washington for three years of study prior to his ordination on June 24, 1943, with fifteen classmates in the Sacred Heart Church on the Notre Dame campus. After ordination, Hesburgh requested an assignment as a chaplain in the armed forces. Instead, he was reassigned to Washington to obtain a doctorate in theology, which he received in 1945. After five years in Washington he returned to Notre Dame and was assigned to teach in the department of theology. In his first few years there, he lived in the dormitories with the undergraduate students and was available day and night for advice and counsel. He wrote his thesis on the place of the laity in the church. It was thought to be the first such serious theological writing on that subject in the history of the Church.

Hesburgh taught moral theology to the general student population. He felt that the religion courses were probably the worst-taught courses at the university and that the existing textbooks were riddled with useless information for young students, including how late one could come to Mass or how early one could leave and still fulfill the Sunday obligation. He preferred to teach ideals, goals, and Christian virtues. Father Roland Simonitsch, the head of the religion department, agreed. He convinced Hesburgh to write a textbook, which Hesburgh titled *God and the World of Man*. It was published by Notre Dame Press in 1950 and sold more than a hundred thousand copies. In the course of his career Hesburgh has written a number of books, including his 1997 autobiography, *God, Country, Notre Dame*, with Jerry Reedy.

Hesburgh considered himself fortunate to be on the faculty of Notre Dame and was content to continue for the rest of his life teaching, writing, and ministering. Father John Cavanaugh, president of the university, had other ideas. In 1948, when Father Simonitsch left his post to finish his doctorial studies in Washington, Cavanaugh appointed Hesburgh chairman of the religion department in charge of more than forty professors. After one year, Cavanaugh elevated the thirty-two-year-old Hesburgh to vice president—in fact, much to Hesburgh's surprise, executive vice president. He did not even know what an executive vice president was. Notre Dame was not sure either, as the institution had never had an executive vice president. Hesburgh's charge was to prepare administrative procedures and job descriptions for each vice president's area of responsibility.

In January 1952 Cavanaugh abruptly announced to Hesburgh that he was sick and on doctor's orders leaving for Florida to get some sun. He expected to be gone six to eight weeks. He asked Hesburgh to "take care of things" in his absence. Cavanaugh brought him up to date on pending matters and then rose from his desk, put his hands under a huge pile of unanswered mail, and, with a big grin spread across his Irish face, dumped the letters in Hesburgh's lap and said, "Well, you can get started on these." In late June, only six months later, when Cavanaugh's six-year term of office was completed, there was no question as to who would be his successor: thirty-five-year-old Father Ted.

Hesburgh envisioned Notre Dame as a great Catholic university, the greatest in the world. The model he used was the Ivy League, and more specifically, Princeton University. Both Yale and Harvard had enormous graduate schools. Princeton was more of Notre Dame's size with a superb undergraduate school and approximately fifteen hundred students in graduate studies. Hesburgh aspired for Notre Dame to be a Catholic Princeton.

Hesburgh never consciously developed a formal administrative style. He appointed the best people he could find for every position and relied on them to do their jobs well. He first sought intelligence. According to Hesburgh, if you put someone in a position of power and that person is not intelligent, you have problems. He also looked for imagination, creativity and enthusiasm. He found them all in Ned Joyce, who graduated magna cum laude in the class of 1937. Joyce was a tall ebullient priest of his own age whom he met three months after becoming executive vice president. When Hesburgh ascended to the presidency, he appointed Joyce, then the university's financial vice president, as his executive vice president. While Hesburgh focused on academics, Joyce reigned over finances, buildings, and grounds, university relations, athletics, and everything else. They served together as president and executive vice president for thirty-five years.

While serving full time as president of the university, Hesburgh joined a number of outside organizations, including the International Federation of Catholic Universities and the Association of American Colleges, serving as president of both groups. In 1956 the Vatican appointed Hesburgh as a delegate to the International Atomic Energy Agency, which laid the groundwork for the landmark Nuclear Proliferation Treaty signed by more than a hundred nations. He served in this capacity for fifteen years.

In 1957, when segregation and racial discrimination became visible, volatile issues, Congress created the U.S. Civil Rights Commission to study the subject, report back, and make recommendations. Some may have questioned Hesburgh's suitability for his appointment to this commission. While Hesburgh grew up in Syracuse, he never knew a black person. He was well into his twenties before he had any significant contact with blacks. Moreover, the student population at Notre Dame was a homogenous lot. Yet he was appointed by President Dwight D. Eisenhower as one of the commission's six members and served for fifteen years.

The commission concentrated on voting as its first major issue. Black voters in Montgomery, Alabama, were systematically denied the right to vote. White voters could be registered en masse but blacks would have to go to some remote place and line up, only to be rejected on a minor technicality. There was not a single black resident of Montgomery County who was registered to vote. The commission successfully subpoenaed a county judge who had refused to let them examine the county voting records. He was George Wallace, later governor of Alabama and a candidate for U.S. president.

The commission also held hearings on other issues, including employment, housing, education, administration of justice, and public accommodations. The Omnibus Civil Rights Act of 1964, a landmark piece of legislation followed by civil rights bills in 1965 and 1968, were seminal laws based in large part upon the work done by the commission.

In 1961 President John F. Kennedy signed an executive order creating the Peace Corps. He gave control to his brother-in-law, Sergeant Shriver, who in turn asked Notre Dame to conceive of a pilot project for the group. Hesburgh offered Bangladesh, Guyana, or Chile. Shriver chose Chile. Hesburgh was instrumental in launching that first Peace Corps project, an effort to teach reading and writing in the rural central valley of the South American country. Hesburgh obtained the permission of the Chilean government necessary to allow the project to begin. Later, Notre Dame trained many of the Peace Corps volunteers.

In 1989 Hesburgh was appointed to the Knight Commission on Intercollegiate Athletics with a task to clean up the moral mess in big-time college football and basketball, which included faking grades and paying student athletes. The Knight Commission managed to transfer control of the sports programs from athletic directors to university presidents. The commission insisted that presidents take responsibility for the rampant cheating occurring in their athletic departments.

Hesburgh was busy with his duties at Notre Dame but still was away so much that he was the subject of a campus joke: What's the difference between God and Hesburgh? God is everywhere; Hesburgh is everywhere but Notre Dame. Hesburgh explained how he was able to multitask successfully: "Over the years I have learned how to handle the multiplicity of problems at the same time. You concentrate your fullest attention on one job while you're doing it, you do the best you can, and then you go on to the next one. When I have said or done something, it is over; I do not worry about it any more. I doubt that I have spent more than a half a dozen sleepless nights in my life. I put my worries aside, I say my prayers and I go to sleep. The real secret to handling the demands upon you is possessing inner peace. No matter what the problems, the tensions, the pressures, one can only help oneself by thinking clearly and acting calmly and resolutely. This cannot be done without inner peace, born of prayer, especially to the Holy Spirit. The Holy Spirit is a light and strength of my life for which I am eternally grateful. My best daily prayer apart from the Mass and breviary continues to be simply, 'Come Holy Spirit.' No better prayer, no better results: much light and great strength."

Hesburgh loves to fly in military airplanes (as a passenger). Through the courtesy of his friends in the armed forces he has flown in bombers, fighters, and highly sophisticated surveillance aircraft. He has flown in a navy torpedo bomber from the flight deck of a carrier and in the back seat of an air force SR-71 at supersonic speed. On that occasion, he set a speed record of greater than Mach 3.35 (more than 2,193 miles per hour), but because they did not exceed that speed in exactly the prescribed manner the feat did not stand as an official record. In the early 1980s Hesburgh was placed on an initial list of civilians slated to go up in the space shuttle. Since he had already passed the astronaut physical and had flown in the SR-71, he thought he had a good chance. There were only two civilians ahead of him: Walter Cronkite and James Mitchener. The 1986 *Challenger* disaster put an end to that civilian space travel initiative. Hesburgh suspects he will not have an opportunity to offer a Mass in space.

Hesburgh offers Mass every day, which commemorates the events the ritual reenacts—the Last Supper and Christ's sacrifice, redeeming the sins of all those who believe in him. The Mass is the central part of the Catholic belief in salvation and of all the services performed by a priest, in Hesburgh's mind, there is nothing more important. Of the many venues in which he has said Mass, he remembered an undistinguished little place in the Rome airport. "I was making a half-hour stopover between planes on my way to Jerusalem when it occurred to me that I would not reach Jerusalem until after midnight. I hurried to this small hotel and, puffing hard, spoke to the desk clerk, a woman. 'I'd like to have a room for half an hour,' I said, 'And it's not what you think it's for.' She laughed and said, 'Well then, why do you want it?' I told her I wanted to offer Mass and invited her to come up and take part if she did not believe me. She said she believed me, and handed me the key. I said Mass, came back down to the desk, and asked her how much I owed. 'Nothing,' she said, 'you have sanctified my hotel.' I told her that I hoped one Mass would do it, thanked her, and hurried off to catch my plane. As the years went on, I discovered that when you make up your mind to do something every day, come hell or high water, your life takes on a new, purposeful fascination: You have this obligation to perform, a personal obligation you must not fail. Since being ordained a priest, I have not failed it, with the exception of one night when I was helping to keep a vigil over a premature baby. I have said Mass with atheistic Russian Communists standing around the altar, with readers such as Rosalynn Carter and Robert McNamara, in an Anglican church that had not seen a Catholic Mass since the middle of the sixteenth century, in a dining car aboard a lurching railroad train, on all kinds of ships, in the middle of an African jungle, in thousands of hotel rooms in more than a hundred countries, and in all five languages that I speak."

Hesburgh retired from Notre Dame in June 1987. During his tenure, the student body doubled, while the faculty tripled. The annual operating budget grew from $6 million to $230 million; the endowment from $6 million to more than a half-billion dollars. Space available in classrooms, libraries, laboratories, offices, and public spaces tripled over the thirty-five years. Almost everything that existed on the campus in 1952 had either been renovated or demolished. Faculty salaries grew from among the worst to among the best in the nation. Endowed and other scholarships rose from $100,000 to more than $60 million annually.

When Hesburgh was asked what he wanted to do in retirement, he replied that he wished to work on five ideas that he believed could change the world and profoundly affect all of humanity:

- Peace in a nuclear age.

- Human rights and justice worldwide.

- Human development in terms of new economic, social, and political structures in the Third World.

- Ecology, the next great threat to the survival and development of humanity.

- Ecumenism, the bringing together in peace of all Christians, as well as all the Sons of Abraham—Jews, Christians, and Muslims, who call Jerusalem a holy shrine to the one true God.

During the latter years of his presidency, Hesburgh founded an institute or a center for study and action in each of those five areas. Those five purpose-directed institutes will remain at the top of his "to do" list as long as he is able to carry on. His primary responsibility is to ensure their survival and growth by raising the necessary operating funds.

Hesburgh believes in the power of a single human being. Citing Albert Schweitzer, Mother Teresa, and others, he said, "One of the greatest modern heresies that I hear from time to time is that in our modern world one person cannot make a difference. I do not believe that for one moment. I know it is factually inaccurate. And I never hesitate to say so, especially to our students at Notre Dame. One person or group of persons can make an enormous difference in our lives and our way of living. History is replete with heroic people who realized that they could make a difference, and did—despite the conventional wisdom of the day."

Although officially retired, Father Hesburgh works regularly at his office on the campus of Notre Dame on the thirteenth floor of the library that carries his name. He often sits at his desk and enjoys a cigar—a violation of library rules—while dispensing advice to countless students, friends, and associates who seek his wisdom. His philosophy: "Do as much as you can, as well as you can, as long as you can. Do not complain about the things you can no longer do."

"Do not put a limit on your dreams," he added. "In other words, you can be anything in this country and become president. President [Barack] Obama proved that. I think twenty-five years before now, no one thought it was possible to have a black president. Secondly, I think anyone who is fortunate enough to be an American citizen ought to give back something. Whatever your field of activity, you ought to be involved in some public or private activity that is for the good of the nation."

To young men who inquire about becoming a priest Hesburgh said his advice is very simple: "I tell them it is the most wonderful life in the world. It is a tough life in a way because you have to go it alone. You cannot get married and have a wife. You have to put spiritual things number one in your life across the board and that's not something everybody wants to take on. On the other hand it has wonderful, you might say, paybacks from the joy that comes from being able to help people. A priest belongs to everybody. You have no private life. The smallest kids can come and they should get your fullest attention. I'm not just a priest for Catholics. I'm a priest for everybody."

In addition to the Congressional Gold Medal, Hesburgh has received the President's Medal, the highest award that can be bestowed at the behest of the president of the United States. Hesburgh is reputed to have received more honorary degrees than any person in history. In 2006 Indiana governor Mitch Daniels honored Hesburgh with the Sachem Award, the state's highest honor.

The multitude of awards are fitting tributes for a man who counseled four popes and six presidents, has held fourteen presidential appointments dealing with the social issues of the time—including civil rights, atomic energy, Third World development, and immigration reform—but who, when asked to name his greatest role, without hesitation says, "Wherever I have been, whatever I have done, I have always and everywhere considered myself essentially a priest."

Carl Erskine

Oisk, the Gentleman from Indiana

It was the third game of the 1953 World Series. The Brooklyn Dodgers were finally playing at home. They had lost the first two outings at Yankee Stadium against the seemingly invincible "Bronx Bombers," and if there ever was a game that Dodgers manager Charlie Dressen wanted to win, this was it.

Brooklyn started twenty-six-year-old pitcher Carl Erskine, Number 17. His stuff was good. He had finished the second half of the season 15-2 and was the designated ace of the pitching staff. He had started the first game, but wildness sent him to the bench early. Erskine felt he had let himself, the team, and the fans down. After all, he was the guy who was supposed to be leading the club to a championship.

Erskine knew the stakes were high, telling his roommate, center fielder Duke Snider, "I've got to pitch like there is no tomorrow. I mean, I cannot flunk again." In the confines of friendly Ebbets Field, he was confident and determined.

Yankee pitcher Vic Raschi could always be counted upon to win close games, and this one would be close. Through the first four innings, neither pitcher allowed a run to score. The game was tied 2-2 in the bottom of the eighth when Dodger catcher Roy Campanella came up to bat. During a television interview with Edward R. Murrow the previous night, he had promised to hit a home run. He kept his promise.

123

In the ninth inning, Yankee Manager Casey Stengel sent up three left-handed pinch hitters. Don Bollweg, a good low fastball hitter, struck out on three fastballs. The next batter, Johnny Mize, had bragged to the Yankee bench, "Don't worry. I've got Erskine's number. You guys are swinging at lousy pitches all day. I'll show you how to hit Erskine." Mize was a splendid hitter who in 1981 was elected to the Hall of Fame. As he came to the plate, a voice over the loudspeaker declared that Erskine had just tied a World Series single-game strikeout record with thirteen. The crowd was exceptionally boisterous even for Brooklyn, and the pitcher missed the announcement. Erskine threw a curve ball to Mize for a strike. Another curve, another strike. Then Mize fouled off a high fastball. Erskine threw another overhand curve and Mize took the bait—striking out and looking bad. The play-by-play announcer informed the crowd and baseball fans all over the world that Erskine had broken the record. Erskine still did not hear. The fans erupted, shouting "Oisken! Oisken!" When Mize trotted back to the bench, Yankees second baseman Billy Martin mocked him. "So that's how you hit Erskine, huh?"

Erskine walked the next hitter, Irv Noren, putting the tying run on first base. Next up was first baseman Joe Collins, who had struck out four straight times and was desperate not to go into the record book himself with a fifth strikeout. Erskine and Collins both knew that with one good swing Collins could be a hero. Collins was determined to at least make contact, and he did. He topped an Erskine curve ball back to the pitcher's mound to end the game. Erskine trotted into the locker room and into the record book unaware until informed by teammate Preacher Roe that he held the record for the most strikeouts in a single World Series game—a record that stood for more than a decade.

Carl Daniel Erskine was born on December 13, 1926, in a small rented house on the west side of Anderson, Indiana, the youngest of Bertha and Matthew Erskine's three boys. At Anderson High School Erskine played on the 1944-45 varsity basketball team at the famed Wigwam, an arena that burned to the ground in 1958 and later was replaced with the second-largest high school basketball gymnasium in the world. Baseball was an afterthought in a state that bred rabid basketball fans. Throughout the season, the Anderson basketball team was rated number one in the state and was featured in *Look* magazine. The team lost in the state tournament because its star, "Jumpin" Johnny Wilson, was injured. In 1946 the year after Erskine graduated, Wilson led the team to the state championship.

Erskine played four years of baseball for Anderson. He had a blistering fastball and an overhand curveball learned from his father, a semi-pro player. On the days he did not pitch, he played center field. Archie Chad, who had coached Anderson's state-championship basketball teams in 1935 and 1937, was the baseball coach. Boyhood friend and basketball teammate Wilson—an African American who grew up in the same mixed neighborhood as Erskine—was an outstanding baseball player, but he also was a championship-caliber track star who was commandeered to that spring sport instead.

Years later, when Erskine shared the Dodger dugout with Jackie Robinson, the man who broke baseball's color barrier marveled at Erskine's open-mindedness. "Carl you don't have any trouble with this black and white thing," Robinson remarked. Erskine responded, "No, Jackie, I don't. My best friend Johnny Wilson ate at my house. I ate at his house. You have to realize that everybody with white skin is not your enemy." Robinson response: "Carl, bigots come in all colors." Erskine believes that Robinson not only changed the face of baseball, but he also advanced the cause of social justice even more so than Martin Luther King Jr.

During the summer following his sophomore year in high school, Erskine played on the American Legion baseball team. At a tournament in East Chicago, he pitched against a team from Hammond, Indiana. Erskine estimated that he struck out twenty batters that day. After the game, two scouts representing the Chicago Cubs offered him a contract but his father insisted that Erskine stay in school. Upon graduation, Stan Freezle, a sporting-goods store owner from Indianapolis who doubled as a Brooklyn Dodger scout, sent Erskine a first-class train ticket in a Pullman car to New York to work out with the Dodgers for a week.

Erskine was smitten. Perhaps in another era Erskine would have donned the Dodger blue, but the United States was at war and Erskine soon had another commitment.

After graduating in 1945, Erskine was drafted and as was the custom given his choice of service. Regaled by letters from his brother Donald in the South Pacific, he also chose the navy. He had been in boot camp a little more than three weeks when the atom bombs were dropped on Hiroshima and Nagasaki, forcing Japan to capitulate. Erskine originally was assigned to a carrier, but when the Japanese surrender became imminent his orders were remanded and he was directed to the Boston Navy Yard. Less than two years later, he was honorably discharged.

Languishing on the navy base, Erskine yearned to play baseball for the local navy team. His request was rejected by the recreation officer in charge, who surveyed Erskine's slight 165-pound frame and replied, "We've got a lot of pitchers already." Years later, a fan at Ebbets Field hailed Erskine near the Dodger dugout. The man offered his hand and said, "Shake hands with the dumbest so and so in the world. I'm the rec officer who wouldn't let you pitch for the U.S. Navy. With guys like me, I'm surprised we won the war."

In 1946, on a Sunday afternoon when he was off duty, Erskine visited Milton, a town outside of Boston where he watched a semipro baseball team practice. After practice, he asked the manager if he needed pitchers. The response: "Well, son, our season is pretty much started here but after we get through practice I'll watch you throw." Erskine was in his navy uniform and he felt that the manager wanted to be nice to a serviceman. Erskine threw a couple of fastballs that the catcher could not even touch. "You gotta curve?" the manager asked. Erskine threw a curveball that went right through the catcher's glove. After watching him throw a few more, the manager put his hand on Erskine's shoulder and said, "Son, what are you doing next Sunday?" Erskine pitched the rest of the summer.

The manager also was a scout for the Boston Braves, and soon Erskine was throwing batting practice for duly impressed major leaguers. The Braves offered him a contract and $2,500 signing bonus. "That was huge," Erskine recalled. "My dad worked all year for that at Delco

Remy, but I didn't want to sign with Boston. I told them, 'I'm only nineteen. My dad will have to sign it.'" Erskine's parents were invited to Boston, even as Erskine called the Dodgers. Owner Branch Rickey, who would have signed Erskine in 1945 but for the Navy, intervened and met Erskine's parents in Boston the night before the 1946 All-Star Game. Rickey was a farm boy from southern Ohio and a spellbinder. After a few yarns he finally said, "I understand the Braves want to sign you. How much do you want?" Erskine asked for $3,000. Rickey had learned of the Braves' offer. He responded "I don't have a good conscious to beat Boston by $500; why don't we make it $3,500?" Erskine signed. Not long after, Erskine was discharged from the navy, made his professional debut with the Dodgers' farm club in Danville, Illinois, and married his high school sweetheart, Betty Palmer.

Erskine met Robinson in 1948, during his second year in the minors. While pitching for the Dodgers' AA farm team in Fort Worth, Texas, Erskine was selected to throw five innings in an exhibition against the major league club. After the game, he was relaxing in the dugout when he heard a voice say, "Where's Erskine? I'm looking for Erskine." He walked to the dugout entrance and saw Robinson standing outside. The 1947 Rookie of the Year stuck out his hand and greeted Erskine with a compliment. "Young man, I hit against you twice today. You're not going to be in the minors very long." By July of that year, Erskine had won fifteen games and was called up by the Dodgers. He joined the team in Pittsburgh and went directly to Forbes Field. When the team bus arrived later, the first player off the bus went straight to Erskine's locker. It was Robinson, who said, "I told you, you couldn't miss." They played nine seasons together.

Erskine's first win in the majors came on July 25, 1948, the same day he joined the Dodgers. He entered late in the game as a relief pitcher and walked two batters before Ralph Kiner hit a sinking line drive to left field. George Shuba made a shoestring catch to end the inning with a double play. The Dodgers went on to win the game by scoring in the ninth inning. Years later Erskine saw Shuba, who was a good hitter but a little shaky with the glove, and asked, "George, did I ever thank you for that great catch off Kiner to help me win my first game?" George said, "Yeah, I remember that play. I trapped the ball."

In 1951 the Dodgers were forced into a three-game National League playoff with the hard-charging New York Giants. *The Wall Street Journal* later reported that the Giants had a telescope in center field and were using it to steal signs and send them via a buzzer system to an agent in the bull pen, who in turn transmitted the signals to batters. In any event, a thirteen-and-a-half-game lead had dwindled to a tie at season's end, forcing the playoff to determine the league championship. The Dodgers lost the first game but tied the series on a Clem Labine shutout.

The Dodgers' pitcher for the deciding game was twenty-game winner Don Newcombe, the team's leading hurler. While Newcombe pitched, Erskine and the other pitchers were in the bull pen. The Dodgers were leading 4-1 going into the ninth inning, but the Giants rallied. They scored a run and had two men on base when Bobby Thomson, representing the winning run, came to the plate. The bull pen phone rang. Erskine and Ralph Branca were up and throwing. Erskine had won sixteen games that year, and he was rested. He would have been the logical choice. Dressen asked if the pitchers were ready. The bull pen coach answered candidly, "They're both ready, but Erskine is bouncing his curve once in awhile." To be effective, Erskine's overhand curve had to be low, so occasionally he buried one in the dirt. Based on the coach's reply, Dressen requested Branca to come into the game and relieve Newcombe. Giant Bobby Thomson sent Branca's second pitch into the Polo Grounds' lower left-field stands for a three-run homer, winning the pennant for the Giants with the infamous "shot heard 'round the world." Tongue in cheek, Erskine said he was saved from disgrace because his best pitch was the curveball he bounced in the dirt in the bull pen that afternoon.

In addition to the overhand curve, Erskine had two more basic pitches: a fastball and a changeup. The Dodgers had a good teaching organization. They taught a four-seam fastball, which when thrown overhand with good velocity causes the seams to rotate so fast that they disappear, giving the ball the appearance of a white cue ball. Erskine also learned the overhand curve and the off-speed changeup, that looks like a fastball without the velocity and is meant to fool the batter.

In 1952 Erskine posted a record of 14-6 and threw a no-hitter against the Chicago Cubs. The next year he enjoyed his best season with a 20-6 record. Although the Dodgers finished first in the National League in 1953 with a record of 105-49, they started 1954 spring training slowly under new Manager Walter Alston. Prior to a preseason game in Jacksonville, Florida, Alston held a team meeting and admonished his players. "I've read a lot of clippings about how great this team is. I haven't seen it," he said. "You guys are pros—you know what it takes to win. I don't give pep talks. You either do it or we get someone else. Meeting's over." Erskine posted an 18-15 record in 1954.

On May 11, 1956, Giants scout Tom Sheehan was quoted in a New York paper disparaging his team's crosstown rivals: "The Dodgers are over the hill. Jackie's too old, Campy's too old and Erskine—he can't win with the garbage he's been throwing up there." Robinson and Erskine read that article before the game against the Giants the next day at Ebbets Field. In the fifth inning, Willie Mays hit a shot to Robinson's left at third base. Robinson made a marvelous clean pickup of the smash on one hop and easily threw Mays out. Erskine went on to pitch a no-hitter. Robinson reached in the hip pocket of his uniform, pulled out the newspaper clipping and waved it at Sheehan, shouting "How do you like that garbage?" Robinson was a fierce competitor. So was Erskine. In 1978 the New York Sportswriter's Association presented Erskine with the Casey Stengel Award, recognizing that Erskine was the only player to pitch two no-hitters in Ebbets Field.

In 1958 the Dodgers moved to Los Angeles. Owner Walter O'Malley was a hard-nosed business tycoon who was responsible for the decision to leave Brooklyn. Peter Golenbock, in his book *Bums: An Oral History of the Brooklyn Dodgers*, quotes a Brooklyn Dodgers fan as saying that the three most hated men in the world were Hitler, Mussolini and O'Malley. It was near the end of the thirty-one-year-old Erskine's career, so he was surprised when Alston picked him to pitch the first game played in Los Angeles in front of almost eighty thousand fans. The 1958 Dodgers were a seasoned team. They had played in five World Series and had been in tight pennant races every year. They were used to big crowds. Erskine remembered the first time he pitched in Yankee Stadium, which held seventy thousand people, and he had noted that more people were at the stadium than lived in Anderson. The Dodgers won the opening game 6-5 and Erskine, who pitched over eight innings, was credited with the win.

In Los Angeles Erskine missed the familiar comfort of Ebbets Field and the lifelong Dodgers fans which included Gladys Gooding. According to Erskine, organist Gooding played "Back Home Again in Indiana" almost as much as she played the National Anthem. She played the song every day when Erskine warmed up or was called in from the bull pen to pitch and every time Princeton, Indiana, native Gil Hodges hit a homerun—and the slugger hit many. The Brooklyn faithful gave Erskine the nickname: "Oisk," a Brooklynese abbreviation of how they pronounced his name: Carl Oisken. Yells from the very close Ebbets Field stands would include, "Hey Oisk, I'm witcha babe, trow it tru his head." Roscoe McGowan, sportswriter for *The New York Times*, referred to Erskine as "that gentleman from Indiana."

Almost from the beginning of his major league career, Erskine suffered from arm pain. It plagued him, but he persevered. Finally, after twelve years in the big leagues, Erskine's sore pitching arm had had enough. He pitched his last game on June 4, 1959, and retired at thirty-two with no job. Erskine accepted an offer from shirt manufacturer Phillips-Van Heusen to move him to New York City to take a position selling a new line called "Pleasure Wear." A few months after he accepted that position his fourth child, Jimmy, was born with Down's Syndrome. Erskine resigned, believing Anderson was a better environment for a young family that included an infant requiring significant attention. He declined opportunities in broadcasting and coaching, which involved extensive traveling. His wife and family needed his support. He and Betty rejected the well-meaning suggestions to institutionalize his young son and moved back home again to Indiana.

Growing up with Wilson prepared Erskine for playing with Robinson, and knowing Robinson prepared him for handling his son Jimmy. According to Erskine, "America had some of the same social attitudes toward people with disabilities that it had toward race relations. I often felt that Jackie came into my life to teach me how to channel energy and anger toward what was happening around me with Jimmy and society's nonacceptance of Down's Syndrome and other birth defects. Jackie and Jimmy—because of traditions, superstitions, ignorance, fear and arrogance—felt the bitterness of rejection. Society considered them second-class citizens or worse."

Upon returning to Anderson, Erskine began a career in the insurance business. He had a slow start, competing with more than two hundred insurance agents in Madison County, but made his mark. In 1963, in the midst of a second successful career, he was asked to serve on the board of the First National Bank in Anderson. Within two years, Erskine was generating more business for the bank than those who were paid to do that same job. Within a few years, the bank asked him to take a full-time position. A year later he was named the executive vice president and a few years after that he was elected president, serving for eleven years in that role. In 1986 the bank merged into Star Bank, a regional player on the Indiana banking scene. Erskine was elected president of the Indiana Banker's Association in 1991, capping a third successful career.

Since returning to Indiana, Erskine has been an active and generous volunteer. He served on the board of the Anderson Chamber of Commerce for years. Erskine was proud to coach the Anderson College (later Anderson University) baseball team for twelve seasons, winning four championships. He chaired fund-raising campaigns for Anderson University, St. John's Hospital, and the YMCA. He is one of the founders of the Hopewell Center, a comprehensive facility serving the developmentally disabled and a major player in the local Special Olympics.

Erskine said, "Young people need to believe in who they are—with or without disabilities. They face many challenges and it is easy to be pulled off course." He understands that they often give in to peer pressure and he stresses how vital it is for children to have peers who can influence them in a positive way.

Erskine spends much of his time with his son Jimmy, who participates in a variety of activities. Jimmy has a full-time job at Applebee's restaurant and is a Special Olympics athlete. Erskine said, "They love him at Applebee's. I have thanked the various managers as they have changed over the years, many times and one of the managers told me, 'Carl, my whole staff interacts better when Jimmy is here. We couldn't run this place without Jimmy.'" Erskine and Jimmy also enjoy fishing the ponds for bass and bluegill.

Erskine always liked music, particularly the harmonica. His grandfather was a musician who played fiddle and banjo. After Erskine retired from baseball, a friend asked him to appear on a radio program with his harmonica. That gig begot additional invitations. In response, he organized a band that plays locally. They call themselves Old Stuff. He also has played the National Anthem at baseball fantasy camps and at an old timer's event in Dodger Stadium.

Erskine's plans to be the first college graduate in his family were constantly detoured—first by the draft, then his baseball career and finally marriage, a job, and family. He did enroll at Anderson College but did not finish his degree. In 1984 Anderson University granted him an honorary degree. He also received an honorary degree from Marian College (now called Marian University) in 1993.

Erskine was one of the "boys of summer," a phrase made famous by Roger Kahn in his 1972 book of the same name, which he coined from a poem by English writer Dylan Thomas. Erskine also wrote two books of his own, *Tales from the Dodger Dugout* (2000) and *What I Learned from Jackie Robinso*n (2005). Erskine was elected to the Indiana Baseball Hall of Fame in 1979 and the Brooklyn Dodger Hall of Fame in 1984. He has three baseballs at the Baseball Hall of Fame in Cooperstown: One each for the two no-hitters and one representing his World Series strikeout record. In 1999 Erskine was named a Living Legend by the Indiana Historical Society. In 2010 Indiana Governor Mitch Daniels presented Erskine with the Sachem award, Indiana's highest honor. Daniels praised Erskine for his dedication to the Anderson community and his integrity in business.

When people comment to Erskine that they were happy he came back to Anderson after baseball he replies, "We never left. We were gone most of the year, but we really never left." The Hoosier State is fortunate to claim Carl Erskine, a famed pitcher and a gentleman from Indiana.

LAWRENCE H. EINHORN, M.D.

A Man of Passion and Compassion

O nly a handful of individuals will ever discover a life-saving medical treatment. Nonetheless, thousands of talented researchers, doctors and others commit their professional careers to that possibility. There is no more challenging foe to them—indeed, to humankind—than that of cancer. Unlike other diseases such as polio, where a single vaccine has essentially eliminated it from worry, cancer is a multi-faceted malignancy of countless permutations requiring many different treatment regimens and approaches.

So it is particularly remarkable that one young assistant professor and clinical researcher made a discovery that eliminated overnight the most deadly cancer threatening young men. In 1973, men with meta-static testicular cancer had a five-percent chance of surviving one year after their diagnosis. Within months of Dr. Lawrence H. Einhorn's innovative use of the drug Cisplatin in combination with other medicines, sixty percent of those treated with his regimen had triumphed over the disease. They were cancer free. Within two years, the success rate had climbed to more than ninety percent and Einhorn's protocol had been adopted by clinicians throughout the world. Einhorn, nurtured in a supportive academic environment at the Indiana University School of Medicine, provided a treatment and hope to hundreds of

135

thousands of men who, otherwise, would have been denied the opportunity to pursue their own dreams into middle and old age.

Lawrence Henry Einhorn was born September 29, 1942, in Dayton, Ohio, to Rosalie and Harry Einhorn. Harry was a general practitioner whose office was in his home. Rosalie was an accomplished violinist who had earned a scholarship to the Julliard School of Music. She chose to set that career aside when she met Harry and became a nurse instead. Young Larry Einhorn inherited perfect pitch, a talent he considers wasteful because, although he enjoys piano and can play tunes by ear, he did not commit the time to become an accomplished musician. Einhorn has two sisters, one older and one younger, neither of whom followed in either of their parents' footsteps. In 1965 Einhorn married Claudette Phillips, whom he met at Indiana University. They have two children, Greg and Leslie.

As a young high-schooler, Einhorn tagged along with Harry on hospital rounds. Einhorn wanted to be just like his father, a bright, hardworking doctor who earned the respect of the community—Einhorn and Einhorn, MDs. Unfortunately, Harry's heart condition forced an early retirement. He died in 1987 after his seventh heart attack, but not before he could take pleasure in the triumph of his only son.

After graduating from Indiana University with a Phi Beta Kappa key in 1963, Einhorn attended medical school at the University of Iowa in Iowa City, a school known for its outstanding internal medicine program. When he graduated in 1967, it was obvious Einhorn would not have an opportunity to practice with his father. Perhaps because of his father's affliction, he contemplated cardiology and chose Indiana University for his internship. The IU cardiology department, led by Dr. Charles Fisch, boasted one of the pre-eminent programs in the country. Toward the end of his year-long internship, Einhorn entered a one-month rotation in hematology/oncology with Dr. Robert Rohn. Einhorn was intrigued by the science. The apparent intractability of the disease piqued his ever-present curiosity and competitive spirit. He felt that cancer was a field where advances would be made and he warmed to the challenge. Einhorn opted to become an oncologist.

Following his internship at Indiana University, Einhorn fulfilled his mandatory military requirement in the Air Force as a first lieutenant, spending two years in Wichita, Kansas, treating the wives of the pilots and kids with runny noses. He declined the Air Force's offer to extend his military career, mustered out as a captain, and again returned to Indiana University in 1970, this time for a one-year residency in internal medicine followed by a one-year hematology fellowship.

Oncology was an emerging field in 1972. There were only four accredited schools for oncology fellowships: The National Cancer Institute in Bethesda, Maryland; Roswell Park Cancer Institute in Buffalo, New York; Memorial Sloan-Kettering Cancer Center in New York City; and University of Texas MD Anderson Cancer Center in Houston. Today, there are about one hundred such centers. Einhorn chose to cap his formal education with a one-year fellowship in oncology at Houston's MD Anderson because of its reputation and because he was acquainted with some of the faculty. He enrolled in the experimental therapeutics program, a curriculum that laid the groundwork for his later thought processes and techniques. Einhorn said he would not have achieved such success in his medical career if he had not attended MD Anderson and learned that progress is made by developing new treatments rather than merely learning how to administer standard therapies. Although ninety-five percent of patients with metastatic testicular cancer were dying at the time, not a single case was referred to the experimental therapeutics program. Those cases remained with the competing general oncology program for reasons that were never explained. Einhorn enjoyed the academic environment. He looked forward to continuing to learn and share his knowledge with others through writing and teaching.

Who could have known in 1973 that after completing his formal education Einhorn would embark on a career almost without parallel—one that would make his name revered in every cancer center in every hospital throughout the world? The educational institutions he attended had reason to predict his success and later proudly proclaimed him as one of their own. Each honored him with its distinguished alumni award: MD Anderson in 1992, University of Iowa Medical School in 2001 and Indiana University in 2006.

Einhorn joined the IU Medical School faculty in 1973 as assistant professor of medicine at age thirty-one. Rohn and Dr. William Bond were the entire oncology department before Einhorn's arrival, and they chose to specialize in treatment of the blood diseases leukemia and lymphoma—no solid tumors. Einhorn's hematology fellowship trained him for the work with leukemia and lymphoma as well as non-cancer ailments including hemophilia and sickle cell anemia. At MD Anderson, he dealt solely with solid-tumor oncology including breast cancer and colon cancer. Einhorn soon narrowed his specialty to solid-tumor cancers that were known to be sensitive to chemotherapy, but not cured by it. That included testicular cancer and small-cell lung cancer.

During the first week on staff, Einhorn met the chief of urology, Dr. John Donahue, a surgeon with a specialty in urological oncology. Donahue welcomed Einhorn, and they enjoyed a genial collaboration and friendship for decades until Donahue retired in 1995. Due to Donahue's reputation, the group saw a disproportionate number of testicular cancer cases. Testicular cancer among the general male population is relatively rare. Only one out of four hundred men will suffer from this disease, but because it strikes only young men, it is the most common cancer among men in their twenties. Testicular cancer surgeries are called RPLND, for retroperitoneal lymph node dissection. After Donahue operated, he referred his patients to Einhorn for chemotherapy—not as a preventative measure, but if the cancer returned. Researchers had discovered a blood marker secreted by the tumors, enabling caregivers to determine if testicular cancer had recurred even before a tumor was noticeable on an X-ray. That early determination provided doctors an opportunity to routinely cure patients with no metastases.

No progress was made when the cancer had metastasized, however. Einhorn was curious. Although ninety-five percent of metastasized testicular cancer patients died of their disease, five percent were cured—and that was five percent more than metastatic colon cancer, breast cancer or lung cancer patients. They were all dying. Perhaps a new therapy could raise the odds of survival. He began a clinical trial with a regimen that combined cancer drugs Adriamycin, Bleomycin and Oncovin. The idea of combining drugs was not just a mad-scientist curiosity. By the time Einhorn began his experiment, the principle of combination was widely accepted under the theory that although one drug may kill ninety-nine percent of the cancer cells, what was left became resistant to that drug and a new drug therapy had to be used. The quest with combination chemotherapy is to wipe out all the cancer the first time.

Chemotherapy side effects were harsh. The hair loss, nausea, vomiting, weakness, tingling in the hands and feet, ringing in the ears, and potential for infection usually were temporary, but there was a lasting effect: a reduction in sperm count that prevented about 40 percent of patients from fathering children. (The sperm bank was a viable option beginning in 1965.) In choosing the combination of drugs, oncologists had to be careful not to use drugs with the same side effects. For example, if each of the drugs has the side effect of low blood counts and infection, combining those drugs would require the doctor to administer a homeopathic and perhaps ineffective dosage. The drugs must also be synergistic, not just additive. And each drug must be approved as an active single agent in order to be licensed by the FDA.

The combination of Adriamycin, Bleomycin and Oncovin produced impressive results. Einhorn was able to triple the recovery rate of his patients. That first study involved fifteen metastatic testicular cancer patients, twelve of whom died. But instead of one survivor, there were three. Einhorn was thrilled. He published his findings in the *Cancer of Chemotherapy Reports Journal*, a major journal at the time.

Einhorn decided to test a new therapy that included Cisplatin, a drug derived from the heavy metal platinum, Element 78 on the periodic table. Platinum is a shimmering silvery-white malleable metal when pure, more notable for its use in fine jewelry. Cisplatin had been used in animals and in-vitro systems, and in 1972 was used experimentally to treat humans. Einhorn had treated a number of patients at MD Anderson with Cisplatin. These patients had melanoma, kidney cancer or previously treated lung cancer. They did terribly. The diseases did not respond, and the drug precipitated more severe nausea and vomiting than any drug Einhorn had ever witnessed. Moreover, it caused kidney failure. Cisplatin was about to be discarded as useless because of its severe toxicity and lack of clinical success. Einhorn saved it from extinction after reading of its limited success with two patients treated for testicular cancer at Roswell Park. Cisplatin had been used as a single agent in a third-line therapy and it killed the tumors, but after six months the cancer became resistant to the drug and brought death to both patients. Einhorn wondered if the effectiveness of Cisplatin could be enhanced as part of a combination therapy.

First, Einhorn found a way to eliminate the propensity of Cisplatin to cause kidney damage. Einhorn knew the standard therapy for dissipating the effect of mercury, also a heavy metal, was to ensure that the patient was well-hydrated, causing the mercury to be excreted into the urine. Einhorn administered a liter of saline fluid before and after chemotherapy in the hope that it would wash away the Cisplatin after it worked its miracle. It did.

Einhorn did not want to test his theory as a third-line therapy. By the time two drugs have failed the patient, it is usually too late for any new drug. Einhorn was determined to give his idea a running start. With what would he combine Cisplatin? The most promising regimen in 1974 was Bleomycin. He also added Velban, like Bleomycin a standard cancer drug at the time. Cisplatin did not lower the blood counts and cause infection, and neither did Bleomycin. Velban did, however, so there was no overlapping toxicity. Because it was an experimental drug, Einhorn had to write a protocol and petition the National Cancer Institute to employ Cisplatin as part of a combination chemotherapy regimen. He referred to it as PVB. The request was rejected with the rationale that if one gave Cisplatin as a first-line therapy, what would be provided as second- or third-line therapy? Einhorn thought the reasoning was stupid and appealed to a higher authority at the institute. About a week later, he received approval to try his regimen.

In August 1974, Einhorn treated his first patient, twenty-two-year-old John Cleland, who had recently graduated from Purdue University. The testicular cancer had metastasized to his lungs and he was near death. He had sores in his mouth and could not swallow his own-saliva. One regimen already had failed—making him a second-line patient, not exactly what Einhorn desired—but he had not been dosed with Bleomycin, Velban or Cisplatin. PVB was administered in four, five-day courses with three-week intervals. Cleland held little hope that PVB would cure him, but he volunteered to participate in the clinical trial with the thought that perhaps it would help someone else.

Based upon the Roswell Park experiments and his own studies, Einhorn knew he could prolong Cleland's life for six months and that the saline treatment would prevent kidney damage, but would this noble experiment destroy the cancer cells permanently? It did. Completely. The scans were clear. They were so remarkably different from Cleland's previous scans that the radiologist was concerned he had confused Cleland's films with those of another patient. Cleland still remains cancer-free after more than thirty-five years. Word spread in the medical community that Einhorn had successfully treated a patient with a new drug therapy. Within months, he was referred twenty patients whose testicular cancer had metastasized. His cure rate shot up to sixty percent. Most of his losses occurred because his patients were receiving second- and third-line therapy or had such massive disease that their debilitated bodies could not respond to the treatment.

In 1975 Einhorn wrote a one-page abstract from which he hoped to present data at the American Society of Clinical Oncology meeting in Toronto. He submitted his abstract in a competition with several thousand papers, of which only four were chosen. His was accepted and with the basis of just twenty patients he gave his account to the plenary session in 1976. At the time he wrote the abstract, most of his patients had been followed for only three to six months. He was fearful that some of the patients would relapse and he would look foolish. Fortunately, their remissions were durable. After the abstract was presented, Einhorn's world changed from one where no one in oncology had heard of him to one where many physicians referred Einhorn their testicular cancer patients and sought his advice. Einhorn typically sees two hundred new testicular cancer patients and five hundred returning patients annually. In addition to his own practice, he responds to approximately twenty e-mails each day from patients and physicians.

Einhorn has treated famous patients, many of whom choose not to go public with their cancer, including professional athletes, congressmen and a Saudi Arabian prince. One of Einhorn's testicular patients was a friend of the president of the New York Stock Exchange and procured for Einhorn an invitation in 2009 to ring the closing bell in recognition of the American Society of Clinical Oncology Foundation, of which he was the past president. The opportunity enabled him to meet CEOs from around the country and raise money for cancer research.

Einhorn's most celebrated patient was Lance Armstrong, the multiple winner of the Tour de France. In his book *It's Not about the Bike*, Armstrong compares his bout with metastatic testicular cancer with being run off the road by a truck. Armstrong is from Austin, Texas, and was initially referred to MD Anderson for treatment. The MD Anderson oncologist prescribed six months of chemotherapy and told Armstrong he would never again be able to competitively ride a bike. Dr. Steven Wolff, a cycling enthusiast who was a professor of medicine and oncologist at Vanderbilt University, suggested that Armstrong consult with Einhorn at Indiana University Medical Center. When informed that Armstrong was considering the Einhorn protocol, the MD Anderson oncologist was dismissive. He said, "You can go to Indiana but chances are you'll be back here. Their therapy won't work for an advanced case like yours." This conversation took place in 1996, more than twenty years after Einhorn had proved his Cisplatin combination was curative.

For Armstrong, Einhorn pursued a variation to his standard therapy. Bleomycin would have no effect on the career of an average twenty-five-year-old, but it was known to cause pulmonary fibrosis, a scaring in the lungs that lowers their ability to carry oxygen. This would destroy the career of a long-distance cyclist who wanted to compete in the Tour de France.

Instead of including Belomycin in the combination drug therapy, Einhorn suggested Ifosfamide, a drug that left no scar tissue on the lungs but caused more patient discomfort when it was administered. Einhorn had tested Ifosfamide in his combination as a substitute for

Bleomycin with the hope that it would produce a higher cure rate, but both drugs had the same cure rate. Armstrong opted for Ifosfamide and suffered more nausea and vomiting, more weakness and tiredness, and more blood transfusions than had he elected the standard treatment. (The severe nausea and vomiting associated with testicular-cancer-fighting drugs has been abated by newer therapies.) Armstrong fully recovered and continued to win races with regularity. He is the most celebrated bicyclist in racing history.

Mondays and Tuesdays are Einhorn's testicular cancer clinic days. Wednesdays he is in his lung cancer clinic. On Mondays and Tuesdays, he is energized. After seeing patients, he reads letters from patients and mothers of young men who have been cured with the Einhorn regimen, thanking him for his care. After seeing lung cancer patients on Wednesdays, he is joyless and frustrated from what he declares a miserable disease. Although his department is engaged in continued research in hopes of developing new effective treatments and better methods of diagnosis, he is not making significant progress. When Einhorn lectures, he often laments that there is a hundred-way tie for first place as the best lung cancer doctor because everyone does pitifully with that disease. In 2010, if a patient has cancer in both lungs and the lymph nodes—a typical pattern with metastatic lung cancer—the five-year survival rate is zero. Still, Einhorn remains upbeat. He feels there will continue to be advances in every cancer each year.

On Thursdays and Fridays, Einhorn writes, teaches, travels and lectures. Fortunately, he loves to travel. His profession takes him around the world to share his research, travails and successes. He has published more than three hundred articles in scientific journals and chapters in seventy textbooks on cancer-treatment research. He often sees overflow patients on Thursdays and Fridays. He understands that when patients are diagnosed with cancer, they want to see an oncologist immediately. His new patients rarely wait as much as a week.

In 2001, Einhorn was inducted into the National Academy of Science, an elite organization established during President Abraham Lincoln's administration to counsel the government on scientific matters. It is populated with about a thousand engineers, archeologists, astronomers, physicists and physicians. Einhorn was the first clinician to be invited into the Academy. Other physician members are engaged in pure research or basic science. The same year, Einhorn was inducted into The American Philosophical Society, an elite society established by Benjamin Franklin to promote useful knowledge. Counted among its inductees are explorers Lewis and Clark, Sir Isaac Newton, Al Gore and Justice Ruth Bader Ginsberg. This prestigious international organization meets twice a year with little purpose other than education and camaraderie.

In 1983 the American Cancer Society awarded Einhorn its Medal of Honor. In 1992 Einhorn received the Charles F. Kettering Prize from the General Motors Cancer Research Foundation. The prize is awarded in recognition of contributions to the diagnosis or treatment of cancer.

Einhorn thrives on the challenge of teaching the bright, young physicians who enter his program as fellows. That love is returned. In 1987 Einhorn was named Distinguished Professor of Medicine. He stated, "You have to have a passion for the field you are in. You want also to have compassion for the patients you are treating—passion and compassion. You can't get anywhere in any field by being lazy and indolent. One of the most important things I try to teach future physicians is to have empathy for their patients. It is important to improve their skills in both listening to patients and talking to them. More often than not, we are confronted with having to deliver tragic news to wonderful people. There are ways of honestly giving bad news without destroying all evidence of hope. I try to emphasize that hope is better than despair."

Einhorn's pioneering work in testicular cancer is attributed to saving the lives of more than two hundred thousand young men over the past three decades. Cisplatin, the drug that came so close to the junk heap, is now the number one drug used to treat ovarian cancer, bladder cancer, lung cancer, cancer of the thyroid, cancer of the thymus, and others. This drug has prolonged the life of millions of cancer patients. If it were not for Einhorn's initiatives, Cisplatin never would have been utilized. That is not enough for this passionate and compassionate physician who believes that practicing medicine is the best job anyone can have and who daily strives to alleviate the suffering and enhance the lives of mankind.

GERALD BEPKO

A Special Agent/A Special Guy

It was the fall of 1968, and chain-smoking, hard-bodied Special Agent Gerald Bepko had just aborted the discreet surveillance of an East Coast gang of semitrailer hijackers. As cover, he and his team of FBI agents had used taxicabs, a United Parcel Service truck, and motorcycles, one of which had broken down. It was placed in the back of the truck, which wound its way through Queens, New York, en route to the FBI office with all federal officers aboard—two in the cab and two in the back with the motorcycle. Bepko rode shotgun. At an intersection near the Long Island Expressway, in the midst of a left turn, their vehicle was struck by a Ford station wagon with such force that it overturned.

Agents scrambled out of the truck in a haze of fumes from a ruptured gas tank. As they sought safety, the agents took stock. Where's Bepko? Then someone noticed his head protruding from beneath the truck. He was barely conscious and seriously injured. His fellow agents righted the vehicle and placed him in an ambulance that raced to St. John's Hospital.

Bepko, who had faced danger during more than three years in the FBI—including the charged environment of Mississippi murder and mayhem during the civil rights movement—had been felled by an everyday automobile accident. The hospital report cited five broken ribs,

a fractured shoulder blade, and a damaged Adam's apple, but it could not record nor even contemplate the far-reaching effect of this trauma. This ordinary mishap set in motion a series of decisions that brought a new career for Special Agent Bepko—and laid out a path for him that would have a profound impact on thousands of men and women for the next forty years.

Born on April 21, 1940, and raised near Jefferson Park on the northwest side of Chicago, Gerald L. Bepko was the only child of Louis Vitus Bepko, a lineman for the Illinois Bell Telephone Company and a proud member of the International Brotherhood of Electrical Workers. The elder Bepko, an avid reader, stressed the value of an education and more than once told his young son that he was trapped in his own job, although he was smarter than his superiors, because he had not earned a college degree. Louis died at fifty-four, when Bepko was only eighteen. Bepko's mother, Geraldine, was devoted to learning but never thought of attending college. She nevertheless worked steadily in a number of responsible jobs that were not normally available to women of her era, retiring as head of statistics for the international division of Zenith Electronics, a large consumer electronics manufacturing firm based in Chicago.

At seventeen, Bepko enrolled at Bradley University, but transferred to Northern Illinois University after one semester because of cost and the ease of commuting from Chicago. At Northern Illinois he lived near campus during the week and spent weekends working in Chicago. After his father died in 1958, Bepko, his mother, and two aunts shared an apartment on the second floor of a flat. His uncle, another aunt, and their daughter lived on the ground floor. In the Bepkos' neighborhood, extended families often lived together. They took care of one another.

Despite Bepko's intelligence, he displayed no brilliance at Northern Illinois. His father's death had a dispiriting impact. Instead of returning to Northern Illinois for his sophomore year he dropped out for awhile to work for a construction company. No one in his family had gone to college and other than the memory of his father's admonitions, there was little emphasis on academic achievement. Lacking a role model to set expectations, Bepko was not a fully engaged student.

Even so, Bepko graduated from Northern Illinois in 1962 after eight semesters of college study with a major in management and immediately enrolled at Chicago-Kent College of Law in downtown Chicago. He had investigated advanced degree programs in business, education, and law. Of the three, law school seemed the most interesting and, for the first time, he became energized about his academic pursuits. Bepko benefited from the prevailing law school admission policies, which were to admit liberally and flunk out a third of each entering class. Bepko and his classmates were warned that lazy students would not make it. He was determined to amend his lackadaisical attitude.

Bepko loved the study of law and, motivated by an interesting and engaging faculty, became a disciplined student. Some faculty members were not much older than Bepko. Many have remained his friends. He honed his sharp mind at law school and excelled. Bepko won a full scholarship after his first semester and graduated first in his class in February 1965. One of his professors, Ralph Brill, boasts of Bepko, "He was the best student I had over a teaching career spanning fifty years."

In 1965 the United States was at war in Vietnam and Bepko was facing the military draft, for which his classification of 1-A designated him as immediately available for armed service. Bepko pondered the Judge Advocate's Corps in the air force and officer candidate school in the army before learning the FBI was a viable alternative.

Dr. No, the first installment of the James Bond movies starring Sean Connery, had been released three years earlier, and Bepko remembered being enthralled by the perilous life of British Agent 007. He applied to the FBI. The agency, led by J. Edgar Hoover, was actively recruiting and preferred candidates with law degrees. While awaiting word from the FBI, Bepko clerked for the Chicago law firm of Ehrlich Bundeson Freidman and Ross. In just a few months, he received a telegram ordering him to report to Washington, D.C., on June 15, 1965, for assignment to the U.S. Marine Corps Base in Quantico, Virginia, site of the FBI Academy.

The rigorous physical training designed to winnow out recruits hardly affected Bepko. He had always been an athlete and was physically fit. In high school he ran track for the varsity team. He loved the outdoors and played baseball and football in the Chicago park leagues during his school years. In addition to exercise, classes were held each day in subjects such as investigative techniques and national security issues. The daily physical and mental demands stimulated Bepko. While others griped about "FBI boot camp," Bepko loved it.

After fourteen weeks of new-agent training, Bepko was posted to Jackson, Mississippi, where racial unrest had turned to violence and the FBI had been assigned an investigatory role. The southern offices were known among the new agents as the "twilight zone." Most of the agents had never been to the South, but they had read about the tense conditions. Lectures on civil rights and FBI strategies had been part of the curriculum. The fall of 1965 was hot in the South in more ways than one.

Jackson is the state capital and the largest city in Mississippi, but compared to the major cities of the north, it was trifling with a population of barely 125,000. Federal agents stood out among the populace and were resented. Bepko, whose name is Czechoslovakian, was especially vulnerable. The people of Jackson did not trust strangers with funny last names. There were no Bepkos in Mississippi.

The year before Bepko arrived, three young political activists—Andrew Goodman, James Chaney and Michael Schwerner—were murdered near Meridian, Mississippi, just ninety-three miles from Jackson. Goodman and Schwerner were white, and Chaney was black. This infamous crime was loosely portrayed in the Academy Award-nominated 1988 movie *Mississippi Burning*, starring Gene Hackman and Willem Dafoe. Mississippi was indeed burning.

Whites were clearly in control in the South, and they meant to preserve that hierarchy. Blacks typically lived in the low and swampy districts aptly referred to as "the bottom area" or just "the bottoms." Bepko was immediately detailed to the bottoms in Vicksburg and assigned to investigate the bombing of a civil rights worker's car. He was busy that fall with a plethora of civil rights cases, often at the risk of his own safety.

The *Mississippi Burning* case was essentially solved before Bepko's arrival, but in that racially charged environment, he was a part of the investigation of a similar case, the death of Vernon Dahmer. Dahmer, a black man who was the head of the National Association for the Advancement of Colored People office in Hattiesburg, owned a general store and other businesses and was a model citizen. With his wife, Ellie, he had six children—four of whom were serving in the U.S. military.

In August 1965, President Lyndon Johnson signed the Voting Rights Act, which eliminated many barriers to voting, including literacy tests. Literacy test requirements had enabled voting registrars to exclude blacks by requiring them to interpret provisions of the Mississippi Constitution. Bepko estimated that only three people in Mississippi could have answered some of the questions posed. In fact, in hearings of the U.S. Civil Rights Commission, chaired by former Harvard Law Dean and Solicitor General Erwin Griswold, a Mississippi voter registrar could not pass the test.

Dahmer was interviewed on the radio just after New Year's Day in 1966. According to Bepko, he implored his brethren to vote, saying, "Today, everybody can vote. Nobody can stop you. Go to the polls and register. If you have a problem, come and see me."

On January 10, 1966, an enraged Ku Klux Klan dispatched a contingent from Laurel, Mississippi, to the bottoms in Hattiesburg. Three carloads of Klansmen firebombed Dahmer's house with containers of gasoline they threw on his front porch and inside his home. Dahmer burst out of the house and onto the flaming porch firing his shotgun. After the perpetrators fled, he retraced his steps through the flames in order to evacuate his family out the back door. Dahmer was taken to the hospital, where he died the next day from smoke inhalation. His lungs had been scorched.

President Johnson demanded that this case be solved immediately. More than thirty agents, including Bepko, worked the leads and gathered evidence that allowed the state to prosecute crimes of arson and murder. Federal charges of conspiracy to intimidate were added. Some Klan members were convicted, but the alleged organizer of the firebombing, Ku Klux Klan Imperial Wizard Sam Bowers, was set free after four trials ended in hung juries. Based on new evidence, the case was reopened in 1998, and Bowers was found guilty of murder and sentenced to life in prison. Because of his initial role, Bepko avidly followed the trial.

Bepko was integral in the investigation of not only the Dahmer case, but also those of other federal crimes, particularly charges of intimidation and violations of the Civil Rights Act. Some of these cases concerned voter registration. That experience prepared him for his next assignment—the James Meredith two hundred mile March Against Fear, the last great march of the civil rights era. The assignment had a lasting impact on Bepko.

In 1961 Meredith had applied for admission to the University of Mississippi and was rejected on racial grounds. The NAACP won a federal suit that granted Meredith the right to enroll, but he was turned away at the doorstep by university authorities and Mississippi governor Ross R. Barnett. A court injunction for contempt removed this barrier, but a white mob again stopped Meredith from entering the university. After a riot in which two people were killed and 375 were wounded, President John F. Kennedy sent three thousand troops to restore order and allow Meredith to register. He graduated in 1963 with a degree in political science and left the state to continue his education.

According to Bepko, Meredith was a fiercely independent, strong-willed, intelligent African American who came back to Mississippi in 1966 knowing what he wanted to do and what he wanted Mississippi to be. He was going to vote in Mississippi, and he was going to run for governor. (He did not accomplish the latter.) "He had defined himself and he had set a vision for himself, and he knew his values and what he wanted to achieve, so he was steadfast and he honored those values so meticulously that it had a tremendous effect on me," Bepko said. "People like Meredith in the face of repression stood up without any goal of personal gain and changed life in the South forevermore."

Meredith planned a nonviolent march, but he must have known his intention to stop in each town and encourage his fellow black citizens to register to vote was sure to incite the local white populace. The scene was indeed ripe for violence. Meredith planned his march from

Memphis, Tennessee, south more than two hundred miles to Jackson. But just beyond Hernando, Mississippi—less than thirty miles into his pilgrimage, and with Bible in hand—he was wounded by a blast from a sixteen-gauge shotgun. Within four hours of the shooting, Bepko was rushed to the march.

For the record, Bepko was assigned to the Meredith march to co-ordinate with local police, Mississippi Highway Patrol, and U.S. Department of Defense personnel on any investigations of federal civil rights violations that might occur. He was also assigned to investigate members of the Klan and other violent racists who already were the subject of FBI inquiries. The Meredith march was a magnet for people who identified with the Klan. Finally, he was tasked with helping to prevent further violence. There was concern that more violence would ignite the powder keg that most knew was beneath the surface in the South, particularly in Mississippi. Formally, it is not within the mission of the FBI to offer individual protection. The FBI is not like the Secret Service, which has a specific protection function, or the U.S. Marshals, who are deployed to secure safe passage. Nevertheless, this was a practical role Bepko played and, according to him, it was based on doing the right thing if something happened in his presence.

Meredith's wounds, although numerous, were not life threatening. After his release from the hospital, he rejoined the march during its last few days and was with the other leaders of the Civil Rights movement at the state capitol for the concluding event. Gunman Aubrey James Norvell was apprehended immediately, confessed to the crime, and was sentenced to five years in prison. In 1997 Meredith presented his personal papers to the University of Mississippi, where they are maintained in the library's special collections branch.

As part of a normal first-year agent rotation, Bepko was transferred in October 1966 to Newark, New Jersey, where he joined a unit investigating truck hijackings, many of which were designated as organized crime activities. There was a spate of these crimes in Newark, a major shipping center. Typically, the driver of a truck would be paid to abandon his vehicle at a designated location. Someone else would drive the truck to a "drop" and disappear. Yet another accomplice at the drop confiscated the cargo and disposed of the truck.

After a few months Bepko was assigned to a small office in Hackensack, New Jersey, referred to as a "resident agency" because it housed only agents—no staff. From this office Bepko worked the truck hijacking leads in Bergen County. Occasionally, he received other exciting assignments. For example, he assisted another agent in work on a cold war national security matter involving a resident of Bergen County. The episode remains classified.

Because of his experience with hijacking cases, Bepko was assigned to the elite "tailgate squad" in New York City in 1968. The label comes from the actual tailgate on the back of a truck and informally describes undercover surveillance work. The FBI owned a variety of surveillance vehicles outfitted with remote-control-activated radio equipment, including taxicabs, motorcycles and specialized cars and trucks. Agents also borrowed trucks from UPS. The FBI recruited informants who notified the agents when goods were scheduled to be at the drop. Surveillance would set up at the drop site and, as the goods were removed, agents would arrest the driver and recover the stolen goods. Bepko packed a pistol with instructions that if he had to discharge it, he was to shoot to kill. That occasion never arose.

It was after just such a stakeout that the traffic accident threw Bepko into the street and pinned him beneath his truck. He remained in intensive care for five days and in the hospital for another ten days or so. Most of the agents smoked, especially while on surveillance detail. Bepko was no exception. In fact, he was a chain-smoker and had a chronic cough. The medication he was given to clear the fluid in his lungs arising from the trauma exacerbated his cough, which caused a great deal of pain to his broken ribs. The nurses told him that if he had not smoked he would not have that problem. He never smoked another cigarette. Although the coughing subsided, the accident permanently impaired Bepko's voice. He quipped, "Before the accident, I could sing like Robert Goulet; now I croon like Mel Torme, 'The Velvet Fog.'"

Bepko returned to active duty in September, but the seeds of his resignation had been planted. Earlier that year he had taken a bride—the former Jean Cougnenc, whom he had met at a "singles" nightclub in New York—and the newlyweds decided to start a family. Living the FBI life in New York was proving too dangerous and not compatible with that goal. "You take stock of your life when something like this happens," Bepko said. He resigned in January 1969 and moved home to Chicago.

In response to a telephone call from Professor Brill at Chicago-Kent, Bepko secured a one-year position at his alma mater teaching courses in corporations and trusts. He had planned to investigate other employment opportunities, but he enjoyed the work and committed to an additional year. Bepko was elated to again be immersed in the study of law and relished the opportunity to share that joy with his students. After deciding it would be his life's work to teach law, he realized he needed to earn an advanced degree to gain a position at one of the finer law schools. In 1971 he earned a master of laws degree from Yale Law School, consistently ranked as the number one law school in the United States.

While at Yale, Bepko sorted through a number of teaching opportunities before opting for a position at Indiana University School of Law–Indianapolis. It was a good fit. His mother-in-law, his mother, and his stepfather lived in Chicago, close enough for the grandparents to visit the Bepkos and their growing family—which by now included toddlers Gerald Jr. and Arminda.

Bepko taught contracts, sales, commercial paper, secured transactions, and consumer law. In 1974 students named him the outstanding new professor. He became a full professor in 1975. The following year he won the Black Cane, an award given to the outstanding professor at the School of Law as chosen by students. Accordingly, his name was placed on the cane that is on permanent display at the school. In 1981 he was appointed dean. During his tenure he authored or contributed to books, wrote articles, and was a popular guest lecturer, particularly on commercial law. He enjoyed stints as a visiting professor at the law schools of Ohio State University, University of Illinois, and Indiana University–Bloomington. During this time he began a parallel career of community service, later serving on the boards of not-for-profits, including Lumina Foundation for Education, Riley Hospital for Children, Economic Club of Indianapolis, United Way of Central Indiana, Greater Indianapolis Progress Committee, Indiana Sports Corp., Indianapolis Chamber of Commerce, and The Children's Museum of Indianapolis. "Looking back, I think of my community engagements as being a defining aspect of my life," Bepko reflected.

In 1986, at forty-six, Bepko was chosen by Indiana University President John Ryan and the IU trustees to become chancellor of Indiana University-Purdue University Indianapolis. Bepko served in that capacity for seventeen years—still teaching for the first decade—and oversaw enormous growth on the IUPUI campus. During his tenure the university erected about twenty-five buildings to accommodate a student body that expanded almost twenty-five percent. At the same time, research income quadrupled—exceeding $200 million.

By 2002, burned out from years of sustaining a rigorous university schedule, Bepko decided to return to the classroom, his first love, to teach and research. He announced his retirement effective at the end of the 2002-03 academic year. Then IU President Myles Brand resigned effective December 31, 2002, to take another position. The university appointed Bepko interim president to give a national search committee time to recruit a permanent replacement for Brand. The new president was inaugurated July 31, 2003. Insiders say Bepko would have landed the president's job, but he declined to apply. "I'm a big-city boy; I prefer Indianapolis rather than the college campus in Bloomington," Bepko said. "I grew up in Chicago and spent a lot of years in New York. I love the intensity and the engagement of an urban campus." After a few months' rest, Bepko returned to the law school to teach—as a volunteer without compensation—a popular course he created titled, "Leadership and the Law."

In 2004 IUPUI created the Bepko Scholars and Fellows Program, the most prestigious scholarship at the school. It is designed to attract students who are committed not only to academic excellence but to community service as well. There are now more than one hundred Bepko scholars.

Echoing his father, Bepko advises his students, "If you don't have a good education in this era, you will have nothing." He worries that the United States is falling behind in the percentage of citizens who have a high-quality education. He also advocates the value of sincerity in all aspects of life. "Integrity and honesty are vitally important to achievement in leadership," he said, "and also for your own personal well-being."

Bepko has received three honorary degrees, including one from IU in 2007 and one from Purdue University in 2009. The third was conferred by Chicago-Kent in 2003 when the commencement speaker was Barack Obama, then a member of the Illinois Senate and a candidate for the U.S. Senate. Bepko recalled that the legislator's speech was excellent, and the brief opportunity Bepko had to speak with Obama made him think the up-and-comer represented a new age of African American leaders. How right he was.

In addition to their two children, the Bepkos have two grandsons, Bradford and Griffin. Bepko, forever an avid Chicago Cubs fan, fills his summer with golf, writing, and an occasional baseball game. He is a devoted family man who is quick to give credit to his partner in life. "I was a real work in process when Jean and I met," Bepko said. "She has been the most civilizing and important influence in my life and is responsible for a large percentage of whatever we have been able to create together."

Bepko has won numerous awards, including the Anti-Defamation League Man of Achievement Award (2005), *Indianapolis Business Journal* Michael A. Carroll Award (2002), Greater Indianapolis Progress Committee Charles L. Whistler Award (2004), Columbia Club's Benjamin Harrison Award for Public Service (1996), Daughters of the American Revolution Medal of Honor (1991), and Indiana Black Expo President's Award (2002). He received the Sagamore of the Wabash from governors of Indiana in both 1993 and 2003. In 2007, in honor of Bepko's extraordinary achievements, the IU School of Law, Indianapolis created the Gerald L. Bepko Professorship in Law, a title to be held by the dean of the law school.

Showing no signs of slowing down, Bepko became the inaugural director of the Randall L. Tobias Center on Leadership Excellence at

IU in 2004. "Being busy on your own terms is the definition of a good retirement," Bepko said. Today he works, primarily without compensation.

Bepko's community focus has benefited businesses as well. He has served on the boards of American United Life Mutual Holding Company, First Indiana Bank, Indiana Energy Inc., Indianapolis Life Insurance Company Inc., USA Group Inc., and State Life Insurance Company Inc.

Louis Vitus Bepko would have been proud that his son took his advice to heart, obtained a superior education, and accomplished the phenomenal career denied him. One can only guess where the life of Gerald Bepko would have led had he not been struck down by a station wagon one fall day in 1968. It might never have brought him to Indiana, where he has distinguished himself as an extraordinary Hoosier.

JIM DAVIS

Cat Conglomerate

Nobody can relate to bugs. It took Jim Davis five years to learn the bitter truth of that statement. Davis had submitted his original cartoon strip, *Gnorm the Gnat*, to several newspaper publishers throughout the United States. *Gnorm* was rejected—swatted, if you will. Typical feedback praised the creator, if not the subject: "The gags are great and the art is good," Davis was told, "but bugs—nobody can relate to bugs."

Gnorm appeared in only one publication, the *Pendleton Times*, a weekly newspaper edited by Davis's high school friend Jerry Brewer. The only fan mail Gnorm received was a letter Davis wrote to himself. At times, Davis questioned whether to accept positions as an art director or a printing-plant production supervisor rather than continue to pursue his chosen career. But Davis, who as a boy overcame chronic asthma and the social stigma of stuttering, was barely fazed by what he saw as a temporary setback. He continued to defer those opportunities as he worked toward a goal of becoming a syndicated cartoonist. He knew he could draw and he understood the business, so Davis held on to his dream—even when Gnorm's dreams ended in 1976.

Still not ready to give up, Davis audited the comics industry. Dogs were doing well—Snoopy, Marmaduke, and Daisy—so he thought, "Why not a cat?" Launched June 19, 1978, Davis's irrepressible car-

161

toon cat, Garfield, by 2002 had found a home in 2,660 newspapers, making it the most widely syndicated comic strip in the world according to the *Guinness Book of World Records*.

James Robert Davis was born July 14, 1945, in Marion, Indiana, ten miles from the family farm. His father, James William Davis, raised corn, soybeans, wheat, pigs, and cows—both dairy cattle and purebred Aberdeen Angus—and founded one of the oldest continuously running 4-H clubs in America. Young Jim's mother, Anna Catherine Davis, was a quintessential farmer's wife and a gifted artist who enjoyed the responsibilities of country life, including taking care of the twenty-five cats who lounged among the barns. Her friends called her Betty because her father had always wanted a daughter named Betty, but he lost that battle with his wife.

Although the family eventually outgrew the farm and the elder Davis found a job at the Owens-Illinois Glass Company factory in nearby Gas City, Jim and his younger brother, Dave "Doc" Davis, enjoyed working with the crops and the animals. If not for chronic asthma, Jim might have made his living milking a cow instead of drawing a cat.

As an asthmatic, Davis spent a great deal of time in bed. He was administered nebulized medicine, including Aeron, which he said "made your heart race two hundred beats a minute. You know, a few puffs of that and you could take on the world for awhile and then you were back in your asthma—and you could only take it so often otherwise, your heart would explode." Inhalers came years later.

In the early 1950s television was not available to entertain children in rural communities. While Jim was physically incapacitated, Betty often gave him a pencil and paper. He loved to draw and make his mother laugh with funny pictures. She was an easy mark. Betty, who had not pursued her artistic talent professionally, was thrilled to see her son exhibit similar skills. Because he stuttered, he was shy—especially in the first and second grades—but he discovered that written expression presented a viable alternative. Davis said his drawings were so bad that he had to label them. When he drew a cow, he wrote the word "cow" and drew an arrow so that people would know what he was drawing. At Fowlerton Elementary School in Fairmount, he could not stop doodling—even while the teacher was speaking. At home, when he did not have drawing paper he drew on newspapers, magazines, wrapping paper, freezer paper, and even the walls. He just kept drawing.

Davis attended Fairmount High School—the alma mater of famous actor James Dean. Dean, who died in 1955 at twenty-four when Davis was ten years old, was a cultural icon who starred in three movies, including, *Rebel Without a Cause.* Paul McCoy, the art instructor at Fairmount, had played trumpet for Tommy and Jimmy Dorsey but tired of the life of an itinerant musician and returned home to teach and direct the school band. He implored Davis to consider more serious art, but the youngster had no such aspirations. He just liked to draw. Whether with a pallet knife, a brush, or a pencil, it was all invigorating to Davis. In high school Davis presented his work for McCoy to critique every week. McCoy pushed Davis to improve. "I didn't think he was ever particularly happy with my work," Davis recalled. "As it turned out, he was very happy. We had lunch together [in 2009] when he visited Indiana. He was ninety-two. He had a ponytail down to his waist and was dressed in black. He came back with all the attitude he had when I was in high school. It was a big thrill to see him and show him the studio."

Davis wanted to attend college at an art school, but his father encouraged him to matriculate at Ball State University in nearby Muncie, reasoning that if his art did not sell, Davis could always get a teaching job with his art degree. Davis had no desire to teach art but he dutifully enrolled at Ball State, where he was accepted in the honors program. He majored in the only art degree offered, art education. He also chose a minor in physical education. The curriculum limited Davis to a few drawing classes and required many art history courses—no cartooning.

Throughout high school and college, Davis made up for the lack of formal cartooning education with his extracurricular activities. At Fairmount, he drew for the school paper, the *Breeze*, penning a panel featuring Herman and Herbie. Herbie was a stereotypical high school freshman, while Herman was always pulling a variety of hijinks, including skipping class whenever possible. At Ball State Davis occasionally created an editorial cartoon for the *Ball State News*, a weekly paper.

In the 1960s commercial illustration was neither practiced nor promoted at Ball State. When Davis spoke with his instructors and fellow students about his quest to become a cartoonist, they derided his aspirations. The art building was filled with artists who were into "serious art."

During his junior year, Davis ruptured a disk in a gymnastics class and was forced to walk with a cane. The sciatic nerve pain was severe and that spring he barely attended classes. He suspended his education the following winter quarter while recuperating from an operation to remove the offending disk. During that time, he secured a job as a pasteup artist at Ad Graphics, a commercial arts studio near the university. Pasteup artists cut out type and glued it back together on boards to be photographed for printed materials. Computers eventually rendered pasteup artists extinct, but Davis enjoyed the experience and was happy to be working in his general area of interest. The money was good—$1.20 an hour. Almost twenty-five years later, Ball State recognized one of its most famous dropouts with an honorary Doctor of Letters degree.

In lieu of a formal education, Davis found a role model in T. K. Ryan, a cartoonist living in Muncie. Ryan originated and drew the syndicated comic strip *Tumbleweeds*, a spoof of the Old West set in the town of Grimy Gulch. During an interview, Davis posed a raft of questions including how Ryan launched his cartoon. Ryan was so impressed with Davis—his curiosity, his art, his cartoons, and his doodles—that he offered him a job as his assistant. Davis accepted the position and in 1969, at age twenty-four, began working in his vocation of choice. He was not allowed to conceptualize or draw a strip, instead, he inked it in after Ryan had completed the drawing and the lettering. Davis also answered fan mail, cleaned the office, and drew in some of the backgrounds. He worked for Ryan until 1978, picking up the discipline of hand-to-hand work with brush and pen and learning the business of generating a syndicated feature.

During his employment with Ryan, Davis began conceptualizing ideas for his own strip. Someone mentioned that it would be great to have a bug strip. Enter *Gnorm the Gnat* and five years of frustration. When the panel was exterminated, Davis brainstormed his next artistic endeavor. Analyzing the comics, including the popular *Peanuts* and *Beatle Bailey* strips, he realized that readers could relate to the weaknesses of humanity in their characters. Still, he knew he did not want to write about humans. Ryan was always incurring grief and losing business for depicting cowboys and Indians in his *Tumbleweeds* strip, in spite of the his effort to treat Native Americans with dignity. Ryan also was ridiculed by feminists about Hildegard Hamhocker, the strip's female character. Davis decided to stay with animals, choosing a cat who thinks he is human.

In the winter of 1977 Davis locked himself in a room at a Holiday Inn and spent a solitary weekend with drawing pads, pens, and pencils. For three days he continually doodled and drew. He created one central character with human failings and then built contrasts from there. The cat was calculating, the owner a daydreamer. The cat was opinionated, the owner wishy-washy. Those differences became the source of conflict and humor. One by one, Davis added a dog and other characters. After three days, Garfield emerged as a fat, lazy, cynical cat who easily is the brightest character in the strip. According to Davis, "Garfield is the composite character of all those cats we had on the farm rolled into one feisty orange fur ball." Garfield, the no-good cat loved by all, was named after Davis's grandfather, James A. Garfield Davis, who himself was named for President James A. Garfield.

Davis submitted *Garfield* to the usual sources—the same ones that had rejected *Gnorm the Gnat*. This time, the reaction was different. The first recipient, the *Chicago Tribune* Syndicate, replied that the strip was excellent but had lost out to another proposal received on the same day from a staff member of the *Chicago Tribune*. The rejection from King Feature Syndicate explained that they already represented a cat panel, *Heathcliff.* The editor enjoyed *Garfield* and advised Davis that

GARFIELD®
by Jim Davis

in order to be a successful comic strip, the main character must suffer. He concluded, "Now this cat, get him hit over the head at least once a week and you are going to get syndicated, young man."

In January 1978 Davis submitted the cartoon to United Feature Syndicate, owner of *Peanuts*. It did not have a cat. Shortly thereafter, the phone rang. It was Lew Little, one of the editors. who said, "We would like to contract your strip, 'Garfield,' but our president thinks that cats should have stripes. We'll pay you if Garfield gets stripes." Davis replied, "Stripes? That's brilliant, it hadn't even occurred to me. You're going to pay me? I love stripes." Today—about 8 million stripes later—Davis rues that decision. "You have no idea how many stripes I've drawn in my lifetime," he said.

United Feature Syndicate agreed to pitch the strip to the newspapers they represented, negotiate a weekly price based on circulation, and send Davis half of what was left after paying for postage, proofing, and printing. Davis was pleased. All he had to do was sit in Muncie, draw the strip, and take it to the mailbox once a week. The strip originally was supposed to debut in 1979, but when a rumor surfaced about the imminent syndication of a striped cat from *Playboy* cartoonist Bernard Kliban, United Feature Syndicate reacted by moving up the deadline. Davis had one month to launch the strip. He scrambled to flesh out his characters, conceive and draw six dailies and a Sunday cartoon, and prepare a sales kit. *Garfield* premiered on June 19, 1978, in forty-one newspapers including the *Chicago Sun-Times* and the *Boston Globe*.

Davis's paycheck for his first month of work was little more than twenty eight dollars, from which he paid an assistant three dollars an hour. He lost money, financing his first year with a loan from the local bank while his market penetration grew. By the end of 1978 he was syndicated to ninety papers and grossing $30,000 per year.

Peripheral markets beckoned. Ballantine Books committed to publish a strip compilation volume of seven months of cartoons—the minimum number necessary to meet its book specifications. Although the syndicate owned the strips and all auxiliary rights, the profit was split fifty-fifty. When his contract expired after fifteen years, Davis purchased all of the rights from the syndicate. That first book, published in 1980, "was the laughingstock of the industry," Davis said. The book was priced at $4.95 during a time when mass-marketed cartoon books were selling for $1.95. The bookstores were unhappy because the oblong shaped book did not fit the standard rack and had to be placed on special displays near the cash register or on the end of aisles. The apparent challenges ended up being extraordinary sales opportunities, and the book flew out of the stores. It turned out that $4.95 was perfect for a gift item.

The first book made *The New York Times* best seller list under the category of trade paperbacks. Its second week on the list, *Garfield* hit number one and stayed there for two years. *The New York Times* referred to the phenomenon as "Cat Chic." Davis issued a compilation every seven months and by 1983, seven of the top fifteen books featured Garfield. A few years later, *The New York Times* created the "Advice, How to and Miscellaneous" category and relegated Garfield books to that list along with titles such as *Thin Thighs in 30 Days* and *Abs of Steel*. Still, the publicity from the books helped sell newspapers, and syndication began to grow at a rate of almost one publication every day. The new readers in turn purchased books. The machine began to feed itself. In addition to fifty compilations, Davis and his staff have written more than a hundred original Garfield books and propelled *Garfield* to become the world's leading syndicated strip, appearing in more than 2,500 papers in more than a hundred languages. One of the advantages of his widely syndicated feature is that Davis continues to receive new ideas from his large readership.

Additional income comes from licensed merchandise including towels and blankets, lunch boxes, and t-shirts. Instead of just a likeness, Davis creates different Garfield art for each premium item. Garfield has appeared in a television series for kids on the Cartoon Network and has won four Emmy awards from the Academy of Television Arts and Sciences in the outstanding animated program category. Garfield also starred in two films for Twentieth Century Fox, for which Davis served as executive producer.

Paws Inc. was formed in 1981 to handle licensing, fan clubs, and other Garfield business concerns. It is a family affair. Among the approximately forty-five employees are Davis's niece Sherry Greer and her husband, Neil Greer, and Davis's daughter Ashley. Davis oversees the operation and his wife, Jill, is the senior vice president of licensing.

In 1985 Davis was recognized by his peers with the National Cartoonist Society's Elzie Segar Award for outstanding contribution to cartooning. Segar was the creator of *Popeye*. In 1989 the Society presented Davis with the Reuben Award for Overall Excellence in Cartooning. That award was named for Pulitzer Prize-winning cartoonist and inventor Rube Goldberg. The National Cartoonist Society named Davis the best humor strip cartoonist of the year in 1981 and 1986.

Davis is often asked why he does not move to Los Angeles or somewhere more convenient to his business—in particular the sources of his peripheral income. No one who has seen Davis in his rural Indiana home need ask that question. His Hoosier roots are deep. He loves being close to his family and feels strongly about giving back to his community. Davis has made numerous charitable contributions to Ball State. His Professor Garfield Foundation collaborates with the university on a Web site (www.professorgarfield.org) where people can interact with Garfield and learn to read. Access is free and available to parents, teachers, and children. Davis spends more than half of his week working on foundation activities. In 1991 he received an honorary doctor of fine arts from Purdue University.

Given his farming background, it is not surprising that Davis is an active environmentalist. In 1990 the National Arbor Day Foundation awarded him the Good Steward Award for his reforestation efforts in his native Indiana. He has developed the land adjacent to his rural office as a solar aquatic system, treating sewage without chemicals by using plants, including roses as filters. "The effluent comes out as drinking water. It's amazing what plants can do," Davis said. "We also import bugs that eat specific impurities in the water, too." His was the first licensed facility in the world that is 100 percent dependent upon this technology.

Davis works in a large family-room atmosphere, complete with a wood-burning fireplace (a concession to saving the environment he has not made). A long conference table in the center of the room leads to a desktop supporting a number of computers and drawing instruments including pencils and felt-tipped markers in different colors—even though Davis works digitally most of the time. The days of drawing the cartoon by hand and pasting it up are over, but Davis still enjoys taking pencil to paper when he's coming up with ideas. He scans his draft onto the computer, then colors and tightens the drawing online. He also is experimenting with and enjoying the transition to creating original drawings on the computer. The drawing is the same—without the graphite. Eventually, Davis intends to do it all on the computer.

When Davis was trying to launch *Garfield*, his only option was to compete with strips that appeared in a finite number of newspapers' funny pages. In the 1990s the field was limited to about three hundred syndicated cartoonists. Today the Internet has increased the opportunities for artists, but it still is tough to make cartooning a profitable profession. Davis declares that a moot point. "Cartoonists love what they do," he said.

Davis recommends that aspiring cartoonists obtain a job relating to art in order to develop drawing skills or journalism in order to hone writing skills. "Learn to draw realistically because regardless of the cartoon style you embrace later on your characters will be more relaxed. They will be more natural," he advised, "You will have a wider repertoire of things you can use as props if you can draw realistically. It helps the cartoon style. Also, learn to draw classically—real figures, real animals. Everything you draw is basically like capturing it with a camera and your muscle memory. You are adding it to your repertoire. Draw all kinds of things. Draw with all kinds of instruments.

"If you make a living at it, you don't have to do anything else. That's all I was ever expecting," he said. "Do what entertains you. Have fun doing it. If you are having fun doing it, people will have fun reading it." He also suggested that cartoonists should be well-read. "The more you read, the more natural depth your product is going to have. There is no way to infuse anything into a comic strip without doing a lot of reading."

When he's not reading or drawing, Davis enjoys golf, gardening, and family. He and Jill have three children: James, Ashley, and Christopher. They also have a cat named Nermal and a dog named Pooky.

Davis continues to closely monitor every aspect of the *Garfield* comic strip. He operates his empire with a simple philosophy: "If we take care of the cat, the cat will take care of us." For more than thirty years, they have taken care of each other and an adoring public. That unique relationship was recognized by Indiana governor Robert D. Orr in 1988, when he presented one of the highest awards Indiana can bestow—Sagamore of the Wabash—not only to Jim Davis, but also to that lazy, self-indulgent cat, Garfield.

DAVID CARTER

Life Is a Yellow Light—Accelerate

J ust after 7 a.m. on May 23, 1997, a team of seven adventurers reached the top of Mount Everest. Team member Ed Viesturs often stated the obvious, "It's optional to get to the summit, but it's not optional to get down. You don't count it unless you get down. Make the round trip." David Carter, the only member of the team who was not a professional climber, almost did not get to count it.

Two weeks before the final push to the summit from Camp I, more than three and a half miles above sea level, Carter had begun suffering from an upper respiratory infection—constantly coughing up phlegm. His condition worsened on summit day while breathing a two-liter flow of supplementary oxygen—dry air. Carter had not slept for more than forty-eight hours, and he was malnourished. While descending, about ten minutes below the summit, he could feel a mass coagulating in his throat. When he realized that he could no longer spit anything out of his mouth, he panicked. He tore off his oxygen mask and started gasping for air, a precious commodity at 28,900 feet.

The first part of the descent is a knife-edged ridge of 1,000 vertical feet. On both sides of the ridge, death is a certainty at the bottom of precipitous vertical drop-offs. This passage does not tolerate mistakes. Viesturs calmed Carter down. He coaxed the oxygen mask

173

back on, and they rested. He promised to stay with Carter, and the ill man relaxed. They arrived at Camp IV (26,000 feet) at 11 a.m. Most climbers sleep at Camp IV after the exhausting summit experience. A Sherpa handed Carter a cup of tea, but he could not swallow. He vomited. Gasping for air, he turned to Viesturs and said, "If I go into this tent I'm dead meat. I'm going to die. I've got to get down." Viesturs and Carter left an hour later with the intention of reaching Camp II (21,500 feet). They did not make it. At 8 p.m. the exhausted climbers arrived at Camp III (23,300 feet). Carter's breathing was more labored. He looked at Viesturs and said, "Ed, I think in a few minutes I'm not going to breathe through this. I can feel it closing." Carter went into respiratory arrest at 8:45 p.m.

David Lawrence Carter was born November 29, 1962, to Jane and Larry Carter. Larry worked practically his entire life in the family business, Carter-Lee Lumber, before retiring in 1997. (The original Lee sold his partnership to Carter's great-great-grandfather, who reportedly told his family that he was too cheap to change the signs.) Jane, a graduate of the Indiana University School of Business, opted to stay home and raise David and his younger brother, John.

While in school, Carter struggled with acute dyslexia, a learning disability that makes it difficult for some people to read and spell. With the assistance of his parents and caring teachers, he gradually overcame his problems. In order to encourage him to read, Mrs. Nichols, his teacher at Northview Middle School assigned him book reports. Carter enjoyed adventure books, particularly mountaineering books. Perhaps he felt a connection between the struggle to overcome a reading disability and the sacrifice necessary to summit a mountaintop. Carter had a special fascination for Everest—or Sagarmatha in Nepali, meaning Goddess of the Sky. Carter had a *National Geographic* poster of Everest on his bedroom wall as a child, and it stayed there until he graduated from college. As a youth, Carter was an Eagle Scout. Backpacking while a Boy Scout gave him a taste of the outdoors—its challenges and pleasures—and piqued his interest in mountain climbing.

At age fourteen on a vacation with his parents to the state of Washington, Carter beheld Mount Rainier for the first time. He was captivated and proclaimed to his father that he needed to scale the mountain—at 14,410 feet one of the highest peaks in the contiguous forty-eight states. It is rated a technical climb requiring ropes, crampons, and ice axes. The next summer father and son summited Rainier and a lifelong obsession was launched. Carter has climbed at least one mountain every year since then.

Carter graduated in 1986 from Indiana University with a degree in political science. He had expected to work in the lumber business, but when the decision needed to be made he knew his heart was in the mountains. He opted to return to Rainier as a mountain-climbing guide. He also guided on Argentina's Mount Aconcagua (22,841 feet), the highest peak in South America, and Alaska's Mount McKinley (20,320 feet), the highest peak in North America. McKinley is Carter's favorite. The locals call it Denali, which means "The Great One." To Carter, it is a special mountain. Carter calls it "the last layman's adventure in the world" because almost anyone in good physical shape with basic mountaineering skills can make it to the top with the help of a guide. An early climber gushed that "the view from the top of Mount McKinley is like looking out the windows of heaven." Carter summited McKinley for the first time in 1982, while a senior at North Central High School in Indianapolis.

In 1991 Carter was retained to guide with an American team on Mount Everest, despite the fact that he had not yet attempted to climb the legendary mountain. Everest can only be climbed after obtaining a permit costing about $65,000 per group. Sherpas may be included in the group at no charge because they are Nepali. In the 1960s, 1970s and 1980s, only a limited number of permits were issued. Climbers had to wait their turns. Beginning in 1990, all those who could afford it were granted access. Most of the climbs since the early 1990s have been commercial expeditions consisting of two or three guides and four to six clients who pay about $60,000 each.

It may seem odd, but it is not unusual for someone who has never attempted Mount Everest to be asked to guide. Carter was designated a junior guide and was tasked with cooking and other supportive roles. During the ascent, he suffered through two bouts of giardiasis, an intestinal illness that is usually transmitted through contaminated water. He lost twenty-two pounds. He trudged on even after breaking a rib from coughing, but when he felt the effects of high-altitude cerebral edema—a severe, frequently fatal form of altitude sickness causing swelling of the brain and accompanied by early symptoms of headache, nausea, and insomnia—he terminated his quest. The best treatment for altitude sickness is an immediate descent. At 26,000 feet he announced, "Hey, I can't go on," and he turned around. The summit lay a scant few thousand feet above.

Carter felt that he did not pace himself on the ascent. He compares his failed attempt to driving the Indianapolis 500 for the first time, "You are a rookie. You are just learning the ropes." When he left Mount Everest in 1991, it haunted him. He thought about it every day. He asked himself, "What would I need to do to summit?" While still guiding in the United States, he sought opportunities to join other Everest expeditions. Finally in 1997 he was invited by Viesturs, who also had been on the 1991 expedition, to join a team sponsored by PBS's *Nova* television production. *Nova* wanted to test the effects of extreme altitude on decision making by quizzing the climbers continually as they continued up the mountain. Carter described the 1997 climb as "unfinished business."

Climbing Mount Everest is one of life's greatest outdoor adventures. It is also an irrational act. The temperature at the summit can be 40 degrees below zero. One cannot leave even a small patch of skin exposed. If you drop a glove and do not replace it, you will lose your hand or your arm to frostbite—if you make it down. Climbing equipment must be carefully chosen for weight, efficiency, and redundancy. The list includes an inch-thick insulated sleeping pad, a down sleeping bag rated to minus-30 degrees, a one-piece climbing suit rated to minus-20 degrees, a climbing harness, rope, food, including high-energy bars, headlamps, helmet, and four to five oxygen bottles each weighing about nine pounds and lasting about five to six hours.

The assault on Everest is accomplished in several stages. There are two main routes and many less frequently climbed paths to the summit. The 1997 team chose the popular South Col route on the Nepal side of the mountain. Base Camp at 17,300 feet is a fifteen- to twenty-day trek on foot from Kathmandu. The team cut that initial time in half by flying into the village of Lukla. At Base Camp they rested and acclimated to the altitude for about two weeks while beginning preparations for the summit.

Just above Base Camp awaits a perilous vertical climb through the Khumbu Glacier known as the Khumbu Icefall. The glacier calves and moves down the mountain at an approximate rate of three to six feet per day. As the glacier moans and groans, blocks of ice—often larger than a home—move, shift, and fall with little advance warning. It was difficult to map a route, but once the route was designated, the climbers placed ladders over the crevasses and used ropes in order to move through as fast as possible. Climbers carried gear up to Camp I through the icefall and then returned to base camp. This is necessary not just to transport gear, but the climbing up and down also is an important part of acclimating to the mountain. The best time to climb the icefall is at night, when the temperature is well below zero and the ice is consolidated. The trip through the icefall usually takes five to six hours. Normally, climbers drop gear at Camp I and then return for breakfast at base camp by 8 a.m. Khumbu Icefall, designated as one of the most treacherous sections of the Mount Everest climb, has claimed the lives of about fifty people. Carter risked seven round trips through the icefall on the 1997 climb. At 19,700 feet, Camp I is about the same altitude as Mount Kilimanjaro, the highest peak in Africa.

When their gear was transported and the climbers were fully acclimated, the team pushed forward to Camp II, a day's journey to 21,500 feet along a relatively flat, gently rising glacial valley on a route known as the Western Cwm. The next day they climbed from Camp II—halfway up the Lhotse face, a steep icy wall—to Camp III at 23,300 feet. It is situated on a seventy-degree plane. Many Sherpas refuse to sleep at Camp III, citing its precarious slope. One slip has sent many climbers thousands of feet to certain death. After a fitful night, the climbing team awoke early and reached Camp IV (26,000 feet) by afternoon to rest for the final push to the summit. Altitude above 26,000 feet is designated the death zone. In the death zone, the body begins to deteriorate and die. It is impossible to acclimate. The longer the stay at this altitude, the more likely a climber will suffer high-altitude cerebral or pulmonary edema. Oxygen dwindles to one-third of what it is at sea level. Breathing becomes an act of desperation. Climbers typically have a maximum of three days to make their summit bid. Sherpas often wait at Camp IV with supplies and hot tea for returning climbers.

That evening Carter had dinner of ramen noodles, two slices of sausage, and a part of a Snickers bar. At 10 p.m. team leader Viesturs led the final ascent. With headlamps affixed, they climbed through the night. No one said a word. The eerie silence yielded only to the sound of climbers sucking in air. Carter recalled, "It was a beautiful night, about a thirty-knot wind. Below us you could see these huge thunderheads in Tibet. The lightning would light up the mountain. You wouldn't hear anything, but you knew all of a sudden it would be like a flash. I'll never forget it. I felt like I was in outer space. I remember looking up at millions of stars. The stars were so bright you could read a book by the Milky Way. Then you would see these hundreds of satellites whipping around. It was really a surreal experience."

In order to reach the summit the climbers had to ascend a steep ridge to the Hillary Step (28,800 feet), a forty-plus-foot rock wall named for Sir Edmund Hillary, who in 1953 with Sherpa Tenzing Norgay became the first to summit Mount Everest. The Hillary Step must be climbed with fixed ropes and is considered the most technically challenging aspect of the climb. Nearer sea level, the Hillary Step would not be a daunting task for an experienced climber, but oxygen and crampons render the climb more difficult. Then there is the altitude. The summit rises a little more than two hundred feet above the Hillary Step, the highest mountain peak in the world. The summit platform of Mount Everest is about twenty feet by twenty feet square. One must stay in the middle to avoid a cornice of unstable snow at the edges and the wind that could blow climbers off the mountain. At the summit there is very little evidence of humans. Whatever is left by climbers in the way of flags and poles is blown off each winter.

While Carter was scaling Everest in 1997, eight people were killed—four on the Tibetan side and four on the Nepali side. On the Nepali side, one man slipped and fell from Camp III, or as Carter put it, he "lost his step and reached maximum velocity." The others died from exposure. Climbers who die are typically left behind. The 1997 team encountered a number of corpses along the route, but all seven members successfully summited the mountain together. One of its members, Tashi Tenzing, was a Sherpa and the grandson of Tenzing Norgay.

At 7:10 a.m. it was Carter's turn to stand on the highest point on earth. Carter remembers having illusions that when he conquered the mountain he would do high fives and feel like a king, like he had just won the World Series. But when he summited he was not filled with exhilaration. He remembers saying to himself, "I've got to get the hell off this." He said, "I was intimidated—like I had just gotten caught with my hand in the cookie jar." He looked around and sat down. He could not talk because he had been coughing, and the only emotion he had was terror. For the first time during the entire expedition, he was frightened. He looked down, and he could see the ridge. He said to himself, "I've got to climb down that thing." Ninety-five percent of the climbing accidents occur on the descent. According to Carter, many who summit do not have sufficient energy to descend safely, "It's like a cat. Any cat can climb a tree but most cats cannot climb down. That's what climbing is all about—making sure you can get down." One in five who attempt Mount Everest pay with their lives—most on the way down.

Descending, Carter reached Camp III at 8 p.m. on summit day and crawled into his tent completely exhausted. By 8:45 his throat closed—no air was going in or out. When he went into respiratory arrest, Viesturs radioed Doctor Howard Donner at Base Camp, who instructed him to give Carter the Heimlich maneuver, a series of under-the-diaphragm abdominal thrusts. That forced enough air from Carter's lungs to create an artificial cough, which expelled some of the obstruction in his airway. Viesturs administered the Heimlich maneuver for about twenty minutes every hour throughout much of the night in order to save Carter's life. A veterinarian by training, Viesturs considered giving Carter a tracheotomy, opening his airway surgically. According to Carter, "If you have a tracheotomy at ultra high altitude, you're going to die. It's because the tracheotomy will collapse, leaving no way to breathe."

Carter was depressed. He felt that his most important obligation to the team was that he should never be a burden. It was the dream team: Viesturs, David Breashears, Pete Athans, Guy Cotter, Tashi Tenzing, and Jangbu Sherpa, the sirdar or foreman in charge of the Sherpa support team. Some had climbed Everest more than once. Viesturs had just made the summit for the fifth time. Carter was friends with them all. He had earned their respect but nonetheless felt a bit intimidated. He did not want to be a liability, but there he was, dying. Viesturs was trying to save his life. Other team members risked their lives descending the Lhotse Face at night from Camp IV to lend a hand. Carter said to himself, "Davey, this is it. We're at the final hour and if you are going to live through this you've got to take this into your own hands." He experienced a burst of energy. He could feel something in his throat—it felt huge. He thrust his middle finger down his throat, coughing and gagging while he worked out the obstruction, a large solid, multicolored bloody mess. He threw it out into the snow, rolled back into the tent, smiled, and said, "I think I just got it out." He could breathe again. It was 1:30 a.m., and he knew he was going to live.

The next morning Carter descended to Camp II and enjoyed a fitful sleep, nervous that the obstruction would return. The following day he traversed the icefall the final time and proceeded to base camp.

Back in Kathmandu, Carter met Elizabeth Hawley, the unofficial chronicler of Himalayan climbing. She is an American who was originally a reporter for *Time*. In 1960 she began interviewing climbers as they returned from Everest and since then has kept detailed records of everyone who has climbed Mount Everest from Nepal. Carter is number 881. In the neighborhood of Thamel in downtown Kathmandu, a bar called Rum Doodle provides a free dinner to anyone who has made it to the top. Successful climbers are issued a Rum Doodle card bearing their photograph. It is like a passport. Carter dropped by for a free meal.

Carter treasures the relationships he has developed with his climbing compatriots and places a higher value on their friendship than reaching the summit. He tries to see Viesturs at least once a year, often at his home on Bainbridge Island, Washington. He also returns to Everest every couple years with friends to trek to base camp. Carter recommends the trek for anyone who likes adventure and wants to see the Himalayans. He said, "It's an incredible trip. It takes about two and a half weeks round trip, door-to-door from Indianapolis. It is not technical, but you must be healthy and in reasonably good shape."

The ultimate hat trick for a mountain climber is to scale the highest peaks on each of the seven continents. Carter has climbed five: Mount Everest in Asia (29,028 feet), Mount McKinley in North America (20,320 feet), Mount Aconcagua in South America (22,841 feet), Mount Kilimanjaro in Africa (19,340 feet), and Mount Elbrus in Europe (18,442 feet). He has not climbed Mount Kosciuszko in Australia (7,310 feet), the easiest of the seven summits—although some say that Carstensz Pyramid in New Guinea (16,023 feet) is the highest peak in the Oceanic continent of which Australia is a part—and Vinson Massif in Antarctica (16,050 feet). He intends to complete those tasks in the next few years.

Carter enjoys his life of adventure. He looks forward to each new experience—going places where he can push himself both mentally and physically. His mantra: Life is a yellow light—accelerate. When not climbing, he is a manager at the family lumberyard, now called Pro-Build. He owes his success in the Mount Everest expedition to surrounding himself with good people—and good climbers. He strives to do the same in his work. His goal is to become a paramedic, an exciting, pressure-filled vocation where often a life is at stake. At home, in addition to his job he spends time working out, either on the Stairmaster, spinning, running, or riding a bicycle. While in college he rode on a Little 500 bicycle racing team.

Carter is married to Marta Heimlich, her name a notable coincidence. They became engaged just before he left for Mount Everest in 1997, and they have one daughter, Vyla. Marta is not a climber, but she likes the outdoors.

"Mountain climbing is a great sport but you need to stay with it. You can never give up," Carter advised. "There are times when you can climb a mountain and there are going to be times when the mountain doesn't want you to climb it. You just have to deal with it, you simply go back and try it again." He cited his experiences on Mount Rainier, which he has summited 55 times in more than 150 attempts. "Mountain climbing is a sport that requires high self-motivation. It's easy in mountain climbing as it is in life to lose focus, get down on yourself, and give up. Never give up."

Carter does not plan to attempt Everest again. "Mount Everest was a real important part of my life but it is just part of my life," he said. "I don't want to be defined by it. What it did was a reality check for me. It made me realize how much I love my family and life. I was haunted by it before. Now that I've done it and had to deal with Camp III when I almost died, it's there and every once in awhile it rears its ugly head, especially when I have a nightmare. It has made me a better person."

Carter succeeded in the ultimate adventure and avoided death at the top of the world. He is possessed of courage, self-confidence, and an indomitable will, yet he remains humble and soft-spoken, a testimony to achievement with class.

WILLIAM COOK

Ready, Fire, Aim!

I t was big news, exciting news, in the town that October morning
in 1988. Bloomington, Indiana had its own man in the *Forbes*
magazine list of the four hundred richest people in America. That
was novel in a community more used to attention for achievers
and newsmakers on its east side, where Indiana University had domin-
ion, than on its west side, Bloomington's industrial row.

Most Bloomington residents who read about him in the newspapers
that morning would not have known Bill Cook if they had sat in a
booth next to him at the folksy Big Wheel restaurant he frequented.
Cook's name had taken on some community familiarity by then, but
not his face, his financial stature, or his unassuming personality. The
fellow who sat in the Big Wheel booth, wearing an open-necked shirt
and cardigan sweater, did not look like a big wheel—he was as common as an old shoe, the few who did recognize him would have said.

Longtime residents remember when Curry Pike was a north-south
road that had to be widened and resurfaced in the late 1950s and early 1960s when some of America's industrial giants chose spots along
it (just outside the western city limits of Bloomington) to build and
thrive—Westinghouse, RCA, Otis Elevator, and General Electric.
Bloomington cheered the arrival of each. In 1963 when an unknown
fellow named Bill Cook moved his unheard-of manufacturing opera-

185

tion into a small house among the giant factories, not a speech was made, not a balloon was popped, and not a ribbon was snipped.

But in the 1980s, when the bloom of Bloomington was fading for many of the megacorporations, their factories shrinking toward shutdowns and pullouts, Cook Inc. was growing from that house to a sprawling campus-style manufacturing operation, the reeling community's employment bulwark.

And in 1988, two and a half decades after he and wife, Gayle, had been the company's entire employee roster for its inaugural year, Bill Cook was designated by *Forbes* as the richest man in Indiana.

The Great Depression was tightening its chokehold on America when William Alfred Cook was born in Mattoon, Illinois, on January 27, 1931, the only child of George and Cleo Cook. At twenty-one, Cleophus Javay DeLong married Harry Orndoff, a young man from a prosperous Mattoon family who already was on the rise as an employee in the thriving railroad business. Just two years later, Harry collapsed at work and died of what today probably would be diagnosed as a congenital heart condition. Cleo was a widow at twenty-three, her apparently settled world and promisingly comfortable financial future abruptly altered. "She went to secretarial school to acquire a skill so she could work," Cook said of the woman who became his mother. "Then she went to Chicago by herself to find a job." She did well as a secretary, working her way to a position in the brand-new, glistening white Wrigley Building downtown, where she reported directly to chewing gum magnate William Wrigley. "It took me a long time to get over Harry," she told Cook's wife, Gayle. Still, in 1923 Cleo married George Alfred Cook, a World War I veteran from Peoria, Illinois who was working as a salesman for Western Electric. Their son was born eight years later.

The family moved to Canton, Illinois, when Cook was entering fourth grade. George landed his family there after he purchased three nearby grain elevators and left the magazine and insurance sales business that had made them vagabonds. Cook had spent his first-grade year attending nine schools in nine different Illinois, Indiana, and Wisconsin towns. Perhaps the process of making new friends every month fostered a sense of confidence and self-reliance in young Cook.

In high school Cook was socially popular, and his leadership skills were evident. He led a student initiative for a community youth center that made it all the way to the city council floor, where he boldly made the pitch himself—an idea whose time had not quite come. A few years later, the center was built.

Canton introduced Cook to Indiana-style appreciations. It was known in Illinois as a "basketball town," one that at the time had made it to the eight-team state tournament finals more times than any other school. Cook was husky—six-feet, two inches tall and 235 pounds— and best known as a center and linebacker in football, but he also played basketball on a Canton High School team that made it to state his junior year.

After graduation from high school, Cook enrolled at Northwestern University. He planned to be a doctor and took the difficult science and math courses that prepared him for medical school admission. Medicine was on Cook's mind when he graduated from Northwestern in 1953, but so was military duty. The Korean War had just ended, but the draft was still on. On August 6, 1953, he went into the army for a two-year hitch. Cook took six weeks of basic training at Camp Pickett, Virginia, and Camp Crowder, Missouri. From there he was posted to Fort Sam Houston, Texas, as an operating-room technician treating military men who were burned in Korea. "Napalm was one of the main instruments of death. It didn't take much to misfire and get our own guys, or a truck would blow up and the gas tanks would spew all over them," Cook recalled. "There were so many bad injuries in that war, particularly from napalm, I didn't think we'd ever use napalm again. Too many got hurt." A decade later, it was a main instrument of death in Vietnam.

Cook's job was to debride burn victims. He used antiseptic soap and rubbed the burn until it bled well, and then he put antibiotics on it and wrapped it up. It was day-in, day-out duty, and yet individual cases stayed in his mind. "You would identify with a guy," he said, recalling a particular patient. "We spent a lot of time trying to keep him alive. He could talk, even though he was dying. We did everything we could to keep him comfortable while he was alive. It was just one of those experiences. I was premed when I went into the military but not when I came out. I identified with the burn patients, and that really got to me. I got involved with those kids. I knew then that I didn't want to become a doctor. I had an interest in medicine, but more in the mechanical parts of medicine."

In 1955, after his army commitment was fulfilled, Cook moved to Chicago and continued his education by working at Martin Aircraft, American Hospital Supply, and Nelson Instrument Company. He took jobs that taught him sales and management but most of all, they taught him not to have to answer to anyone at all in running a company. He sat down for a self-assessment, writing in a notebook he still has what he saw as his strengths and his shortcomings, what fields he could enter, and how. At Nelson Instrument, Cook made an important connection of a different kind. He met owner-inventor Lloyd Nelson's second cousin, Gayle Karch. Cook instantly fell in love. They were married four and a half months later on September 21, 1957, and they have one son, Carl, born in 1962.

In 1957 Cook and Beta Theta Pi fraternity brother Brian Baldwin put their minds and names together and formed Balco, a company that manufactured and distributed shot glasses. They set up shop in Chicago. The glasses had a 35-millimeter picture on the bottom, held in place by a filter. In the middle of glass, a lens magnified the picture. Cook remembered, "They were called 'art photos,' but they were just nudes. We got the pictures from California—eight hundred of them. Gayle and I and her cousin sat in her cousin's living room going over all eight hundred pictures, evaluating them, to pick out four. It took us quite a long time one evening. But there was a problem with these shot glasses. It seems the filter we used to hold the film to the bottom of the glass didn't hold too well, and the film began to curl. Pretty soon we found out there were fifty thousand shot glasses out all over the United States with the film curled at the bottom. When the curling problem developed, we got out of that business, closed the doors of that shop, and discontinued our mailbox." They had invested $15,000 in the enterprise and lost it all.

They tried another business together—this time a little more orthodox. Baldwin, an engineer, also had worked for American Hospital Supply. Their mutual experiences made them aware of a market for disposable hypodermic needles, which were just beginning to gain acceptance over reusable needles. They found a building on Chicago's north side, and Cook painted the inside walls and lined up some equipment. Manufacturing Process Laboratories Inc. was ready to go. "It was a successful company," Cook said. "We turned out about two million stainless steel hypodermic needles a day, a lot more needles than I ever wanted to see again." American Hospital Supply was one of its leading customers. After five years, Cook sold his stock in MPL to Baldwin for $15,000.

The Cooks tired of Chicago and were ready to go it on their own. They moved to Bloomington in the middle of the winter of 1963 because, according to Cook, "It wasn't snowing there." He was thirty-two years old. A laboratory invention by an obscure Swiss radiologist came just in time to be the impetus for Cook's own career launch. It was the 1950s when Doctor Sven-Ivar Seldinger—32 himself at the time—discovered a revolutionary medical means of catheterization, inserting a tiny catheter into the patient's blood stream and guiding it into the arteries where dye is released, delineating the problem for detection and cure. As Cook likes to say, "It separates the surgeon from his pocketbook."

The Seldinger method meant one of medicine's common terms and practices was about to become obsolete. Instead of exploratory surgery called "cut-down entry," cutting through flesh and muscles into an artery wall to see if a problem within the body could be cured—those answers could be found with only a needle hole as an entryway. Within a few years, the Seldinger method was being taught in medical schools, and younger surgeons in particular were picking it up quickly.

Doctors in general—not to mention the entrenched and wealthy giants of the medical equipment industry—were not nearly so quick to grasp the business potential of the advance. The product niche Cook had picked involved making and selling Seldinger-method kits to hospitals, which up to that time had to fashion their own needle, catheter, and wire guide sets. On July 1, 1963, Cook Inc. was officially launched from a newly rented Bloomington apartment. The birth of the company was announced in the July 5, 1963, issue of the *Indiana Investor*, under New Indiana Corporations Formed Week Ending Friday, June 28:

Cook Inc., 2305 E. 2nd St., Bloomington, 1,000 shares
(Resident Agent) William A. Cook
(Purpose) Merchandising

The Cooks kept the initial investment down, to avoid starting with high debt. Gayle said, "At first we bought components for the catheters and the wire guides, then we started making some from scratch, then a few more, and a few more—inexpensive small items that we put together. We didn't need investors."

The Cooks rented a three-bedroom apartment for $165 a month, and it was in the Cooks' third bedroom where entrepreneurial history was made. Every morning, Cook Inc. President Bill Cook—after eating breakfast with Gayle—closed the spare-bedroom door behind him and went to work. The man who eventually led his whole company into a tieless work culture was unyielding with himself during its nascent months. "I wore a coat and tie simply because I wanted to keep formality in the office," he said. Gayle, too, was dressed professionally when their day began. "We just kept up the routine that we knew eventually we would have if things were successful." Behind that door, one at a time, Cook built Seldinger units. "All I needed was a blowtorch, a soldering iron, and a few little tools I could make myself," he said. Outside the room, Cook was the salesman and Gayle the quality-control supervisor and bookkeeper.

Two months after the incorporation papers were filed, Cook Inc. received its first purchase order: Illinois Masonic Hospital wanted two "Seldinger Wire Guides" for $3.50 each. The invoice from the order is a framed treasure for the Cooks. And when that order was filled and the first payment check came in, a tradition began. "Every time we got paid on an invoice from a shipment, we'd go out to have a hamburger at McDonald's," Cook said.

Cook also was the company pilot. All during the 1960s, Cook flew himself, first in a Mooney single-engine propeller airplane that he owned a one-third interest in and later in his own Mooney. The Mooneys cruised between 165 and 170 miles per hour. One day he'd be in one place and the next day someplace else. He would go from Fargo to Minneapolis, maybe, then to Oregon. To this day there are customers who never knew he did not have eight or ten employees running around. He was at a meeting in Florida and someone said, "How many salesmen do you have?" Cook did not want to tell them, so he just said, "Well, we're doing pretty well." But he was it.

After a year Cook Inc. began adding employees. In its second year the company moved to Curry Pike. Annual sales topped $1 million by the company's seventh year, $100 million after another thirteen. In 2006, forty-three years after its humble beginnings, the worldwide Cook medical-products empire had its first $1 billion sales year. Today Cook Inc. is among the world's best-known and most respected names in medical devices and supplies.

Cook often is asked for business advice. He has taught seminars at Rose-Hulman Institute of Technology, a prestigious engineering school in Terre Haute, Indiana. In the course of these activities he authored a pamphlet titled *The Leader Determines Company Behavior*, in which he lays out some basic tenets—some values for living—that would be taught in a Cook classroom:

> • Don't be in a hurry to begin your life's work; take time to look around as an adult. Experiment. Be a job hopper or a professional student for a while. Taking the time now to find out what you want from life will be a fantastic learning experience. I was thirty-two years old before I quit going to school and job-hopping, and I have never regretted it. But, remember, it may befuddle your parents for a time.

> • Never plan too far ahead, or too precisely, because you can lose sight of your goals and dreams. Dreams can die because

"plans" make them seem insurmountable. A business or a personal plan is a perfect excuse for not seeking a better, alternative direction. When I see people making long-range plans, I see so many pitfalls that can make those plans go awry. I see it in government, I see it in everyday business life: people making long-range plans and making investments in something that, halfway down the road, they find doesn't work. A lot of that has to do with not concentrating on the element of today—always thinking about tomorrow. I think you always have to have a little of tomorrow in mind, but you shouldn't plan too heavily and make decisions that way. Concentrate only on today, solve today's problems, and don't worry about what's going to happen tomorrow until tomorrow. I call it segmental thinking.

• Plans made by a committee remove part of the responsibility that should be yours alone. If I make a plan, if I have an insight for a goal, it's mine. If you have committee goals, you have everybody's ideas of what they think the goal ought to be. That's one of the reasons I think the federal government doesn't work too well: too much committee and not enough people assuming responsibility, and taking responsibility, for a job.

• Know history, because the past helps you foresee your future. As you get older and you rely upon your past, it certainly helps. How did you get where you are? You don't make mistakes when you rely on history. There are too many places where you repeat mistakes again and again and again and again.

• Try to keep your family above the business. There was a time in my life when I kept my business in front of my family, a little bit. There were times during the early years when I could not be around, when I was gone for long periods of time. But you do have to work hard to make your dreams come alive and be real. If you are going into a creative occupation, you have to expect to be a workaholic where time means little to you.

• Always be competitive. You always want to compete, not necessarily with others, sometimes with yourself. But most certainly you want to compete against your competitors. You don't want to like your competitors too much. You want to be friendly to them, but you don't want them being your friend. And if you can buy them, do so.

• Ready, fire, aim. Ready means preparation. Get yourself ready to do something, then do it. If you screw up, you go back and see what happened. What I call "aim" is hindsight: You find out where you screwed up, and you can correct it much easier. A lot of people would rather sit and prepare. They can prepare all their life. You've got to feel a little uncertainty, a little risk, and then say, "Okay, I'm ready to risk this. And when I'm done, I'll figure out: Did I do it right, or did I do it wrong?" One of the key elements is: Did you make your risk with good common sense, based on history?

Reading the pamphlet gives one a feeling of "being there," of sensing that Cook lived and learned the wisdom he imparted and knowing he still has more to learn and more to teach as he continues his career.

Cook shares his enormous wealth generously but specifically. A science building on the Northwestern campus bears the Cook name. So does a football stadium at Rose-Hulman. So does the state-of-the-art music library at the renowned Indiana University School of Music and the basketball practice facility dedicated to the instruction and preparation of men and women student athletes, the result of more than $45 million in gifts the Cooks have given to the university where Gayle was Phi Beta Kappa as an arts major and Cook served as a trustee. His generosity is having a similar effect on his other hometown—Canton, Illinois. A new Cook Inc. plant graces the skyline of downtown Canton, one of forty-two in the Cook Inc. empire.

In the 1990s the Cooks invested millions in financing a Bloomington team that in just nine years evolved from idea to world champion of the summertime youth activity called drum corps (for kids sixteen to twenty-two). Cook plunged in after seeing the effects of drum corps discipline and artistry on a young Purdue University marching band participant named Carl Cook. After nine years the Star of Indiana drum corps unit that Cook backed morphed into a touring music show and ultimately a Broadway production called *Blast!*—which won both an Emmy award and a Tony. Cook has been out of the drum corps business longer now than he was in it, but it's going to take a whole lot longer than that before that world will ever forget those names: Star of Indiana and Bill Cook.

The Emmy and Tony are among the treasured Cook honors and rewards. So are gold medals—unprecedented for a nonphysician—awarded him by the Society for Interventional Medicine and its European counterpart, the Cardiovascular and Interventional Radiological Society of Europe. His honors list, with governors' citations, national awards, and university honorary degrees, naturally is long. Cook has received honorary degrees from Northwestern, IU, Rose-Hulman, Marian College (now Marian University) and Vincennes University. In 2004 at a black-tie event in Bloomington, the American Heart Association gave the Cooks its Cor Vitae Award for contributions to cardiovascular health care. Bill and Gayle received Indiana Living Legend recognition by the Indiana Historical Society in July 2006 and at a star-spangled ceremony in Washington's Constitution Hall, the Horatio Alger Society named him one of its 2010 national honorees.

As individuals and as a couple, Bill and Gayle Cook have been honored as preservationists by the National Trust for Historic Preservation, the National Park Service, Historic Landmarks Foundation of Indiana, and the Indiana Department of Natural Resources.

The Cooks' proudest endeavor in the use of their prosperity has been in the restoration of the West Baden Springs Hotel, once on the National Trust's list of the eleven most endangered historic properties in the United States. This led to what preservationists nationally call "The Save of the Century." It might be the only luxury hotel in the world—might have been then, might still be now—where the "rooms with a view" are the ones facing in. The round hotel has six floors, with a corridor separating inside and outside rooms. A person walking that corridor finds a constantly adjusting compass woven into the carpeting. It is the inside rooms that can look out into the atrium, with its 31,416 square feet of floor space and 2.73 million cubic feet of airspace—and its dome, exquisite and stunning then and now. It all almost became extinct. It is a National Historic Landmark that once was known as the Eighth Wonder of the World. On May 23, 2007, a ribbon was cut in front of the main entrance, and the West Baden Springs Hotel officially opened to its first paid occupants in seventy-five years. The cost to the Cooks was about $75 million. On the night of June 23, 2007, the grandest of all the Cooks' restorations glistened in its considerable glory. Gala was the word used for the event that brought one thousand people out that night to celebrate the return to life of the West Baden Springs Hotel. Gala fits that event, but understates. "It was the highlight of my life," said Cook.

Every year, *Forbes* magazine duly chronicles achievement based upon accumulated wealth. If *Forbes* would have included in its criteria an analysis of the impact on the health of our nation and the humanitarian deployment of wealth, the rank of Hoosier Bill Cook visionary, inventor, industrialist, philanthropist, preservationist, and billionaire, would be even higher.

GEBISA EJETA

Geneticist on a Mission

L ike most children in his Ethiopian village, Gebisa Ejeta grew up in a one-room thatched roofed hut with a mud floor. Behind a partition, fire was used to cook what little food that could be coaxed from the earth—mostly teff, an African cereal grass, along with wheat and chickpeas. His parents, like the generations that preceded them, were illiterate farmers. Seasonally or in bad crop years, hunger was a persistent problem. Meals were never available to enjoy—only for sustenance.

Despite his humble origins, Ejeta dreamed of somehow eliminating the suffering of malnourished children. For much of the last forty years, he has devoted his waking hours to a quest to ensure that the children of Africa need no longer starve.

Ejeta concentrated on improving sorghum yields. For centuries, sorghum has been one of the world's five principal grains. Sorghum is versatile. It can be roasted like popcorn or boiled like rice. It also can be ground to make bread and brewed to make both alcoholic and nonalcoholic beverages. The flour from sorghum can make porridge. Ejeta calls sorghum "a staff of life" for millions of people. The crop is as important to Africa as corn and soybeans are to the United States. The vital but vulnerable sorghum plant has been perpetually plagued by its dual nemeses: drought and the deadly parasitic weed striga. The

consequences have been widespread food shortages, visiting death to millions. After thousands of experiments and countless failures, Ejeta developed Africa's first commercial hybrid variety of sorghum resistant to both drought and striga. The quest was won.

On June 11, 2009, U.S. Secretary of State Hillary Clinton announced that Ejeta had won the World Food Prize for his research. The award is considered by many as the Nobel Prize of agriculture. His work was cited as dramatically enhancing the food supply of people throughout Africa in their constant struggle with the scourge of starvation. According to U.S. Secretary of Agriculture Tom Vilsack, Ejeta had put himself in the company of the greatest researchers and scientists in the world.

The only child of Ejeta Dassa and Motu Ayano was born on June 1, 1950, in the communal farming village of Wollonkomi, population 1,500—not large enough to warrant identification on most maps of Ethiopia. The unimproved road connecting the village to the world was used by occasional visitors and travelers who stopped briefly in Wollonkomi midway on their journey from the capital of Addis Ababa to Ambo, a town known for its mineral water. The village rarely engaged in commerce with other communities. The child was given the name Gebisa (guh-BEE-suh), which in the tribal Orono language means "blessed." According to custom, his surname was his father's first name: Ejeta (eh-JET-tuh).

Only a few of the children of the village attended church school, where they learned to read and write the official Ethiopian language, Amharic. In the evenings they studied Geez, the language of the Ethiopian Orthodox Church in which Ejeta and his family worshiped. Ejeta learned to read in Geez and to understand the scriptures. The early childhood academic discipline likely was a catalyst for the development of his young, fertile mind.

At age nine Ejeta left the church school to study at the home of a neighbor who shared with some villagers the cost of a high school dropout hired to teach enough rudimentary English, arithmetic, and science to complete the equivalent of third grade. The next year, at the urging of his mother, Ejeta began fourth grade at Aleka Kidane Wold, a boarding school in Addis Alem, where all subjects were taught in English. Ejeta walked twenty kilometers to school each Sunday evening carrying a weekly ration of food and returned home after school on Friday to help with family chores and to restock on supplies. Bus service was available, but he could not afford the twenty-five-cent fare. He was a good student and ably advanced through the grades. "My mother is an illiterate woman, but my mother is a woman with great vision and hopefulness. She is a person who believed that through education her only child would get out of that kind of life. More than any other person, the one who is responsible for my being the person I turned out to be is my mother," Ejeta said.

In Ethiopia after the eighth grade, qualifying students may choose among four boarding schools according to areas of special interests: business, technical, agriculture, and academics. As a teenager, Ejeta continued to question whether it was possible to break the cycle of starvation that visited upon his countrymen. He chose to study at Jimma College of Agriculture in the western part of the country. The school was established by Oklahoma State University under the U.S. government's Point Four Program, a project that gave economic aid to poor countries announced by President Harry S. Truman in his inaugural address in 1949. For the first time in his life, he was provided a consistent diet of nutritious food.

Ejeta graduated from Jimma with distinction in 1968 and qualified for acceptance to the government-subsidized Alemaya College (later named Haramaya). There, he met Bruane Gebrekidan, the school's plant geneticist. According to Ejeta, "He was the one who guided me to the plant sciences and to plant genetics, the one who convinced me about serving humanity through science." Ejeta graduated from Alemaya at the top of his class in 1973 with a bachelor's degree in plant science.

Entering high school, Ejeta was a small boy but perhaps as a result of better nutrition at school he experienced an extraordinary growth spurt his first two years and achieved his adult height of six feet, seven inches.

It was no wonder that he was encouraged to play basketball and volleyball. He competed in high school and all four years of college. In his final year of college, Ejeta, the tallest player on the team, was selected to play center for the Ethiopian National Basketball Team.

After graduation, Ejeta joined the Alemaya faculty as a junior member with the expectation that he would get a scholarship to study overseas. He intended to earn master's and PhD degrees and return to teach at the college, but when he was provided a grant to study in Canada later that year, he opted not to go. He was already consumed with his research on sorghum. There was much at stake.

In 1973 on the other side of the world, Purdue University Professor John Axtell and his students sifted through more than nine thousand varieties of sorghum in the Purdue collection and discovered a strain of high-lysine sorghum in a variant originating in Ethiopia. Lysine is an essential amino acid, and the increased concentration added nutritional value to the sorghum. Axtell made plans to travel to Ethiopia and personally collect samples of the crop. He coordinated his visit with Doctor Brhane Gebee Kidan, a professor at Alemaya and Ejeta's supervisor. Upon Axtell's arrival, Kidan assigned Ejeta to work with him for a week. The American was so impressed that he invited Ejeta to come to Purdue as a graduate student and paid research assistant.

Ejeta arrived at Purdue in the summer of 1974 and enrolled in the master's program in the Department of Agronomy, specializing in plant breeding and genetics, specifically sorghum. Of Axtell, Ejeta said, "He was my mentor and the one who actually discovered me. He literally picked me out of Africa and brought me to Purdue as a graduate student. He saw attributes in me that I didn't even know I had." Ejeta also cited Lowell Hardin, professor emeritus of agricultural economics, as an important mentor.

Axtell was well known in academic circles and had been invited to meetings and conferences worldwide. But in the spring of 1976 he found himself in conflict. He had been invited to two conferences at the same time, one in Tanzania and the other in Vienna. He arranged for Ejeta to attend the conference in Tanzania. Ejeta accepted the invitation to return to Africa and seized the additional opportunity to spend a month in his native village. He looked forward to visiting his widowed mother, but he had another motive: a girl, Senait Workale-mahu. He had dated her while he was at Alemaya and they had been carrying on a written correspondence since he left the country. He agonized over the risk that he would be detained if he visited Ethiopia because Emperor Haile Selassie had been overthrown by a Communist junta, a regime hostile to the western world. Love won out. The couple, without the luxury of a long courtship, married in Addis Ababa, processed the necessary paperwork, and traveled together to Purdue. They have five children, four girls and the youngest, a son. The children enjoy athletics. None has expressed an interest in agronomy.

Ejeta earned a master's degree in 1976 and a PhD in 1978 while working as a teaching assistant in plant genetics and research. He planned to return to Ethiopia and use his skills to enhance the quality and quantity of the agricultural output of his native country, but it was not meant to be. Ethiopia was still under Communist rule and, as Ejeta said, "The country went to pot when the Communists took over. By the time I had finished my work at Purdue, it was no place to go back to." As the years passed, his Hoosier roots grew deeper and his desire to return to Ethiopia waned, but since the Communist regime was overthrown in 1991, Ejeta has visited his home village of Wollonkomi at least once a year.

In 1979, with the assistance of Axtell, Gebisa found an exciting opportunity. He joined the International Crop Research Institute for the Semi-Arid Tropics, headquartered in Hyderbad, India, and funded by the United Nations Development Program. After a few months in India he was stationed in Wad Medani, Sudan, a difficult place to live with a wife and an infant daughter.

In Sudan Ejeta's team searched for genetic variances of sorghum with specific traits that helped it resist drought at different stages of plant development. Then, the team created new genetic combinations through conventional breeding methods, testing more than three thousand hybrids. Within five years Ejeta helped the team develop, test, and deploy the first commercial drought-resistant sorghum hybrid in Africa; however, as his oldest daughter reached school age and the family grew—then consisting of four daughters—he and his wife opted to return to America.

In 1984 Ejeta joined the faculty at Purdue as assistant professor of plant breeding and genetics, and continued his research with vigor. His university team designed a novel approach that led to understanding a series of biological phenomena, eventually resulting in the solution of a seemingly intractable problem: the curse of the weed striga. The researchers unlocked the biochemical means by which striga interacts with sorghum and chokes its growth. Sorghum releases a chemical compound during its development that the striga seeds use as a cue to germinate. It also releases another compound that striga requires to produce rootlets, which attach to the roots of the sorghum plants and eventually rob the sorghum crop of its nutrients. One striga plant can produce as many as a half million new seeds that can potentially remain viable for up to twenty years, resulting in a very quick spread and massive yield losses of the sorghum crop.

"When I started trying to work on this everybody was surprised because we don't have an environment in the United States where I could grow a plant and see whether or not it was resistant to striga. The risk of unleashing striga on crops grown in the United States was not worth the benefits that could be derived from the experiment," Ejeta said. "It looked very foolish until I came up with an idea that maybe under laboratory conditions I could see where there may be a mutant or a variant of the host plant that may not produce enough of these chemicals—and if it did not produce these chemicals, I hypothesized, that the plant would escape or be resistant. So when we built an agricultural research building at Purdue. I received permission from the U.S.D.A. [U.S. Department of Agriculture] to introduce the parasitic weed for use in the containment facility." Because striga is known to attack corn, a mainstay in Indiana, Ejeta's team is required to change clothes to work in the laboratory and to undergo thorough decontamination procedures upon leaving.

Ten years after Ejeta picked up his research at Purdue, eight tons of drought-tolerant and striga-resistant sorghum seeds produced at the university's agricultural research farm were distributed to a dozen African countries, including Ethiopia. Farmers reported yields as much as four times larger than traditional sorghum crops. The World Food Prize Foundation ultimately recognized Ejeta's achievement and its enormous impact, bestowing its highest honor, the World Food Prize. Founded in 1986 by Nobel Laureate Dr. Norman E. Borlaug, the prize is awarded annually to individuals whose efforts significantly contribute to improving the quality, quantity, and availability of food in the world. The prize also recognizes contributions in any field involving the world's food supply, including agricultural science and technology, manufacturing, marketing, nutrition, economics, poverty alleviation, political leadership, and the social sciences.

During the week of the World Food Prize presentation ceremonies, high-level dialogue is held on food security and general agricultural issues. The best minds in the field are brought to the international headquarters of the World Food Prize Foundation in Borlaug's hometown, Des Moines, Iowa, to speak during the three-day conference. In years past Ejeta had been honored to present. When he received a call in April 2009, he thought it was another invitation to speak. Citing a busy schedule, he politely declined to attend the event. World Food Prize Foundation president Kenneth Quinn replied, "We would like you to come out this year because you are the 2009 World Prize Laureate."

Always humble and soft-spoken, Ejeta responded to the press, "I'm pleased that the selection committee found my work significant enough to choose me. . . . It is a great honor." Others were more effusive. Purdue president France Córdova said, "Dr. Ejeta is proof that one person can make a big difference in the world and in helping solve its grand challenges. His efforts to meet the challenge of world hunger represent the best in Purdue research." Jay Akridge, Purdue's Glenn W. Sample Dean of Agriculture, agreed: "Dr. Ejeta's research has improved the food supply for more than half a billion people in several African countries. His work is a powerful demonstration of the difference agricultural research can make in creating a more secure and consistent food supply for millions of people. We're obviously very proud of Gebisa and are thrilled that he was selected to receive the 2009 World Food Prize."

At the October 15 ceremony, Ejeta received a sculpture created by world-renowned designer Saul Bass and a $250,000 cash prize. The sculpture, which is given to each winner, is an earth-colored bowl made of alabaster resting on a slate base with a pewter sphere sitting in its center. From the sphere, a wedge was removed, and the exposed interior was cut with a leaf design. The sphere symbolizes the world; the leaf design, its food; and the bowl, the nourishment of its people. In 2010 Ejeta announced that he would use the $250,000 grant to support educational and community service projects benefitting African children. His first project will be to build a new school in Wollonkomi so that every child in his native village will have access to educational opportunities and a means to break the stranglehold of hunger.

In a celebration on the Purdue campus, Córdova declared October 22, 2009, Gebisa Ejeta Day. On that day, the Purdue community discussed the issue of fighting hunger. The night before, Purdue students held a hunger banquet to illustrate how food availability and consumption varies around the world. Banquet guests drew a ticket assigning them to a high-, middle- or low-income tier as determined by world development report statistics. Then they were served a meal representative of what people in those income levels would eat each day. The fifteen percent of the guests in the high-income tier enjoyed a gourmet meal. The twenty-five percent in the middle tier dined on rice and beans, and the sixty percent in the low-income tier waited in line for small portions of rice and water. Organizers hoped that activity would motivate students to find ways to end poverty and hunger.

In the wake of the World Food Prize, Ejeta was treated to two homecomings. The first was in July 2010 on a visit to his mother in Wollonkomi. Hundreds of residents waited for him to appear. He also spoke to the children of the village as a part of a separate recognition ceremony. In November he accepted an official invitation from the government of Ethiopia for a series of celebrations. One of the events of the week was a symposium at which he and his invited guests discussed agricultural development in Africa and in Ethiopia specifically. At the end of that day, President Girma Woldeghiorgis held a dinner in Ejeta's honor with all the delegates at the conference and presented him with the Ethiopian Medal of Honor, the highest award that can be bestowed upon a scientist. During that week there also was a regional celebration in Wollonkomi where fifteen thousand people appeared to express their thanks for the difference he made in their lives.

The World Food Prize has given Ejeta a much larger platform. He speaks throughout the world, and he uses those opportunities to advocate for greater food security in developing countries. One of his goals is to spread basic agricultural training to millions of poor farmers. He believes that simple agronomic practices common in the West, such as planting seeds at the right time and controlling weeds, could revolutionize African agriculture. According to Ejeta, "One of the problems in developing countries is not conducting scientific research but delivering the results of that science to the farm community so that it can be adopted–taking the technology to the farmers." Ejeta would like to see farmers not only produce enough to feed themselves but somehow create a profit motive so they would produce a surplus and then to connect that surplus to a delivery system. In the Sudan and other countries where Ejeta has worked, he has been involved with various programs to capitalize these kinds of agricultural enterprise activities—creating an environment in which science can really make a difference.

Ejeta is an advisor to the Bill and Melinda Gates Foundation and its Alliance for Green Revolution in Africa, an agricultural initiative that works with African government, farmers, and others to reduce hunger and poverty through agricultural development. He took a sabbatical from Purdue in October 2006 and spent a year in Nairobi, Kenya, to design and begin implementation of the program. He traveled with his wife and seventeen-year-old son, who took a year off from school. Ejeta has ongoing relationships with the Gates Foundation and the Rockefeller Foundation, as well as other international organizations and endowments. All are volunteer positions. By partnering with leaders and farmers across sub-Saharan Africa and educational institutions in the United States and abroad, Ejeta has personally trained and inspired a new generation of African agricultural scientists that is carrying forth his work.

At Purdue Ejeta is a distinguished professor of plant breeding and genetics. He teaches at the graduate level. He is also a role model and mentor. According to Ejeta, "The fortunate part of what we do at the university is multifaceted. The same research that we do to advance science to help humanity is also a tool for educating graduate students so they continue with ideas still left in mind. The need out there is great, so there is more to do. We need to extend the results of our work to more programs and more nations. We need to build stronger human and institutional capacity in African nations to help people feed themselves. We need to encourage the development of similar advances in maize, millets and other crops of Africa." He tells his students and his children that he never thought he was bright, so he erred on the part of effort. Focus and effort made a difference in his life. There are not a lot of insufficiencies that one cannot overcome with hard work.

In testimony before the U.S. Senate Committee on Foreign Relations on March 24, 2009, Ejeta remembered, "I was nurtured with lots of love but on a diet less than adequate even for body maintenance, let alone for growth and intellectual development. All nutritional and developmental indicators might have suggested that I was destined not for my current physical stature or the modest professional successes I have attained, but for failure and perhaps for disaster. And there by the grace of God, in what feels like a destiny nothing less than providential, I am invited to sit here today before this distinguished committee, in this hallowed institution of this great nation, to provide this testimony as a notable scientist with some distinction and repute. This is a very long journey from that village in west- central Ethiopia where I am sorry to report has not changed much since the days of my childhood."

Ejeta is devoted to not only affect change in his village, but to continue to affect change throughout the world. Gebisa Ejeta, a transplanted Hoosier and world-renowned geneticist, is on a mission to beat back the plague of hunger. He is already one of few people in the history of our earth who has saved the lives of millions of his fellow man.

Angelo Pizzo

Storyteller

In the lore of Hoosier high school basketball, steeped with tradition and pride, one game—no, one moment—stands above all else: Bobby Plump's last shot. That basket in the waning seconds of the 1954 Indiana state championship game crowned Milan, one of the smallest schools in the tournament, victorious over basketball powerhouse Muncie Central. Although more than a half century has passed, some southern Indiana old-timers still mark time by that event, replacing Pearl Harbor Day, a joyless focal point of the prior decade.

Two years before "The Shot," four-year-old Angelo Pizzo moved with his family from Chicago to Bloomington, Indiana less than an hour's drive from Milan and well within the aura of that legendary feat—recounted every year at tournament time. Growing up, Pizzo loved two things: movies and Hoosier basketball. In 1981 he endeavored to merge his two loves.

In the afterglow of Indiana University's 1981 romp through the National Collegiate Athletic Association tournament under Coach Bob Knight, Pizzo was inspired to capture the "Milan Miracle" in a fictionalized account. Although he had attended graduate school in film studies and worked in the television and movie business for a decade, he had never written a screenplay. Five weeks of research and a year of

209

writing produced a bulky script of twice the normal and acceptable length. Pizzo shared his creation with trusted filmmaking mentor Phil Mandelker, who responded with what Pizzo referred to as the most unforgettably traumatic and painful conversation in his creative life. In a hurried call from New York's John F. Kennedy International Airport on his way to Paris, Mandelker pronounced the script hopeless. Pizzo threw his script into the back of his closet, where it sat for years, and but for the cajoling and encouragement of another friend, author Scott Berg, would have been forgotten. With encouragement and assistance from Berg, Pizzo extracted a producible script from that first effort. Rising from the back of Pizzo's closet, *Hoosiers*—the movie that almost was never made—garnered nominations for two Academy Awards and was named by an ESPN expert panel as the number one sports movie of all time.

Physician Anthony Pizzo was recruited from the University of Chicago in 1952 to establish the pathology lab at Bloomington Hospital; he also served as county coroner. He enjoyed politics and was elected to the Bloomington City Council and the Indiana Senate. He and his wife, Patricia, had seven children, starting with Angelo, born on January 9, 1948. Patricia enjoyed staying home and managing the busy household.

Patricia gave Angelo the first nudge into the performing arts. A friend in the theater department at Indiana University convinced her that nine-year-old Angelo could be an actor and recruited him to a play role at the nearby Brown County Playhouse. He had good reviews and enjoyed the work. He did readings, musicals, and ballets and later, much to his chagrin, was kidded by his high school football teammates for playing a part in *The Nutcracker*. As a teenager, he became more self-conscious and was concerned about how girls thought of him. At fourteen, he announced to all who would listen that his career in the theater was finished. Pizzo dropped out of all extracurricular activities, not just acting. Although his grades suffered, he graduated.

In 1967 IU was required to accept all in-state students, so Pizzo enrolled and was placed on academic probation. He chose to major in political science. Politics, often the subject of dinner conversation, intrigued him. As a preteen, he had been fascinated with John Kennedy's 1960 presidential campaign. Pizzo's vague goal after earning a degree in political science was to move to Washington, D.C. At IU he joined Sigma Nu fraternity and enjoyed the social life. Understanding that if he did not perform well he would flunk out and miss all the fun, he achieved a perfect 4.0 grade point average his first semester at college. While in school, he volunteered for Birch Bayh's U.S. Senate campaign in Indiana and Robert Kennedy's presidential bid.

As a child Pizzo loved adventure stories. He read the classics, including *Three Musketeers*, *The Man in the Iron Mask* and *Tom Sawyer*. In college, Pizzo transferred that love to film. His elective course opportunities were filled with film history courses. He saw every movie available. Although he was passionate about films, the idea of actually making a living in that field seemed remote.

Pizzo did not go to Washington after graduation. He spent much of the next year in Aspen, Colorado, working for a property-management company while rooming with his fraternity brother and best friend David Anspaugh, who was a ski instructor. Pizzo then moved to Hawaii and managed a record store, still contemplating his career. That contemplation became a crisis, a conflict between what he was trained for—political science—and what he loved, film. He held long discussions with friends and family, including his father, whose passion was medicine. When he told his father that movies were the only thing that he really loved, his father replied, "Figure out how to make a living at it." Pizzo accepted that advice and now counsels, "Consider the amount of time that you spend in your workday. It takes up a significant part of your waking life. Why waste it performing something you don't care about. Find something that you have a passion for, something that means something to you, and then you will have a much more rewarding life."

At twenty-three, Pizzo decided to earn a master's degree and a doctorate so he could teach film at a university. The University of Southern California had begun a new department in the film school titled, History, Theory and Criticism—exactly what Pizzo was looking for. On his return from Hawaii in January 1972, Pizzo nailed his interview at USC and was accepted for the semester beginning in September 1973. He returned to Bloomington and spent the year preparing for USC, taking additional film courses and buying every book about films that he could find.

While in graduate school Pizzo met television producer Grant Tinker, who was married to Mary Tyler Moore and whose company, MTM, produced her show. Tinker was beginning the last season of the *Mary Tyler Moore Show* and offered Pizzo three hours of work per week as an unpaid assistant, for which USC granted him three hours of credit toward his graduate degree. It was the first time Pizzo had gotten close to an actual production. Watching every show sitting next to Tinker, he began to think that film production was not alien territory. Perhaps his role in films was to be a producer.

After that experience, Tinker suggested that Pizzo meet Philip Mandelker, who was developing thirteen one-hour drama episodes for television and who was looking for someone to provide research for the series. Mandelker, a New York native, set his dramas in blue-collar Flint, Michigan, with a large Irish-Catholic family and a dog named Detroit. Pizzo took the position. Two weeks later, Mandelker's assistant quit and Pizzo was offered the job. Pizzo was two hundred pages into writing his doctoral thesis on the genre theory of film criticism, but Mandelker was undeterred. "You'll have to put it aside," he implored. "I'll need you fourteen to fifteen hours a day, seven days a week. I will teach you everything you will need to know about making television movies. Everything—casting, editing, composing, directing—everything." Pizzo was granted a six-month sabbatical and put all his doctorial papers in a box. They are still there. Mandelker and Pizzo completed thirteen episodes over the next six months. The show, called *The Fitzpatricks*, aired during the 1977-78 season against *Laverne and Shirley* and *Happy Days*, the top two shows at the time—a slot referred to in television parlance as The Dead Zone.

The Fitzpatricks was canceled, but the Mandelker/Pizzo relationship remained strong. Mandelker facilitated an offer for Pizzo from Time-

Life Films president David Suskind to become director of development. In that capacity he developed ideas to sell miniseries and movies of the week to the television networks. Once the ideas were sold, it was Pizzo's responsibility to hire writers and to supervise the writing and the production. The position lasted six years. After working a short stint in a similar position for another company, he was rehired by Time-Life in the position of vice president of production for feature films. The tables were turned, rather than pitching ideas to networks, he was buying film ideas from others. The film-production unit made about five movies a year. In 1981 the company exited the business and paid Pizzo a severance package.

Pizzo again found himself at a crossroads. This time he had some money, but he still had no idea what he wanted to do. Another long discussion with his father ensued. While at USC Pizzo had thought about writing an antiwar movement script, but he believed that there was no market for that kind of movie. It was 1981. IU had just captured the NCAA championship and Pizzo had a different idea: *Hoosiers.*

Unlike most states, in the 1950s Indiana held a single-class basketball tournament that allowed all schools to compete for the same championship. It was one of America's largest and most popular high school tournaments. School consolidation was still in its infancy, so most Indiana high schools of the era had small enrollments. Often these rural schools advanced several games into the tournament but inevitably fell in the regional to larger urban schools. In 1952, twenty-four-year-old Marvin Wood was hired as coach at Milan, which had 161 students. Wood angered many when he closed practice to outsiders, an act that removed one of the major forms of leisure-time entertainment for the town's basketball-crazed population. Wood taught the team patience rather than the run-and-gun approach of the previous coach, culminating in a four-corner, ball-control offense that he called the "cat and mouse."

In 1954 Wood and his talented and disciplined team advanced through the tournament to the final game in storied Butler Fieldhouse, where they faced heavily favored perennial power Muncie Central. After three quarters the game was tied 26-26. Plump, who had uncharacteristically shot only two for ten from the field, froze the ball unchallenged for more than four minutes during the fourth quarter. With the score tied at 30, Plump hit a fourteen-footer from the right side as time expired to seal the win, denying the Bearcats a fifth state title. The next day as the team returned home from Indianapolis, forty thousand people descended on Milan, population 1,150, to congratulate the Indians. No school with an enrollment of less than five times that of Milan's ever won the tournament again under the one-class system, which was abandoned in 1997.

Pizzo began to create a script for *Hoosiers* in 1981, but it did not go well. At Time-Life, he had always emphasized to writers that they should compose from an outline, but it just was not working for Pizzo. He wrote scenes over and over again until he threw most of them away. In desperation Pizzo called his friend John Young, a writer and producer that he admired. Young gave him valuable advice: "The biggest obstacle to many writers is self-consciousness and if you struggle with that, if that's an issue, then don't reread anything. Just go from one scene to the next, to the next, to the next. Discover things along the way about characters that will change the way you think about them. Never go back and read what you've written until you finish your story." Pizzo liked that advice—and it worked.

Pizzo nervously shared his creation with Mandelker, his friend and mentor, who delivered the hurried and brutal rejection with little explanation. Pizzo then returned to Los Angeles to take a position developing projects for Paramount. One night at a dinner party, Pizzo found himself sitting next to Scott Berg, a Pulitzer Prize-winning biographer. During dinner, Berg asked Pizzo about his writing. Pizzo said, "I wrote this script. It was a terrible mistake." Berg replied, "Really, why do you think that?" Pizzo said, "Well it's an awful script. I had somebody read it for me who told me so." Berg begged Pizzo to allow him to read the script, but Pizzo was too embarrassed to share it with him. After many inquiries over a number of months, Pizzo finally broke down and gave Berg the script. Within days he called Pizzo and said, "There's a great movie here. It is just long. We need to cut it." In fact, the actual script for *Hoosiers* was in that draft; it just had to be edited. Berg sat down with Pizzo for two or three weekends and suggested how to cut the script. Then Pizzo gave it to Anspaugh, who had just won an Emmy Award for directing an episode of *Hill Street Blues*. Anspaugh liked it, too, and Pizzo learned an important lesson: "Never give any one person the power to judge you. Not one person, not twenty and never be defined by someone telling you what you can't do." Pizzo's agent liked the script as well, but cautioned that it was a small regional film and that major studios would not be interested. He suggested that Pizzo and Anspaugh try investors in Indiana. With the assistance of Governor Robert D. Orr, they met with a number of people in the movie industry in Indiana, including Cindy Simon-Skjodt, daughter of and assistant to real-estate magnate Mel Simon, also a movie producer. She said her family was not interested.

When Anspaugh was giving ski lessons in Aspen, one of his students was actor Jack Nicholson. A friendship was forged. Capitalizing on that relationship, Anspaugh and Pizzo sent him the script and persuaded him to play the leading role. *Chinatown* (1974) had made Nicholson one of the biggest stars in the business. With Nicholson attached, the script attracted interest from many studios. But scheduling conflicts kept Nicholson from participating. After a number of actors turned them down, they showed it to Gene Hackman, who committed to the movie. Hackman had won critical and popular acclaim in 1971's *The French Connection*, but had failed to achieve similar success with his subsequent films. Hackman was not Nicholson, and many studios rejected the film with him as the lead. Anspaugh and Pizzo finally found film financier John Daly, who agreed to finance the film at an estimated cost of $7 million. Daly was from England but had started a production company in Los Angeles and had a distribution contract with Orion Pictures. Later, it was revealed that when Daly read the script, he cried. His father was an alcoholic who embarrassed him at his soccer games. He related to the Shooter character in *Hoosiers*, an alcoholic played by Dennis Hopper, whose film credits included *Easy Rider* (1969), *Apocalypse Now* (1979) and *Blue Velvet* (1986).

Hoosiers rated high in a test screening in Costa Mesa, California. Nonetheless, Orion was reluctant to green light a national release. The movie, which Pizzo insisted be shot entirely in Indiana, was given a test release in the state beginning on Thanksgiving 1986, with the understanding that if it did not perform it would not go much further. Pizzo and Anspaugh went to radio stations and newspapers throughout Indiana to beg people to attend. It also helped that the picture had garnered glowing reviews in national magazines and newspapers. The Indiana release was a major success and the movie earned its national release beginning with a world premiere at the Circle Theater in Indianapolis. After the premiere, Lieutenant Governor John Mutz presented Pizzo the Sagamore of the Wabash Award, at the time, Indiana's highest honor. Years later, the movie in which Orion had so little faith was selected by the Library of Congress for its National Film Registry.

In order to qualify for the Academy Awards, a movie must play in a theater in either Los Angeles or New York for at least one week before the end of the year it is released. Because Orion felt there was a zero chance that the picture would garner any nominations, it did not schedule the national opening until January. Undaunted, Daly leased a theater in Los Angeles and opened it himself in December 1986. The movie was nominated for two Oscars: Dennis Hopper for best supporting actor and Jerry Goldsmith for best composer.

Angelo was invited to the Oscars, but he had a conflict. Oscar night coincided with the final game of the 1987 National Collegiate Athletic Association basketball tournament, in which IU was a contestant. There were higher-rated teams in the tournament that year, and Pizzo was certain that IU would be eliminated before Final Four weekend. Anspaugh and Pizzo accepted seats for the Academy Awards next to Hopper and Goldsmith. They arranged for their tuxedos and a limo and were set to attend until IU miraculously made it to the final game. As faithful Hoosier fans, they opted to forego the ceremony and hosted a party at Anspaugh's home with television sets tuned into both the Academy Awards and the basketball game. *Hoosiers* did not win an Oscar, but the Hoosier basketball team won the NCAA championship, beating Syracuse 74-73 on a last-second shot by Keith Smart.

After *Hoosiers,* Pizzo was in demand. Orion paid him to rewrite a few of its scripts and to research and write according to his own preference. Pizzo began a project set at the Indianapolis 500. He followed the racing circuit for five months, got to know the drivers, traveled with them, and wrote a script. But Pizzo was unable to interest a major actor, which doomed the effort. His script went nowhere.

In 1990 Daniel "Rudy" Ruettiger pitched Pizzo his life story—the story of how he refused to give up his dream of playing football for the storied University of Notre Dame despite significant obstacles. The first time they met, Pizzo turned him down, telling Ruettinger, "I'll never do it. I don't want to do another sports movie set in Indiana and I hate Notre Dame football." But Ruettinger never gave up. He continued to inundate Pizzo with Notre Dame material, including videos. At about the same time, Anspaugh met with a producer and told him about the concept. The producer said he had just had lunch with the president of Columbia Pictures, Frank Price, who had attended Michigan State University, but said his biggest disappointment in life was that he was not accepted to Notre Dame. They pitched the movie to Price and he took it.

Pizzo spent six weeks on and around the Notre Dame campus in South Bend, Indiana researching and writing the script. *Rudy* was released in October 1993 with the tagline, "When people say dreams don't come true, tell them about Rudy." The next year, *Rudy* won the Studio Crystal Heart Award at the Heartland Film Festival in Indianapolis. A column in the September 20, 2010, issue of *Sports Illustrated* hailed *Rudy* as one of the best sports movies of all time. Pizzo won more than respect as a result of that project. While filming on the Notre Dame campus, he met Greta Lind, a professional actress who played Mary, the coed in charge of the Notre Dame pep squad. They married and had two sons, Anthony and Quinn. Both boys are promising athletes. Neither has shown interest in making movies.

Pizzo is sought after and paid handsomely to rewrite scripts. In his estimation he has rejected 95 percent of those opportunities, preferring to concentrate on "originals." In 2004 Pizzo and his family moved from Los Angeles back to Bloomington. Pizzo refers to the return home as "one of the most important decisions I've made in my life." Pizzo was looking for something he could not find in Los Angeles, a place where his sons could grow up with midwestern values like he did, with a sense of community—family. That extended family dines together just about every Sunday night. Since moving back to Indiana, Pizzo has enriched his community. He serves on the boards of the Heartland Film Festival, the New Harmony Writers Project, and the Kinsey Institute.

In 2005 Pizzo made a third movie, *The Game of Their Lives*, (released on video as *The Miracle Match*) based on the true story of the 1950 U.S. soccer team, which against all odds beat England 1-0. Unlike *Rudy* and *Hoosiers*" where things fell into place "like magic," as Pizzo put it, *The Game of Their Lives* was a production that started out looking like it had a bright future until everything went wrong. The film was released in only five markets and had only a small marketing budget. It flopped. Pizzo laments the fact that he knew more about making movies going into *The Game of Their Lives* than he did about *Hoosiers*, yet the outcome was disappointing. The *Hoosiers* budget was $7 million, *Rudy* was $14 million, and *The Game of Their Lives* was $28 million. The budgets, however, had an inverse relationship to the success of the movies.

Pizzo now works from home at a desk constructed from the gymnasium floor of the old IU Fieldhouse. He points out to guests that three national champions regularly played basketball on the top of his desk. Although his three produced movies were conceived around sports teams, Pizzo maintains that sports movies are not necessarily his niche. He points to common themes including persistence, human relationships, and dreaming big and concludes that sports are not the only genre that can carry that message. Although Pizzo came to his craft almost by accident, he would ply no other trade. He said that writing is an arduous, difficult, and painful profession but, he added, "When I think about retiring, not doing writing any more, it's inconceivable. I will do it as long as I'm alive because nothing gives me greater satisfaction than when I'm on the last page of a completed screen play. Of course, there's always a terrifying part of it and that's when I'm on the first page knowing there are one hundred and twenty blank pages to follow that have to be filled with magic. It's one of the most awful feelings in the entire experience. I've met a lot of writers over the course of the years and yet to come across a good writer that didn't find writing very, very difficult. Because they write from a deeper place, a place of vulnerability, a place of pain. I never met a writer who said he really loved writing and was really any good."

In 1995 Pizzo received the Governor's Art Award for contributions to the arts and in 1996 the Thomas Hart Benton Mural Medallion Award as a distinguished IU alumnus. Although he never finished his doctorate at USC, in 2000 he received an honorary Doctor of Humanities degree from Franklin College. In 2010 Pizzo received the IU College of Arts and Sciences Distinguished Alumni Award. He also was honored that year with the St. Vincent Silver Medal by the Indiana Basketball Hall of Fame, which cited him for his outstanding contribution to high school basketball. Recipients of the Silver Medal are considered to be Hall of Fame inductees. He joined Milan's Coach Wood and Bobby Plump among Indiana's basketball heroes—a fitting tribute for Angelo Pizzo, Indiana's Hoosier storyteller.

MITCH DANIELS

My Man Mitch

"Hey Mitch, a plane just hit a New York office building." Mitch Daniels, director of the federal Office of Management and Budget, glanced at the television set in the reception room. It was September 11, 2001, shortly before 9 a.m. Daniels continued the meeting in his office in Washington, D.C.'s Eisenhower Building, located directly across from the executive parking lot and only a sixty-second sprint to the Oval Office. Daniels had traversed that lot to advise President George W. Bush on many occasions.

About fifteen minutes later, United Airlines Flight 175 shattered Tower Two of the World Trade Center. This was no accident. At OMB evacuation was the instinctive response. There was no alert system in the Eisenhower Building, no beep, no buzz, no intercom, and no alarm. Elementary schools had better warning systems than buildings in the White House complex. Somehow the word was passed.

As occupants hastened to the pavement, an explosion riveted their attention just down Seventeenth Street, where black smoke was pouring from the direction of the Pentagon. Was the United States under attack? Daniels's cell phone was inoperative. He ran to the OMB annex around the corner and used a landline to call his driver. "John, where are you?" John Fielding was in his office in a far corner of the Eisen-

221

hower Building, possibly the only American who was not aware that something was awry. Daniels said, "John, run to my office, which is wide open, grab the in-box, my briefcase and my gym bag. Get those three things and try to get the car out through the crowd. I'll meet you at Eighteenth and G." Fielding picked him up at the designated intersection and drove Daniels to his apartment on Connecticut Avenue, where he established communication with his deputies and other officials. That afternoon, Fielding deposited Daniels a few blocks from the White House. Daniels talked himself through a White House defense perimeter, hastily set up by soldiers, and established an operations center in the Roosevelt Room in the West Wing by about 4 p.m.

Daniels's principal deputy—former Secretary of the Navy Sean O'Keefe, who later became administrator of the National Aeronautics and Space Administration—was the only one of his staff members to secure admission to the White House. Together, they encouraged federal government departments to begin thinking about the tasks they were required to perform. For example, it was the responsibility of the Department of Transportation to guard the airports. Daniels and O'Keefe tallied the funds necessary for each department to respond to the developing catastrophe. Later, they used their offices to facilitate those requests for authority and funds.

Over the next few days, Daniels was Bush's chief liaison in discussions with Congress on financial and related issues, including the concerns of New York City and the domestic airlines. Extraordinary cooperation took place—a demonstration of collegiality that has rarely graced the halls of Congress before or since. Democratic and Republican leadership were on the same page. During this uncertain period in the nation's history, Daniels demonstrated innovative thinking and bold decisive action—leadership skills that less than a decade later catapulted him onto the short list of Republicans mentioned as likely candidates for the office of president of the United States.

Mitchell Elias Daniels Jr. was born April 7, 1949, in Monongahela,

Pennsylvania, to his namesake and Dorothy "Dottie" Wilkes Daniels. The elder Daniels, a regional manager for pharmaceutical company Pitman-Moore, accepted a transfer from Georgia and moved his family to Indianapolis in 1958 while Mitch Jr. and his younger sister, Deborah, were in elementary school. Daniels graduated from North Central High School in 1967 and was named a presidential scholar by President Lyndon Johnson as part of a program established in 1964 to honor the nation's most distinguished graduating high school seniors. While at North Central, Daniels whetted his appetite for politics by successfully winning the office of student council president.

In 1971 Daniels graduated from Princeton University's Woodrow Wilson School of Public and International Affairs, where he was acclaimed not only for his intellect but also for his skill at—as he put it, probability and geometry, but more commonly known as poker and pool. Prior to graduation, Daniels pursued his fascination with politics, serving as a summer intern for Indianapolis mayor Richard Lugar. Upon graduation, Daniels postponed plans for law school, opting instead to work on Lugar's re-election committee. He continued to work for the Indiana Republican Party, assisting in Lugar's failed attempt to unseat U.S. Senator Birch Bayh in 1974. The next year he joined the mayor's staff as his primary assistant.

Daniels ran Lugar's successful 1976 senatorial election campaign. When Lugar took office the following January, Daniels moved to the nation's capital and served six years as the senator's chief of staff. When Lugar won its chairmanship, he asked Daniels to shift to the job of executive director of the National Republican Senatorial Committee, a group that helps the party's current and prospective candidates with everything from budget planning to research and strategy. While in Washington, Daniels married Cheri Lynn Herman from New Albany, Indiana in 1978. He attended night law school at Georgetown University, graduating with honors in 1979.

In 1984 Daniels accepted an invitation to join President Ronald Reagan's administration and within a year was named chief political officer and adviser to the president. Daniels learned from Reagan to keep a close eye on key departments and not to ever get distracted from the important things he was trying to work on.

Three years later, Daniels returned to Indianapolis to accept the position of chief executive officer of the financially stressed Hudson Institute, a think tank founded in 1961 by futurist Herman Kahn. The policy-research organization, which has since moved to the nation's capital, aims to do innovative analysis promoting global security, prosperity, and freedom. During his tenure Daniels revitalized the institute with an extensive reorganization of its research programs and a broadened fund raising base. The motivation for his move was more personal, though. He and his wife, Cheri, wanted to raise their four young girls—Meagan, Melissa, Meredith and Maggie—in Indiana.

In 1988 Indiana Senator Dan Quayle was elected vice president on George H. W. Bush's presidential ticket. Quayle agreed to resign his Senate seat so that Governor Robert D. Orr could choose a Republican replacement before Governor-elect Evan Bayh took office. Orr offered the seat to Daniels. According to Daniels, it was a stunning opportunity. He had never held public office. It was the kind of challenge he would normally relish, but he just could not accept. His family had only been back in Indiana for a year and a half. His hours were normal. He felt that all the things were occurring that were supposed to happen at this time in his life. However awesome this possibility was, it came at the wrong time. They would not consider disrupting the family. It was unthinkable. He said, "No." The appointment went to Daniel Coats, a member of the U.S. House of Representatives representing Indiana's Fourth Congressional District.

In 1990 Daniels was enticed to leave the Hudson Institute for the corporate world. He was named vice president of corporate affairs for Eli Lilly and Company. Headquartered in Indianapolis, Lilly is a global, research-based pharmaceutical company founded in 1876. Daniels knew working for Lilly was an extraordinary opportunity—and an extraordinary responsibility. The fact that he was recruited at that high level was counter to the Lilly culture. "I told myself, don't shoot off your mouth, but after you think you understand things well enough to have an opinion, you have a responsibility to speak up and try to contribute your best judgment—not to be a yes man," said Daniels. When management presentations were requested, Daniels had expressed views about the health-care marketplace and the changes he felt were needed. The concept of managed care was emerging and Daniels opined that the customer was changing. He noted that Lilly's competitors were responding to the new marketplace.

Not long after Daniels joined the firm, Lilly underwent a restructuring. Manufacturing, sales, and marketing for North American pharmaceuticals were placed in one business unit. Before, each function had been in its own silo. After only one month, the chairman of the new division abruptly resigned. Company President Vaughn Bryson delivered a jolt to Daniels, telling him, "I want you to be the next president of North American Pharmaceutical Operations." Daniels was astonished. He had only been employed at Lilly for three years.

Not long after Daniels's promotion, there was a major disruption in the Lilly executive suite. Bryson was ousted, reportedly for making radical changes to the company without consulting the board. He was replaced by board member Randall Tobias. It was traumatic to a company that had always experienced orderly change at the top. Daniels was an admirer of Bryson and he loved Lilly. He was worried how this palace coup would affect the company, and he wrongly assumed that he would be fired because he was so closely associated with the prior administration. Tobias left Daniels in place.

Daniels cites his work at Lilly as a very intense and formative experience. "It was business on a major scale, complete accountability," he said. "Even though Lilly was working hard to globalize, North America represented 60 percent of the sales of the company and more than 70 percent of the margin of the company. North America meant everything. In addition, those four years were tough. The pharmaceutical business runs on new products. If you have a new product, properly patent-protected, it is hard not to make money. If you do not, it is very difficult. We had no new products until the very end. You had to learn how to do everything—how to squeeze a nickel, how to turn an underperforming asset into some cash or some better asset, how to make more sales somehow happen out of the same tired product line. It was an incredibly stretching experience." After four years, Daniels was again promoted, this time to senior vice president of corporate strategy and policy. Daniels was eleven years into a successful career as an executive at Lilly when another call for public service intervened. This time Daniels answered the call.

In January 2001 Daniels accepted the invitation of President George W. Bush to serve as his budget director. The OMB's major missions are to assist the president in overseeing the preparation of the federal budget and to hold accountable the executive branch agencies. In this role he was a member of the National Security Council and became a member of the Homeland Security Council after its creation in October 2001. The National Security Council, established in 1947, is the president's principal forum for considering national security and foreign policy matters with his senior advisers and cabinet officials. The Homeland Security Council is composed of cabinet members and senior White House officials whose departments have principal interests in homeland security policymaking. It is responsible for assessing the country's objectives, commitments, and risks, then making recommendations to the president with respect to homeland security policy. Bush dubbed Daniels "the Blade" in recognition of his budget-cutting prowess. Daniels enjoyed the sobriquet. Congressmen calling OMB looking for funding for their favorite causes were treated to the Daniels wit. When left on hold, they were teased with the Rolling Stones hit, "You can't always get what you want."

After two and a half years as head of the OMB, Daniels left the Bush administration to run for governor of Indiana. The task was daunting. No candidate from Indianapolis had ever been elected governor in the nearly two centuries of Indiana statehood, and the Daniels name was relatively unknown—far less so than the incumbent, war hero Joe Kernan. Daniels campaigned throughout the state in a white recreational vehicle covered with signatures of supporters and his trademark "My Man Mitch" campaign slogan, a reference to another nickname bestowed by Bush. Daniels visited all ninety-two counties at least three times and spent most nights as a guest of fellow Hoosiers. He kept detailed notes from his experience across Indiana, which he collected in a book titled, *Notes from the Road—16 months of towns, tales and tenderloins.* He dedicated the book to his father, who died just prior to the election:

> For Mitch, Sr.
> (February 8, 1923—August 5, 2004).
> He didn't quite make it to
> the end of the road, but no one ever
> gave a traveler better directions.

In the preface, Daniels explained his strategy:

> Having reached a decision to run for political office, something I had never expected to do, I resolved to go at it a little differently. There was much about modern politics I had long found unsatisfying and even distasteful: its domination by handlers and consultant mercenaries, reducing candidates to mouthpieces; the descent of public discourse into trivial issues and cooked-up character assassination; and, in particular, the retreat of campaigning to the television and the tarmac.

> Over recent decades, personal contact has practically disappeared from our politics. The handlers, who make more money the more resources are committed to advertising, are quick to tell candidates not to bother with public campaigning, aside from stunts for the news media, and cameo appearances at an airport or two. Best to spend your time sitting at a telephone, groveling for dollars to buy more ads demonizing your opponent and expressing your staunch commitment to whatever issues the polls say are popular this year.

> And, obviously, the mercenaries all say, there is no percentage

in visiting smaller towns. There are no TV cameras there and, besides, just do the math. If a candidate spent every available day seeking out voters, and every one of them influenced several others, it still wouldn't amount to a fraction of the votes necessary.

But we hit the Road [sic] anyway. As an unknown and untested quantity in Indiana politics, I knew I would have to earn my way. Others started far ahead in credibility and recognition and, besides, if this fool thing was worth doing at all, I figured I might as well throw myself totally into it.

Indianapolis Star columnist Matthew Tully, called Daniels's 2004 campaign "a rousing, inspired affair. On the road for more than a year, hitting tiny towns that most Hoosiers had never heard of, Daniels set the standard for running a statewide campaign in Indiana. He raised plenty of money and ran many commercials but in many ways rejected typical campaign tactics. He took his message to the people and laid out a long policy agenda. Even his fiercest critics acknowledge the campaign was politics at its best." Daniels wrote his own speeches and kept his politics positive and clean. Quoting Reagan, he said, "Remember we have no enemies, only opponents." In 2004 Daniels was elected the forty-ninth governor of Indiana, defeating Kernan with 53 percent of the vote.

The Daniels administration was populated by design with Lilly employees. According to Daniels, "You don't progress at Lilly unless you are honest and have a good work ethic and you are decent to people. I wanted my administration to have this ethos." One of his most important accomplishments as governor was returning Indiana to fiscal solvency. On his first day in office, Daniels created the Office of Management and Budget to look for efficiencies and cost savings across state government. In 2005 he led the state to its first balanced budget in eight years and, without a tax increase, transformed the $600 million deficit he inherited into a surplus of $370 million. Daniels used the surpluses generated in 2005 and 2006 to repay hundreds of millions of dollars the state had borrowed from Indiana's public schools, state universities, and local units of government in previous administrations.

Daniels believes that government should limit itself to those obligations that it really must perform and then do them very well. It is not surprising that by 2010 Indiana had the fewest state employees since 1982 and per-capita cost of state government in Indiana was the sixth lowest in the nation. Rating agencies Fitch and Moody's joined Standard and Poor's in giving Indiana a AAA rating, the highest possible. Indiana was one of only nine states with an AAA credit rating from all three ratings agencies. All three agencies credited Indiana's fiscal management through difficult economic times as a primary factor in the state's high credit rating. With its AAA credit rating, Indiana was able to borrow money at lower interest rates than states with lower ratings. Indiana school corporations also benefited because their ratings are tied to the state's credit rating.

When Daniels was elected, he declared that his number one priority was job creation. Daniels supported legislation establishing the public-private Indiana Economic Development Corporation, became chairman of its board, and ordered it to "act at the speed of business, not the speed of government," to attract new jobs. During its first year, the IEDC closed more transactions than its predecessor agency had in the previous two years combined convincing 485 businesses to commit to creating more than 60,000 new jobs and investing $14.5 billion into the Indiana economy. In 2006 the IEDC topped its 2005 results in only ten months and earned Indiana the distinction as the only state in the nation to land three high-profile automotive investments— from major manufacturers Toyota, Honda, and Cummins. In 2007 the IEDC announced its third consecutive record-breaking year for new investment and job commitments in Indiana. During this period Indiana was ranked as one of the leading states in biofuel productions with fifteen plants, including the world's largest soybean biodiesel plant.

In 2008 Daniels was named "Public Official of the Year" by the independent magazine *Governing* for his achievements as governor. He also received the Manhattan Institute's Innovator Award for his creative public policy initiatives, including the lease of the Indiana Toll Road. Dubbed "Major Moves," it was the largest privatization of public infrastructure in the United States, generating nearly $4 billion for reinvestment in the state's record breaking ten-year transportation and infrastructure program. He also championed the Healthy Indiana Plan to provide healthcare coverage for uninsured Hoosier adults and conceived of the sweeping property tax reform in 2008 that resulted in the biggest tax cut in Indiana history. Also that year, Daniels was reelected to a second and constitutionally limited final consecutive term by an eighteen-point margin, receiving more votes than any candidate in state history. According to one survey, his approval rating in 2010 was 70 percent, placing him among the country's most popular governors.

As governor, Daniels often is asked to speak to students. He advises young adults to read all the history that they did not learn in school. He also encourages people to have lots of children, calling it, "the great experience of life and the best way you can pay back what you owe your country." Daniels's view of the world as he has come to embrace it used to be called "liberalism." "Liber" in Latin means freedom and liberty. He believes in a government that protects the liberty of an individual and enhances the opportunity for that individual, acting as a free and moral human being, to maximize his human potential. "It's their job to do it," he said. "It's not society's job to care for them from cradle to grave but to try to create the conditions and protect the freedoms that allow people to make of themselves what they can and what they want to."

Daniels understands the importance of and is committed to staying physically fit. He played intramural sports in high school. By college, he was smoking cigarettes. "I remember I got out of college and people had started to write these books about running and I remember saying to myself, 'Well, you know college was fun but I have to get myself in shape, quit smoking cigarettes and start running.' I had some old beat up tennis shoes. I didn't know that there was such a thing as a running shoe. It makes my feet sore to think about this now. Then Lugar got very interested in it—a terrific role model. He put up a chart on a wall and you'd take a marker and put your mileage up there every week, try to beat the boss," said Daniels. As governor he created INShape Indiana, an initiative designed to help Hoosiers make healthier choices about food, physical activity, and tobacco. Since its inception in 2005, the program has partnered with hospitals and health-related not-for-profit organizations, private industry, and other government agencies.

Daniels is an avid Brooklyn Dodgers fan, a mania he acquired as a child. For his seventh birthday, his parents purchased a mixed breed Airedale/Scottie from the Humane Society for five dollars. Its name was Tutti Frutti, but Dottie Daniels could not picture yelling that out the back door. So young Mitch named him Duke after Dodgers centerfielder Duke Snider, his all-time favorite baseball player. Ironically, Daniels' wife, Cheri, has a major league baseball heritage. Her grandfather was Hall of Fame second baseman William Jennings Bryan "Billy" Herman. Cheri keeps herself fit by often walking as many as fifty miles per week. Her athletic ability may run to the exotic. As first lady, she won watermelon seed spitting and cow milking contests at the Indiana State Fair. For his part, Daniels also enjoys riding a motorcycle and often is spotted on one of his Harley-Davidsons—always wearing a helmet.

Daniels has emerged as a key national voice in the Republican Party. He has declared that Republicans need to campaign to govern, not just to win. "We need a credible program and a tone that's friendly and inviting and that gives you some chance of unifying people around some action," he said. "It's time to move on to an honest discussion about what we can afford as a nation and how to pay for it."

When asked whether he would run for president in 2012, Daniels at first staunchly denied any interest in higher office and dismissed local and national speculation about his ambitions for a possible presidential bid. He expressed his reluctance to subject his family to the savagery of presidential politics. He also reminded observers of his promise to Hoosiers that he would serve out his term.

In leaving the door slightly ajar, however, he cited a number of issues he would tackle as president. In a June 2010 interview in the *Weekly Standard*, Daniels said that the next president would have to call a truce on social issues until the economic issues are resolved. Daniels favors a deficit-reduction plan that would include reformation of the Social Security system, a health care fix, examination of defense spending, and tax simplification.

Indiana has not provided a president to the nation since Benjamin Harrison in 1888. Daniels could end that drought. He would make a remarkable president, blessed as he is with towering intelligence, extensive state and federal government experience, and solid midwestern values. Hoosiers would be proud to elevate "Our Man Mitch" to the world stage.

MICHAEL S. MAURER served
as Secretary of Commerce under
Governor Mitch Daniels. He
is a regular columnist for the
Indianapolis Business Journal and
an irregular contributor to the
New York Times crossword puzzle.
He lives in Carmel, Indiana with
his wife, Janie. The Maurer's
have three children and eight
grandchildren. Contact Maurer at:
mmaurer@ibj.com.